SECRET AGENCIES

WITHDRAWN

Yale University Press / New Haven and London

Secret Agencies

U.S. INTELLIGENCE IN A HOSTILE WORLD

Loch K. Johnson

Designed by Nancy Ovedovitz and set in Times Roman type by The Composing Room of Michigan, Inc., Grand Rapids, Michigan. Printed in the United States of America by Vail-Ballou Press, Binghamton, New York.

Library of Congress Cataloging-in-Publication Data
Johnson, Loch K., 1942-
Secret agencies: U.S. intelligence in a hostile world / Loch K. Johnson.
    p. cm.
Includes bibliographical references and index.
ISBN 0-300-06611-2 (cloth: alk. paper)
        0-300-07654-1 (pbk.: alk. paper)
1. Intelligence service—United States.   I. Title.
JK468.I6J66   1996
327.1273—dc20   96-8610
                        CIP

A catalogue record for this book is available from the British Library.

The paper in this book meets the guidelines for permanence and durability of the Committee on Production Guidelines for Book Longevity of the Council on Library Resources.

10 9 8 7 6 5 4 3 2

To the memory of Les Aspin (1938–95), friend and mentor

There are many elements that go into every important decision.
In the first place, you must try to grapple with the facts.
What is the actual situation?
Secretary of State Dean Rusk to Eric Goldman (January 12, 1964)

CONTENTS

Contents

PREFACE

This book examines how, and how well, the intelligence agencies of the United States have been used by government officials since the end of World War Two to guard and advance the global interests of the nation. My purpose is to help inform the American people about the hidden side of their government. For democracy relies on a knowledgeable citizenry to provide general guidance to those few individuals who make foreign policy decisions on their behalf.

America's secret agencies engage in three primary missions. First and foremost, they are expected to gather and interpret information from around the world (referred to by intelligence officers as collection and analysis). Second, the agencies are expected to protect U.S. government secrets from espionage by other governments (counterintelligence). Third, from time to time they have been directed to oppose the nation's adversaries through the use of aggressive clandestine operations abroad (covert action). Throughout the Cold War (1945–91) the Soviet Union was the nemesis of American foreign policy and hence the number-one target of the intelligence agencies. The containment of Soviet-inspired communism was the preeminent objective that shaped America's relations with the rest of the world and provided the raison d'être for the secret agencies.

In an earlier study, *A Season of Inquiry* (1985), I wrote about the beginning of a new era for American intelligence ushered in by a series of spy scandals. In the benchmark year 1975 government investigators had accused the secret agencies of conducting espionage against American citizens, the very people they had been created to protect. Probes by the executive and legislative branches chronicled a long list of Orwellian excesses: spying on civil rights activists and Vietnam War dissenters, plotting the assassination of foreign leaders, and running unsavory clandestine operations meant to undermine or destroy regimes considered anathema to the interests of the United States—even democracies (Chile is only the most well-known case).

In the light of this jarring breach of trust, U.S. intelligence agencies would no longer enjoy the same breadth of discretion in the conduct of covert operations around the globe as they had had before. Henceforth officials within the executive branch—and, in a dramatic expansion of supervision, the legislative branch as well—would attempt to hold the nation's spymasters to a higher standard of accountability. *A Season of Inquiry* traced the debates about the future of intelligence that took place during the "Year of Intelligence," as some officers of the Central Intelligence Agency (CIA) remember 1975, or—for the more embittered—the time of the "Intelligence Wars." Scandal had forced both the president and the Congress to grapple with the dilemma of how to tighten control over the secret agencies without stifling their initiative and morale in the struggle against America's external enemies. A unique experiment in intelligence accountability had begun.

My second study of intelligence, *America's Secret Power* (1989), examined the effectiveness of the new accountability during its first decade, including the performance of neophyte House and Senate intelligence oversight committees, the stringent approval and reporting requirements for sensitive operations, and the new Intelligence Oversight Board (IOB) set up in the executive office of the president. The verdict: even after ten years, the new relationships remained rough-hewn—and they had failed altogether to prevent the Iran-contra affair of 1986–87. Nevertheless, the new methods of democratic control had worked most of the time, and clearly they represented a vast improvement over the open-ended authority granted the secret agencies throughout the earlier era of tolerant neglect (1945–74).

America's Secret Power explored a number of problems that continued to disturb the balance between accountability and effectiveness for the baker's dozen departments and agencies that make up the so-called intelligence community (IC). Seven major "sins of intelligence" emerged from the study, the most damning of which was the failure to provide policymakers with objective information. The book identified a variety of pathologies that weakened the core intelligence mission of information collection and interpretation. It also explored the elaborate relationships that had evolved since the end of World War Two between the secret side of government and other American institutions, particularly the media and the universities.

In the same year *America's Secret Power* was published, history offered up one of its rare sea-changes in world affairs. In November 1989 the Berlin Wall was brought down suddenly, and the Soviet Union soon came tumbling after. In a quick succession of astounding and exhilarating events, the Cold War was over. These events, culminating in a splintering of the Soviet empire in 1991 into its constituent republics and once-captive nations, brought to the forefront troubling questions about U.S. intelligence capabilities. How could the secret agencies have failed to anticipate the dissolution of America's deadliest international rival? What would happen to the clandestine service now that the Cold War was over?

The present book carries forward my research into the netherworld of intelligence, further unfolding topics taken up earlier and setting out in new directions as well—among them the debate over whether the United States should engage in a more aggressive use of economic espionage against allies and enemies alike. I consider a range of ethical questions surrounding the use of covert operations, while continuing to follow the thread of intelligence accountability that weaved through the companion volumes. I offer an updated appraisal at the close of a second decade in this noble—and often shaky—experiment meant to bring some semblance of democracy into the darkest corners of American government.

I begin by examining what is meant by "intelligence," why nations with global interests consider it important to have secret agencies, and how the use of intelligence is beset with existential vexations (chapter 1). Chapter 2 brings a broad historical overview of America's secret operations abroad from the Cold War to the present. The purpose of this chapter is to indicate how the emphasis placed on the different intelligence missions by the government has fluctuated over the years. The moral implications of clandestine operations are assessed in chapter 3, where I offer a set of guidelines for a more ethical approach to the use of secret power.

The question of intelligence accountability, a central concern for any probe into the interstices between secrecy and democracy, is taken up in chapter 4 with a close look at how well overseers have monitored the intelligence agencies through Congressional hearings. Chapter 5 contrasts the U.S. approach to intelligence with that of other countries.

The issue of intelligence and economic security is the focus of chapter 6. The key question here is: Should this nation's secret agencies aid the American business community in its struggle for success in the global marketplace against adroit foreign competitors like Japan and Germany? The book concludes in chapter 7 with an evaluation of how well America's intelligence agencies fared during the Cold War against the USSR, a totalitarian state bristling with nuclear weapons and endowed with powerful secret services of its own. Have the American people been well served in their quest for peace and security in a world marred by violence, intrigue, and uncertainty? Do the billions of taxpayer dollars spent on intelligence over the past fifty years add up to a wise investment or a foolish waste of money?

The methodology in this and my other books has been straightforward: study everything of a serious nature that has been written on the subject—a steadily burgeoning literature of government documents, periodicals, and scholarly treatises—and interview as many intelligence professionals and outside experts as possible.[1] The interviews have been with men and women at all levels of the secret agencies and with their overseers in the executive and legislative branches, as well as with a wide range of academic specialists from the United States and abroad.

A unifying theme binds together this corpus of research. The information provided to policymakers by the intelligence community often contributes vitally to the making of sound decisions, giving the secret agencies a role of unquestionable importance to the nation's well-being. Yet the evidence clearly reveals that, at the same time, the intelligence agencies have the capacity not only to safeguard democracy but to subvert it as well. Moreover, the information they have provided to the nation's leaders has at times been wrong, as a result of errors in judgment or bias in reporting—or because many things about the world are simply unknowable. Thus the intelligence agencies indeed warrant the support of Americans, but they also require a close watchfulness—even wariness.

This book has benefited greatly from discussions with intelligence officers and overseers, most of whom have requested anonymity for professional reasons. I thank them profusely for their patience and generosity. Some of the thoughtful people with whom I have spoken can be openly thanked, though, beginning with Les Aspin, the former secretary of defense and chairman of the Commission on the Roles and Capabilities of Intelligence. He was a wonderful source of encouragement for this project; he read and commented on portions of the manuscript as I went along, and was especially helpful with chapter 7. His premature death in 1995 was a tragedy for the country and for the many of us who valued his friendship and keen analytic mind.

Others I am pleased and able to thank openly include James A. Barry, David D. Gries, Arthur S. Hulnick, Carol Minor, Kay Oliver, Hayden B. Peake, Donald P. Steury, and Michael A. Turner of the CIA's Center for the Study of Intelligence and its Office of Academic Affairs; Harold P. Ford, Joseph S. Nye, Jr., and Gregory F. Treverton, all formerly with the National Intelligence Council; Douglas J. MacEachin, formerly deputy director of intelligence at the CIA; George J. Tenet, a former senior intelligence official on the National Security Council (NSC) and presently the deputy director of central intelligence; the late James J. Angleton, chief of CIA counterintelligence; John T. Elliff, Senator Wyche Fowler, Richard H. Giza, Thomas K. Latimer, Senator Sam Nunn, and Paula L. Scalingi, former legislative overseers; Elizabeth Rindskopf, former general counsel of the CIA; Frederick P. Hitz, the CIA's inspector general; Dean Rusk, former secretary of state; former intelligence officers George Carver, Dr. Ray S. Cline, Jack Davis, and Walter Pforzheimer; and each of the directors of Central Intelligence from 1966 to 1995—Richard Helms, James R. Schlesinger, William E. Colby, George Bush, Adm. Stansfield Turner, William J. Casey, William H. Webster, Robert M. Gates, and R. James Woolsey—who kindly subjected themselves to the author's questioning.

I also want to express my appreciation to several scholars, friends, private analysts, and reporters who have allowed me to bend their ears on the topics in this book, often guiding me in a better direction than the one I was traveling: Christopher Andrew, Richard K. Betts, Steven Emerson, Louis Fisher, Randall Fort, John Lewis Gaddis, Roy Godson, Allen E. Goodman, Michael Handel, Glenn P. Hastedt, John Hollister Hedley, Karl F. Inderfurth, Rhodri Jeffreys-Jones, Robert Jervis, Frederick M. Kaiser, Anne Karalekas, William M. Leary, Mark M. Lowenthal, Fred F. Manget, Ernest R. May, Harvey Nelsen, Jay Peterzell, John Prados, Harry Howe Ransom (esteemed mentor), Jeffrey T. Richelson, Harry Sepp, Frank John Smist, Jr., Robert David Steele, Stafford T. Thomas, Richard R. Valcourt, Wesley K. Wark, H. Bradford Westerfield (who generously and with great insight read an early draft of the manuscript), and David Wise. No doubt they will object to some of the conclusions I have reached in these pages; but perhaps they will see their good influence here and there, too. The annotations throughout this volume are further testimony of my debt to the individuals mentioned here, along with a much wider group of intelligence specialists.

I would like to express my deep gratitude, as well, for the support I have received from the University of Georgia. My interview trips to Washington, D.C., were made possible by funding from Thomas P. Lauth, the head of the Department of Political Science; Wyatt W. Anderson, dean of the College of Arts and Sciences; and Robert L. Anderson, the associate vice president for research. I am grateful as well to Rick Dunn and Amy Fletcher, doctoral candidates at the university, for their research assistance; to Chuck Grench, Otto Bohlmann, Susan Laity, and Richard Miller of Yale University Press for their guidance and encouragement; and to the following journals and publishers for permitting me to draw on materials I have previously published: Frank Cass, Simon & Schuster, the University of Oklahoma Press, St. Martin's Press, the *American Intelligence Journal*, the *American Journal of International Law*, *Foreign Policy*, the *Journal of Strategic Studies*, and the *International Journal of Intelligence and Counterintelligence*.

Above all, I want to thank my wife, Leena, and my daughter, Kristin, for the cheerful tolerance they have displayed toward the research trips that took me away from the hearth and the long hours spent huddled before the pale screen of a word processor at home. Their unwavering love and devotion have sustained me through the solitude and frustrations that accompany the writing of a book.

ABBREVIATIONS AND ACRONYMS

ABM	anti-ballistic missile
ACIS	Arms Control Intelligence Staff
AFIO	Association of Former Intelligence Officers
AG	Attorney General
AWACS	Airborne Warning and Control System
BMD	ballistic missile defense
BNL	Banca Nazionale del Lavoro
CA	covert action
CAS	Covert Action Staff (CIA)
CE	counterespionage
CHAOS	codename for CIA domestic spying operation
CI	counterintelligence
CIA	Central Intelligence Agency
CINC	commander in chief
CISPES	an FBI counterintelligence program
C/CATF	chief/Central American Task Force
CMS	Community Management Staff
CNN	Cable News Network

COINTELPRO	Counterintelligence Program (FBI)
COMINT	communications intelligence
COMIREX	Committee on Imagery Requirements and Exploitation
CORONA	codename for first U.S. spy satellite system
COS	chief of station (CIA)
CPSU	Communist Party of the Soviet Union
CRS	Congressional Research Service (Library of Congress)
DA	Directorate of Administration (CIA)
DAS	deputy assistant secretary
DCIA	Director of the Central Intelligence Agency
DCI	Director of Central Intelligence
DDA	Deputy Director for Administration (CIA)
DDCIA	Deputy Director of the Central Intelligence Agency
DDI	Deputy Director for Intelligence (CIA)
DDO	Deputy Director for Operations (CIA)
DDS&T	Deputy Director for Science and Technology (CIA)
DEA	Drug Enforcement Administration
DECA	Developing Espionage and CI Awareness (FBI)
DEIB	*Daily Economic Intelligence Brief*
DGSE	French Intelligence Service
DI	Directorate of Intelligence (CIA)
DIA	Defense Intelligence Agency
DID	*Defense Intelligence Daily*
DINSUM	Defense Intelligence Summary
DO	Directorate of Operations (CIA)
DOD	Department of Defense
DS&T	Directorate of Science and Technology (CIA)
ELINT	electronic intelligence
FBI	Federal Bureau of Investigation
FBIS	Foreign Broadcast Information Service (CIA)
FOIA	Freedom of Information Act
GAO	General Accounting Office (Congress)
GATT	General Agreement on Tariffs and Trade
GEO	geosynchronous orbit
GNP	Gross National Product
GRU	Soviet military intelligence
HEO	high-elliptical orbit
HPSCI	House Permanent Select Committee on Intelligence
HUMINT	human intelligence (espionage)
IA	Intelligence Assessment
IC	intelligence community
ICBM	intercontinental ballistic missile
IG	Inspector General
IIM	Interagency Intelligence Memorandum

Abbreviations and Acronyms

IMF	International Monetary Fund
INR	Bureau of Intelligence and Research (State Dept.)
INTELINK	an intelligence community computer information system
IOB	Intelligence Oversight Board (White House)
IRS	Internal Revenue Service
ISC	Intelligence and Security Committee (Britain)
JCS	Joint Chiefs of Staff
ITT	International Telephone and Telegraph Corporation
JCS	Joint Chiefs of Staff
JETRO	Japan's external trading organization
KGB	Soviet secret police and foreign intelligence service
KH	Keyhole (satellite)
LEO	low-elliptical orbit
MASINT	measurement and signature intelligence
MIRV	multiple independent reentry vehicle
MITI	a Japanese economic planning group
MRBM	medium-range ballistic missile
MRC	major regional conflict
MVD	Soviet Ministry of Internal Affairs
NAFTA	North American Free Trade Agreement
NATO	North Atlantic Treaty Organization
NEC	National Economic Council (White House)
NEO	noncombatant evacuation operation
NFIP	National Foreign Intelligence Program
NIMA	National Imagery and Mapping Agency
NIC	National Intelligence Council
NID	*National Intelligence Daily*
NIE	National Intelligence Estimate
NIO	National Intelligence Officer
NISC	National Intelligence Study Center
NOC	non-official cover
NPC	nonproliferation center
NPIC	National Photographic Interpretation Center
NRO	National Reconnaissance Office
NSA	National Security Agency
NSC	National Security Council (White House)
NSCID	National Security Council Intelligence Directive
NTM	National Technical Means
OEOB	Old Executive Office Building
OMB	Office of Management and Budget
OOTW	operations other than war
OPA	Office of Public Affairs (CIA)
OPC	Office of Policy Coordination (CIA)
OPEC	Organization of Petroleum Exporting Countries

op sec	operational security
ORD	Office of Research and Development (CIA)
ORR	Office of Research and Reports (SOVA predecessor)
OSINT	open-source intelligence
OSS	Office of Strategic Services
OSWR	Office of Special Weapons Research
OTA	Office of Technology Assessment (Congress)
OTR	Office of Training (CIA)
PAC	Political Action Committee
PDB	*President's Daily Brief*
PDD	Presidential Decision Directive
PFIAB	President's Foreign Intelligence Advisory Board
PHOINT	photographic intelligence (imagery)
PLA	People's Liberation Army (China)
PLO	Palestine Liberation Organization
PM	paramilitary
PRC	People's Republic of China
RADINT	radar intelligence
ROSE	Rich Open Source Environment—CIA computer software
SA	Special Activities Division, DO/CIA
SAC	Strategic Air Command
SAM	surface-to-air missile
SHAMROCK	codename for NSA domestic wiretap
SIGINT	signals intelligence (special intelligence)
SIRC	Security Intelligence Review Committee (Canada)
SIS	Strategic Intelligence Service (Britain)
SLBM	submarine-launched ballistic missile
SMO	support to military operations
SNIE	Special National Intelligence Estimate
SOG	Special Operations Group (paramilitary covert action)
SOVA	Office of Soviet Analysis (CIA)
SSCI	Senate Select Committee on Intelligence
SVRR	Russian intelligence service
TECHINT	technical intelligence
TELINT	telemetry intelligence
UAV	unmanned aerial vehicle
UN	United Nations
USC	United States Code (statutory identification system)
USG	United States Government
USIB	United States Intelligence Board
USTR	United States Trade Representative
VC	Viet Cong (pro-Communist faction in Vietnam War)
WMD	weapons of mass destruction

SECRET AGENCIES

CHAPTER 1

THE MEANINGS AND METHODS OF INTELLIGENCE

In a full-page magazine advertisement that offered financial counseling for the perplexed consumer, a New York bank presented readers with a drawing of a man in a rowboat. Blithely oaring his way along a sparkling river, he seemed completely unaware of the gathering currents about to sweep him over a waterfall. The copy advised, "Moving ahead without looking ahead could prove to be the greatest risk of all."

As with boating in unfamiliar waters, steering a nation through the treacherous tides of history can also be a perilous enterprise. Responsible leaders in every nation seek knowledge—and, ideally, foreknowledge—of the world around them. For with a better understanding of global affairs, they are apt to protect and advance more effectively the vital interests of their citizens.

THE FOUR MEANINGS OF INTELLIGENCE

A prudent awareness of the dangers and opportunities that confront a nation can be achieved only through painstaking collection of information about key events, circumstances, and personalities worldwide. This gathering of information, followed by its careful sifting, lies at the heart of "intelligence" as that term is applied to affairs of state.

More formally, professional intelligence officers define strategic intelligence as the "knowledge and foreknowledge of the world around us—the prelude to Presidential decision and action."[1] At this global level the objective is to acquire an understanding of the potential risks and gains confronting the nation from all compass points. At the more restricted level of tactical intelligence the focus turns to an assessment of likely outcomes in specific battlefields or theaters of war—what military commanders refer to as "situation awareness."

From this point of view (and it is by far the most common usage) intelligence is *information,* a tangible product collected and interpreted in order to achieve a sharper image of political and military conditions worldwide. A typical intelligence question at the strategic level would be, "If a coup toppled the Russian president, who would be among the field of leading contenders to replace him, and what political and military views do they have?" Or at the tactical level, one can imagine General H. Norman Schwarzkopf demanding during the Persian Gulf War in 1991, "I want the precise location of Iraq's Republican Guard—and I want it now!" To prevail in battle, a nation must have data on the enemy's terrain, roads, airfields, ports, waterways, and bridges. "Can that bridge support a tank?" "Is the runway long enough for a C-47?" "Is the beach firm enough to support an amphibious landing?" "Is aviation fuel available on the island?" Even the types of local parasites cannot be overlooked if troops are to be properly inoculated against infectious diseases.

What makes intelligence different from other forms of information are the strands of secret material woven into it. As Abram N. Shulsky emphasizes, intelligence often entails "information some other party is trying to deny":[2] agent dossiers locked in Kremlin safes; telephone conversations between Beijing commanders and artillery units of the People's Liberation Army (PLA) on maneuvers near Changchun; the flight plans of cocaine-filled Caravelle jets from Colombia headed for landing strips in Mexico along the Texas border.

Still, much of the information gathered and analyzed by American intelligence agencies is drawn from open sources in the public domain, such as Iranian television broadcasts, Japanese economic reports, or editorials in *Rossiiskaya Gazeta* and the hundreds of other new Russian newspapers. Allen Dulles, the chief of intelligence from 1953 to 1961, testified before the Senate Armed Services Committee on April 25, 1947, that about 80 percent of intelligence analysis is based on the public record—although CIA old-timers hasten to add that he was including in this figure information gathered by diplomats and military attaches.

Whatever the precise mix of covert and overt information in intelligence reporting during the Cold War, both are necessary ingredients for good analysis. The overt information provides a context for the covert—a way of putting the clandestine "nuggets" into perspective. Yet classified studies (some by reputable outside scholars on contract) that have looked at the "added value" of clandestine reporting conclude that policymakers really do gain information from the secret agencies beyond what can be found in the *New York Times*, the *Economist*, or *Foreign Policy*.[3]

Nonetheless, many policymakers prefer the public literature, because it is written in a felicitous style and, since it is unclassified, can be talked about openly. Few, though, are prepared to relinquish their access to the *President's Daily Brief* or *PDB* (if they are lucky enough to be one of the thirteen policy elites to receive it), the *National Intelligence Daily* (*NID*), the *Defense Intelligence Digest* (*DID*), or the many other publications prepared by the intelligence agencies.

Policymakers understand that intelligence sources offer unique access to data on terrorist activities or enemy weapons systems, for instance, via worldwide coverage by agents in almost every capital and via surveillance satellites. Most important, decisionmakers know they can talk back to these "newspapers," asking intelligence officers to follow up with tailored oral briefings or written reports. In a word, intelligence is responsive to their needs.

During the Cold War much of the information sought by policymakers was secret ("denied") and had to be acquired through clandestine means. Espionage thus became a defining feature of intelligence-as-information. Even if the bulk of what was reported by intelligence officers came from open sources, it reached far beyond the policymaker's usual brief sampling of the daily Washington newspapers and the *New York Times*.

Since the end of the Cold War the intelligence agencies have tended to concentrate on the secret pieces of the global puzzle. Sensitive to the charge (however wrong) that it adds little to what the newspapers report, the intelligence community has made a concerted effort to demonstrate the value added from its clandestine tradecraft. The overt/covert mix also depends on the subject. With respect to terrorism, counternarcotics, and proliferation—or "hard targets" like North Korea or Iran—the overwhelming percentage (75 to 90) of all the material in intelligence reports is likely to come from clandestine sources. In contrast, political and economic subjects are often well reported in the public media, and the secret agencies turn to these sources too for a reliable context in which to place their covert findings (anywhere from 10 to 40 percent of the total).

One intelligence analyst has observed that roughly 60 percent of the sources used by his technical branch of the CIA are open, including scientific journals, computer databases, newspaper articles, and reports from the CIA's Foreign Broadcast Information Service (FBIS), which translates thousands of foreign periodicals and newspapers into English. Another 25 percent is based on insider information, that is, hard-to-find "gray literature" (such as technical-conference proceedings), diplomatic reporting, contract studies, and surveys financed by the intelligence agencies. Only 15 percent of its information comes from mechanical and human espionage—though, it should be kept in mind, this information often proves the most valuable.[4]

From another vantage point intelligence may be considered a *process*: a series of interactive steps formally referred to as the "intelligence cycle."[5] At the beginning of the cycle officials plan what information to target around the world; then they order the information to be collected and organized—or "processed" in the narrower sense of that word—for close study (analysis) by experts.

Once the expert analysts have assessed the information, it is disseminated in the last step of the cycle to top policy officers in the executive branch and selected members of Congress with foreign policy responsibilities. An illustration of this usage of the word *intelligence* might be, "Analysts in the Directorate of Intelligence (DI), the CIA's analytic shop, play a vital intelligence role as they attempt to interpret the goals and *modus operandi* of Islamic radicals."

From a third perspective intelligence may be thought of as a set of *missions* carried out by the secret agencies. The first is collection and analysis, a shorthand phrase for the full intelligence cycle;[6] second, counterintelligence, the thwarting of secret activities directed against the United States by foreign entities (usually hostile intelligence services);[7] and third, covert action, the secret intervention into the affairs of other states[8]—sometimes called "special activities" or, for the benefit of the occasional Latin scholar who might come across the Special Activities Division (SA) crest at CIA Headquarters, "Actiones Praecipuae." An example of this usage might be, "What mix of secret intelligence operations—collection-and-analysis, counterintelligence, and covert action—might be most effective to prevent North Korea from developing an arsenal of nuclear weapons?"

Finally, the term *intelligence* is used from time to time to denote the structures or *organizations* that carry out these core missions. Intelligence in this in-

Meanings and Methods

stance refers to the actual network of officials and agencies involved in the gathering, processing, interpreting, and disseminating of information, as well as those who plan and implement counterintelligence (CI) and covert action (CA). Using this sense of the word the president might remark, "Make sure intelligence is present at the Tuesday meeting of the National Security Council." Or a battalion commander might say, "Get intelligence on the line; I need the exact coordinates of Serbian artillery near Bihac."

The establishment of intelligence as an organization in the United States has a long history, beginning with George Washington—one of the few presidents with a deep and abiding interest in the subject.[9] As general during the Revolutionary War he had his own secret code number ("711") and made use of an effective network of spies led by Paul Revere and including Nathan Hale.

Intelligence organizations have played a role in each of America's military conflicts since the Revolutionary War.[10] General Ethan Allen Hitchcock formed a highly successful spy ring in the U.S. Army during the 1840s that helped lead to victory in the war with Mexico. Allan Pinkerton assembled a talented team of spies for the Union Army during the Civil War, and Rose O'Neil Greenhow ("Rebel Rose"), a resourceful agent for the South, contributed to the Confederate success at the first Battle of Bull Run. The outbreak of war in Europe in 1914 stirred some modest efforts in Washington to create a more sophisticated secret service for the nation, but only with the onset of World War Two did this objective receive the full attention of President Franklin D. Roosevelt. In June 1942 he ordered the formation of a new intelligence agency, called the Office of Strategic Services (OSS), which vigorously pursued each of the intelligence missions against the Axis powers.[11]

Still, as the former secretary of state Dean Rusk remembers, the U.S. intelligence services during World War Two remained bare-boned. "When I was assigned to G-2 [Army Intelligence] in 1941, well over a year after the war had started in Europe," he once told a Senate subcommittee, "I was asked to take charge of a new section that had been organized to cover everything from Afghanistan right through southern Asia, southeast Asia, Australia, and the Pacific. . . . Because we had no intelligence organization that had been giving attention to that area up to that time, the materials available to me when I reported for duty consisted of a tourist handbook on India and Ceylon, a 1924 military attache's report from London on the Indian Army, and a drawer full of clippings from the *New York Times* that had been gathered since World War One. That was literally the resources of G-2 on that vast part of the world a year after the war in Europe had started."[12]

At the end of the war President Harry S Truman turned toward the task of modernizing the government's intelligence organization. The attack by the Japanese air force at Pearl Harbor on December 7, 1941, had caught the U.S. Navy by surprise and caused extensive destruction to the Pacific fleet. This "day of infamy," in President Roosevelt's phrase, is still considered the most disastrous intelligence failure in American history.

Until the attack the U.S. military was unaware that the Japanese possessed a new type of aerial torpedo that could navigate the relatively shallow waters of Pearl Harbor. Nor did government officials have reliable information about the likely targets of a Japanese air attack; conventional wisdom at the time pointed to the Philippines as the probable site. Moreover, the fragments of information obtained by U.S. military intelligence that did point to Hawaii were never adequately analyzed and coordinated within the government; the president and other high officials were never given access, for example, to decoded intercepts of Japanese military communications that indicated that Pearl Harbor could be in jeopardy.[13]

With the establishment of the CIA by way of the National Security Act of 1947, President Truman hoped to improve the capabilities of the United States to anticipate security dangers. His objective was to upgrade the collection, analysis, and—especially—the interagency coordination and dissemination of information useful to policymakers as they dealt with world affairs. Above all, the goal was to have no more Pearl Harbors. At the time Truman gave little thought to counterintelligence or covert action; indeed, mention of these missions was omitted altogether from the National Security Act, although they would soon take on a life of their own as U.S.-Soviet hostilities deepened.

The Cold War sired and nourished strapping espionage bureaucracies in both the United States and the Soviet Union. Today, America's spy empire—the intelligence community—consists of thirteen major and several minor secret agencies. According to various newspaper accounts, the IC employs over 150,000 people and, in recent times, has spent some $28–30 billion a year.[14]

Beneath the president and the National Security Council (NSC) in the intelligence chain-of-command stands the director of Central Intelligence or DCI. This chief intelligence officer is in charge—titularly at least—of the entire secret government. (Appendix A provides a list of the seventeen men who have served in this position since 1947.) The DCI simultaneously heads "the Agency," as the CIA is called by insiders, and in this capacity is referred to as the DCIA (director of the CIA).[15]

The CIA is the best known of the secret agencies. Its headquarters are in the Washington, D.C., suburb of Langley, Virginia, in a campus-like setting along the banks of the Potomac River—known sarcastically by some intelligence officers outside the CIA as "Langley Farms."[16] The DCI has his main office on its seventh floor, but he also occupies a suite on the third floor of the Old Executive Office Building, or OEOB, next to the White House. The CIA is mainly responsible for the analysis of strategic information and has also been granted control over the planning and conduct of covert action. (Counterintelligence is a responsibility shared by all the intelligence agencies, in coordination with a new—and still inchoate—National Counterintelligence Center, established in 1994 in the wake of the Aldrich Ames spy scandal.) The CIA's organizational chart (as of 1995) is presented in figure 1.1.

The CIA's major companion agencies include the National Security Agency (NSA), located at Fort Meade, Maryland, responsible for codebreaking and electronic eavesdropping; the National Reconnaissance Office (NRO), with quarters in newly constructed buildings near Dulles Airport in the Virginia countryside and chartered to coordinate the development and management of surveillance satellites; the National Imagery and Mapping Office (NIMA), which supervises the photographic side of foreign surveillance; the Defense Intelligence Agency (DIA), also in the DOD and in charge of military intelligence analysis; and the four military intelligence services, each gathering tactical intelligence from all corners of the globe. Each of these entities is under the command of the secretary of defense (as well as the DCI—a sure prescription for blurred lines of authority) and as a result are considered the nation's military intelligence agencies.[17]

On the civilian side of intelligence stand (along with the CIA): the Bureau of Intelligence and Research (INR), at the Department of State; the FBI's intelligence units, housed within the Department of Justice; the Department of the Treasury, home of the Secret Service and the Internal Revenue Service, both of which have an intelligence component; and the Department of Energy's intelligence corps, which (among other duties) tracks the flow of fissionable materials around the globe.[18] Together, these military and civilian agencies comprise the largest organization for the production of information in the history of civilization (see figure 1.2).[19]

AN ENCOMPASSING VIEW OF INTELLIGENCE

Regardless of how the term is used—as product, process, mission, or organization—intelligence is widely considered America's "first line of defense."[20] The assumption behind this perspective is that sound choices for U.S. foreign policy depend on decisionmakers having the most accurate, complete, and timely information possible about the capabilities and intentions of other na-

Figure 1.1 The Office of the DCI and the Central Intelligence Agency

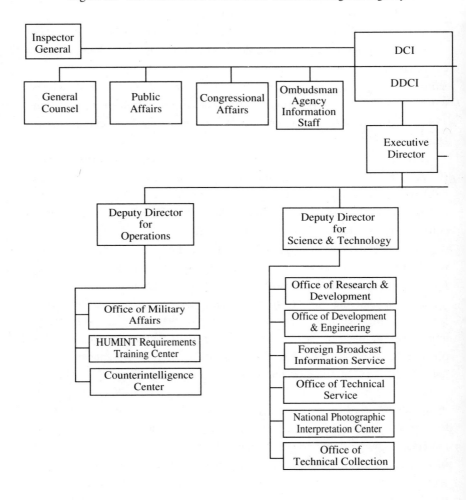

Source: Adapted from "Director of Central Intelligence Command Responsibilities," Office of Public Affairs, Central Intelligence Agency, December 1994.

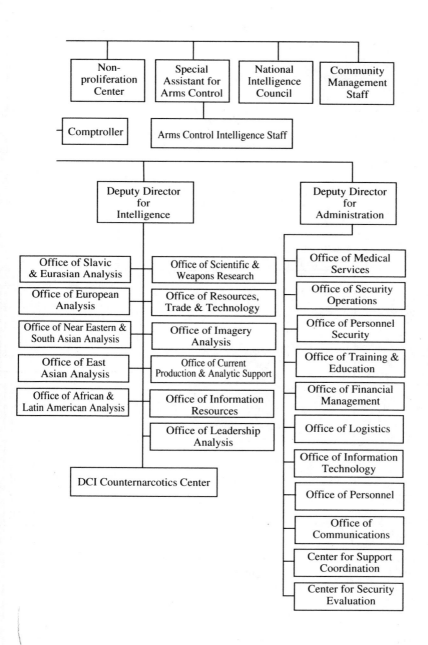

Non-proliferation Center	Special Assistant for Arms Control	National Intelligence Council	Community Management Staff

Comptroller

Arms Control Intelligence Staff

Deputy Director for Intelligence

Deputy Director for Administration

Office of Slavic & Eurasian Analysis

Office of Scientific & Weapons Research

Office of Medical Services

Office of European Analysis

Office of Resources, Trade & Technology

Office of Security Operations

Office of Near Eastern & South Asian Analysis

Office of Imagery Analysis

Office of Personnel Security

Office of East Asian Analysis

Office of Current Production & Analytic Support

Office of Training & Education

Office of African & Latin American Analysis

Office of Information Resources

Office of Financial Management

Office of Leadership Analysis

Office of Logistics

DCI Counternarcotics Center

Office of Information Technology

Office of Personnel

Office of Communications

Center for Support Coordination

Center for Security Evaluation

Figure 1.2 The United States Intelligence Community

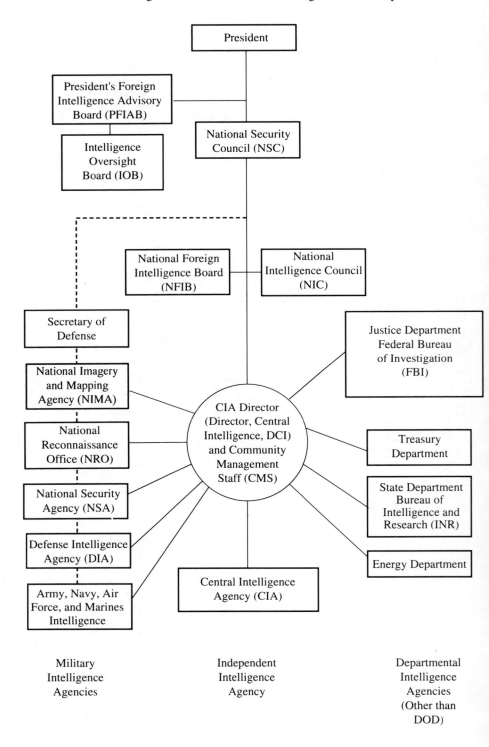

tions or factions. This is not an easy assignment on a vast planet where nations keep their political ambitions closely veiled and hide their development of new weapons inside heavily guarded buildings and even, as in North Korea, in deep underground caverns.

At bottom the intelligence community, with its intricate worldwide network of mechanical and human spies, has but one overmastering objective: to safeguard the United States and its international interests. This can mean anything from promoting democracy to ensuring access to foreign oil and preventing internal subversion—an important mission of the domestically oriented intelligence agencies, like the FBI. To achieve these goals, it is first necessary to acquire and understand information about the potential threats and opportunities; consequently, reliable facts and analysis are seen by many scholars and government practitioners as the sine qua non of effective decisionmaking. "Every morning I start my day with an intelligence report," President Clinton has remarked. "The intelligence I receive informs just about every foreign policy decision we make."[21]

A former secretary of state has suggested why decisionmakers often display a healthy appetite for information of all kinds, including intelligence: "The ghost that haunts the policy officer or haunts the man who makes the final decision is the question as to whether, in fact, he has in his mind all of the important elements that ought to bear upon his decision, or whether there is a missing piece that he is not aware of that could have a decisive effect if it became known."[22]

The situation in the Persian Gulf in August 1990 provides an illustration of how vital intelligence can be to policy officers. No question pressed more heavily on those in the White House and the Pentagon during that month than the exact size and strength of the Iraqi military units that were headed south to invade Kuwait. An effective American response would have to rely substantially on accurate intelligence about the troop and weapons strength of the Iraqi forces. Drawing on a combination of intelligence sources (including the order-of-battle expertise of an Iraqi military defector), the CIA and the DIA quickly provided answers.

In this instance of "competitive analysis" the two agencies disagreed dramatically on the potency of the Iraqi military. It took another two months of data scrubbing before it became clear that the DIA figures had been based on outdated information from the Iran-Iraq war and consequently were inflated. Yet even in those frustrating instances where the secret agencies disagree, the debate that ensues gives a more reliable result than if leaders were able to turn to only one agency for an answer. Out of this particular interagency disagreement came a useful cross-checking of sources and methodologies which eventually produced a highly reliable order-of-battle assessment. Regrettably, a president will not always have the luxury of waiting so long before dispatching troops into battle. Nor will the United States always possess the resources—even in more robust economic times—to provide intelligence support for every possible military contingency the country may face overseas. Even the idea (endorsed by the bottom-up review conducted by Secretary of Defense Les Aspin in 1994) of fighting simultaneously two so-called major regional conflicts (MRCs)—say, in North Korea and Iraq—would stretch American intelligence support and warfighting capabilities to the limit.

Defense Secretary William J. Perry, Aspin's successor, questioned the feasibility of the 2MRC concept in public hearings. "It's an entirely implausible scenario that we'd fight two wars at once," he conceded before the Senate Defense Appropriations Subcommittee in 1994.[23] Yet demands for intelligence support for military operations (referred to as SMO in the Pentagon) extend even beyond the prospect of two major wars. Intelligence support is needed for small-scale interventions (like Haiti and Somalia) as well as "Operations Other Than War" (OOTW in Pentagonese), which include dispensing military and humanitarian aid, staging counternarcotics operations, noncombatant evacuations (NEOs), and United Nations (UN) peacekeeping operations, as well as counterterrorism operations, interdicting weapons of mass destruction (WMDs), and assisting foreign forces.

Each of these activities stands to benefit from good intelligence support; and this is only the Pentagon's list. The civilians in the government who deal with foreign affairs have their own intelligence requirements, too, from information on trade matters to support at international environmental conferences—all tugging at the same finite resources. The tension between uniforms and suits—tactical intelligence for the military field commanders and strategic intelligence for the president and the rest of the civilian part of the government—lies at the heart of the current debate over future directions for American intelligence.

The president, as the commander in chief and the highest civilian officer in the government, is caught in this cross fire between contending intelligence requirements. Added to the complexity of the rival claims on the intelligence dollar is the fact that most of the time, happily, the United States is at peace. Yet when war comes, the nation must be ready. In the first instance, the president can tilt toward the civilian side of intelligence, using the assets of the intelligence community to gather and analyze information that may head off a war. In the second instance, however, he must tilt toward success on the battlefield, with the fewest American casualties possible. (Zero-body-bag wars is the quixotic goal of some military planners in whose heads dance visions of remote-control, penny-arcade weapons.) These are quite different postures (despite some overlap); as a result, sorting out the nation's future intelligence needs is hampered by turf battles within the bureaucracy.

Given these multiple dimensions of intelligence, how shall it be defined? If one prefers a narrow dictionary definition, the idea of intelligence as product— *secret* information—is apt to be most satisfying. As we have seen, however, this perspective leaves aside a good many activities carried out by the secret agencies. For that reason, in this book I prefer a broader perspective. Regardless of one's favorite definition, the most important point is to have an understanding of what duties the secret agencies actually perform. In this spirit, one can say that intelligence has to do with a cluster of government agencies that conduct secret activities, including counterintelligence, covert action, and, foremost, the collection and analysis of information (from a mixture of open and covert sources) for the illumination of foreign policy deliberations.

THE METHODS OF INTELLIGENCE

Human beings have always needed information to secure their livelihood and their safety—the location of the best fishing stream, the site where firewood might be gathered, when deer herds were likely to appear. During the Cold War the presence of nuclear warheads and rapid-delivery systems held out for Americans—and perhaps for all humankind—the prospect of sudden extinction. This ominous condition made accurate information about the intentions and capabilities of the well-armed adversary, the USSR, more vital than ever.

In this current "information age" we are constantly bombarded by facts, opinions, speculation, rumor, and gossip from every direction. Television carries into our homes each night unsettling images of squalor and death from around the world (not to mention our own backyard). Computers draw us into an interactive milieu where e-mail gives, and expects in return, ever more rapid exchanges of information. The cellular telephone assures that a flow of information will follow us everywhere: into the car, the mall, the meetingplace. What effect has this rising tide of information—and its secret undercurrents we call intelligence—had on decisions made in the high councils of government?

Foreign policy decisions are preceded in most cases by the gathering and interpretation of information by government officials about the costs and benefits that may accrue to their nation from various options. In prehistoric times, people were touched by only small eddies of data about the world around them:

hints of changing weather in the cloud formations, the scent of game, the sound of a twig snapping at night that warned of an intruder. In our own time, American leaders stand in the middle of a deep and rushing stream of information from across the globe—from newspapers, computers, radio, telephone, and especially television. As Ronald Steel observed in 1995, "We would probably not be involved in any of these areas [Somalia, Rwanda, the Balkans] were it not for the power of television to bring the most horrifying images into the American living room."[24]

The form of some information that comes to the president and other top officials has changed little from the early days of the republic: whispers from the First Lady, ruminations over drinks in the Georgetown parlors, the counsel of confidants offered in the privacy of the Oval Office. Yet consider these dramatic changes: thousands of high-resolution satellite photographs arrive each day in the offices of intelligence analysts; data in the form of signals intelligence (SIGINT) pour into the receiving antennae at the NSA; live, ghastly pictures of the carnage in Rwanda and Bosnia fill the television screens in the White House and most every other house; a deluge of citizen opinion jams Internet terminals throughout the government, including the warrens of the Old Executive Office Building, where NSC staffers prepare their influential option papers on foreign affairs. The advance of technology has produced a downpour of information that falls relentlessly on intelligence officers and policymakers alike.

Information Collection

Sophisticated spy machines, designed for the purposes of broader and faster information collection, have exercised a fascination on those in public office. Over the years since 1947 the managers of the secret agencies have successfully promoted a steadily rising investment for technical intelligence, or TECHINT.

By definition TECHINT refers chiefly to IMINT and SIGINT. IMINT is the acronym for imagery intelligence, also called photographic intelligence (PHOTINT), electro-optical intelligence, or, in plain English, photography. SIGINT, also known as "special intelligence," encompasses the interception and analysis of communications intelligence (COMINT)—say, two drug dealers talking to one another via cellular telephones in Colombia—and electronic intelligence (ELINT), such as the electronic signals associated with radar jamming.[25]

Foreign radios, satellites, cellular telephones, and land-line and fiber-optic communications all are inviting targets for SIGINT collectors hoping to learn the intentions of adversaries. Electronic eavesdropping can be the key to averting war. For example, it could tip off the attack plans of a belligerent nation that might be countered by stepped-up diplomacy or a show of military strength. It may also save the lives of individual Americans abroad. Recently a U.S. ambassador was forced to plan an evacuation because of a civil war that was spreading through the country in which he was stationed. A SIGINT intercept disclosed that a team of assassins had learned of the proposed evacuation route and intended to slay the ambassador, his wife, and children. Warned of the trap, the ambassador and his family took a different route to the airport and escaped.

Another of the technical "ints" is MASINT, which stands for measurement and signature intelligence. MASINT exploits the physical properties of foreign targets (an enemy missile, for example) through the use of special technical sensors. These properties might include energy emitted from a nuclear warhead, mechanical noises, or telemetry intelligence (TELINT), the collection of data emitted by weapons as they are being flight-tested, which reveals their specifications.

Prior to the advent of the U-2 spy airplane in the 1950s, the most important TECHINT efforts against the Soviet Union came from radar sites in Turkey and Iran (collecting RADINT, or radar intelligence, a form of MASINT), from EC-135 and RC-135 aircraft lumbering along the perimeter of the USSR, and from camera-laden, unmanned balloons drifting across Soviet airspace. Some of the balloons made it to Japan and the Pacific, but most crashed somewhere in the vast Soviet territory.

The U-2 is an imagery collector and the most outstanding of the early TECHINT innovations.[26] Developed in an accelerated program to obtain reliable data on the extent of the feared "bomber gap," this sleek spyplane—the so-called Black Lady of Espionage—made its debut with a flight over the Soviet Union on July 4, 1956. A series of twenty-nine additional U-2 flights deep into the USSR during the late 1950s and early 1960 (brought to a halt for six months beginning on May 1, 1960, when the Soviets shot down over Sverdlovsk a U-2 piloted by Gary Francis Powers) provided IMINT impressive enough to persuade American leaders that the Soviets had far fewer long-range bombers than initially feared. The Bison and Bear aircraft simply were nowhere to be found in the anticipated numbers on Soviet airfields.

Evidence regarding the next alarm—a "missile gap," stemming from concern over a possible acceleration of the Soviet ICBM program—remained inconclusive.[27] Following the U-2 shootdown in 1960, President Dwight D. Eisenhower had promised his Kremlin counterpart, Nikita Khrushchev, that he would curb further U-2 flights over Soviet territory, so the answer to the missile debate would require a different approach: satellite photography from the more secure confines of space. With a new sense of urgency, the government rushed forward with its nascent satellite program.

After a frustrating concatenation of technical disasters, in 1960 the United States at last placed a reliable surveillance satellite in space (Project CORONA). The first CORONA image, taken on August 18, 1960, was disappointingly fuzzy but clear enough nonetheless to discern a Soviet airfield at Mys Shmidta. Unfortunately, most of the satellite photos taken in 1960 were dark and difficult to read; during 1961, however, the spy cameras improved greatly, and their pictures of military installations in the USSR did indeed disclose the existence of a missile gap—but one that favored the United States.

By the 1970s America had launched several types of satellites into the heavens—some as big as a Mack truck. A few relied on electro-optical technology, others on infrared sensors and radar. Some circled the planet in a low elliptical orbit (LEO), others in a high elliptical orbit (HEO), and a few remained in a stationary posture over a single nation or region (achieved by orbiting in synchrony with the earth's own spin velocity, called geosynchronous orbit or GEO). The perigees and apogees ranged from less than one hundred to more than twenty-four thousand miles in space. Together, the constellation of satellites ("platforms") offered an exciting new TECHINT blend of collection cameras and sensors that allowed several perspectives of the same target.

Harold Brown, the secretary of defense during the Carter presidency, has commented on the value of this intelligence synergism:

> Our national technical means [NTM, the accepted euphemism at the time for satellites and other TECHINT machines] enable us to assemble a detailed picture of Soviet forces, including the characteristics of individual systems, by using information from a variety of sources. . . . We regularly monitor key areas of the Soviet ICBM test ranges. We monitor missile test firings with a wide variety of sensors: cameras taking pictures of launch impact areas; infrared detectors measuring heat from the engine; radars tracking ICBMs in flight; and radios receiving Soviet telemetry signals. . . . The use of multiple sources complicates any effort to disguise or conceal a violation.[28]

The technological advances were fairly steady and remarkable from 1956 to the 1980s, though always punctuated by setbacks. By 1963 the "Keyhole" or KH cameras (a generic term for spaceborne image collectors, just as "Talent" refers to cameras aboard aircraft like the U-2) could peer from remote space into newly dug Soviet missile silos. In the 1970s the "Rhyolite" generation of satellites tracked missile telemetry with ever greater accuracy and, joined by its cohorts "Chalet" and "Jumpseat," achieved major breakthroughs in COMINT. The infrared and radar satellites of the late 1960s and the 1970s were especially important innovations because, unlike electro-optical photography, they are able to penetrate through cloud cover and the darkness of night (relying on star glow alone to provide the necessary definition). The KH-11 imagery satellite launched in 1976 presented as a gift to incoming president Jimmy Carter one of the greatest advances of all: real-time imagery of the USSR and other foreign targets. The main points of friction now were the processing and interpretation of the images, not their delivery to earth.

Into the 1980s the TECHINT wizards in the intelligence community and their colleagues in the private sector spun out more devices for watching American adversaries more closely. The speed with which data were moved from satellite platform to earth-bound photointerpreters accelerated, new cameras provided wider swaths of coverage, and engineers produced an expanded range of camera angles for greater comprehension of such matters as a missile's dimensions. Further, the lifespan of the satellites rose from a few days to months, then years; and the number of ground stations increased to process more rapidly the stream of data from space. Failed launches that so plagued the early days of the spy satellite program became a rarity.[29]

Spy satellites have their limits, of course. Despite their sophisticated phototechnology, they do not have x-ray vision and cannot see through roofs. Moreover, nations like Russia and China have learned how to track their orbits. Foreign regimes often halt their use of sensitive communications and telemetry testing and hide their weapons as the "birds" pass overhead. The North Koreans solved this problem by locating their most sensitive weapons facilities underground. Yet the reconnaissance satellites have contributed in a major way to making the world more transparent and therefore safer from the dangerous hysteria that has frequently arisen over the possible machinations of unseen enemies.

The recruitment of human spies who can steal secrets from vaults or overhear important conversations among foreign adversaries is still a high priority for America's secret agencies. During the Cold War, however, spending on TECHINT far outdistanced spending on old-fashioned espionage (known as human intelligence or HUMINT).[30] A strong proclivity exists among those who make budget decisions for national security to focus on warheads, throw weights, missile velocities, fuel range, and the specifications of spy satellites—things measurable.

Briefings to legislators who hold the intelligence purse strings are ineluctably accompanied by state-of-the-art visual aids: flashy four-color slides ("grabbie graphics," a CIA specialty), videotapes, and CD-ROMs. They portray satellites outfitted with all the latest bells and whistles, and clad—like the Great Gatsby's famous motorcar—in shiny metal and glass that mirror a dozen suns as they rotate the earth.

Unlike the traditional human spy (whose identity is a tightly held secret—no pictures allowed), the spy satellite has a tangible presence. Not only can the DCI show it off with slides during closed-door hearings, he can also pass around the photographs it has produced: startlingly detailed displays of the enemy's missile sites and tank deployments; infrared tracings of "hot" radioactive material flowing through the pipelines of a weapons factory deep within the territory of a nation whose leaders claim that the facility is merely a pharmaceutical laboratory; radar impressions, taken at night or through cloud cover, of fighter aircraft bearing missiles on a remote runway. Satellite cameras neither lie nor defect to the enemy, while their human counterparts (recruited by trolling bars in foreign capitals) have been guilty on both counts. Technical intelligence is, in a word, *trusted* by collectors, analysts, and policy officers alike.

One result of this growing reliance on TECHINT has been the acquisition of more and more information collected at ever faster rates. And the intelligence agencies have worked to improve the mobility of the collection platforms and achieve greater flexibility in reorienting their instrumentation toward fresh targets at a moment's notice. The aspiration is to create a "surge capacity" that will allow the quick shifting of platforms toward whatever newly threatening targets may suddenly arise—Somalia today, Suriname tomorrow.

Once information is captured by an intelligence platform, the ability to send the data hurtling back to Washington for processing has also been tremendously accelerated. Film from the early CORONA satellites had to be catapulted from space back toward earth, then plucked out of the ether by ponderous C-119 and C-130 aircraft—which sometimes failed to snare the precious eighty-four-pound capsules as they descended by parachute toward the Pacific Ocean.[31] The data were flown home while fidgeting photointerpreters awaited the next batch of black-and-white images. Now, as a result of modern digital communications, the trip from satellite to Stateside takes only moments.

Recent technological advances have improved overt information collection too. Intelligence officers are turning increasingly toward new computer-based information search tools (like Lexis-Nexis) and the daily reporting of information from around the world by private companies (like Oxford Analytica), along with the burgeoning use of the Internet, facsimile machines, and e-mail. Academe, business, the media, and government are busy harnessing these powerful tools of information management.[32] At the CIA, an impressive system called ROSE (Rich Open Source Environment) allows agency analysts to tap into more than two thousand full-text on-line journals, from the *African Economic Digest* to the *Yale Law Review*.

Recently a program called INTELINK, based on Internet technology, has been introduced as a means of spinning the government's secret agencies into at least a limited web of classified-information exchanges, to be supplemented eventually with access to the ROSE materials. After a number of false starts, the infrastructure for modern computer information management is growing steadily and drawing the analytic side of the secret agencies closer together than ever before. The CIA now has secure e-mail facilities to maintain contact with its stations around the world; and fax intelligence, sent over secure lines, has become a favorite means by which intelligence officers communicate with policymakers.

In spite of efforts by the intelligence agencies to keep up with technological advances in communications, close observers suggest that in some respects they have fallen behind the private business sector—and even some college dormitories—in desktop information management. Inside the State Department, for instance, the INR's e-mail system is self-contained (for security purposes). This prevents intelligence officers from sending classified e-mail to the diplomats they are supposed to support—not to mention adding to INR's sense of isolation in the building. Policy officers in the OEOB, an antiquated (if charming) structure, are similarly without secure e-mail connections to the intelligence agencies; NSC staffers must hike over to the Situation Room in the basement of the White House to read classified cable traffic. Impressive recent progress aside, the IC's communications infrastructure still has a long way to go before analysts are connected to each other, to collectors, to open-source data banks, and to the policy community in a sophisticated network of work stations.

While technology has undoubtedly made the task of information collection more efficient, human beings continue to play a vital role. The case officer engaged in HUMINT overseas must carry out the sensitive agent-recruitment operations abroad and attempt to calculate the intentions of foreign leaders.[33] For as Ephraim Kam has emphasized, an adversary's most important secrets "often exist in the mind of one man alone . . . or else they are shared by only a few top officials."[34] This kind of information is accessible, if at all, only to an intelligence officer with ties to someone inside the closed councils of the target government.

"No matter how good our technology, we'll always rely on human intelligence to tell us what an adversary has in mind," President Clinton has acknowledged. "We'll always need gifted, motivated case officers at the heart of the clandestine service. We'll always need good analysts to make a clean and clear picture out of the fragments of what our spies and satellites put on the table."[35] In the early days of tracking the Soviet target, when TECHINT was still in its infancy, HUMINT sources—even though good ones were rare—sometimes proved of great value. Colonel G. A. Tokaty-Tokaev, for example, defected to the United States in 1948 with useful information on the state of the Soviet ICBM program; and Colonel Oleg Penkovsky's espionage on behalf of the United States and Great Britain during the 1960s was an even greater windfall.

During the Carter administration the nation was reminded again of the importance of HUMINT when Iranian student militants took American diplomats hostage inside the U.S. embassy in Tehran. In planning a rescue operation, satellites could provide excellent eagle-eye pictures of Tehran but could not see inside the embassy or find precisely where the hostages were being kept. "We had a zillion shots of the roof of the embassy and they were magnified a hundred times," remembers one of the rescue planners. "We could tell you about the tiles; we could tell you about the grass and how many cars were parked there. Anything you wanted to know about the external aspects of the embassy we could tell you in infinite detail. We couldn't tell you shit about what was going on inside that building."[36]

The question of intelligence targeting further illustrates the cardinal role of the human being in matters of intelligence gathering. The most important targets for the intelligence community are those nations or factions that present a danger, or potential crisis, for the United States (so-called Tier 0 nations in current jargon). Yet while North Korea, Iraq, Iran, and other "rogue states" are easy enough to place into this category, will U.S. leaders have the sagacity to anticipate what other targets should be at the top of the list in the immediate—let alone the long term—future?

"When I became Secretary of Defense [in 1993], I served several months without ever giving Rwanda a thought," recalled Les Aspin. "Then, for several weeks, that's all I thought about. After that, it fell abruptly off the screen again and I never again thought about Rwanda."[37] Knowing where to position the nation's high-tech intelligence platforms is not a simple task, since countries have an annoying habit of leaping suddenly from Tier 4 (the outer fringes of the targeting list) to Tier 0—Grenada, Panama, Kuwait, Yugoslavia, and Somalia, among other recent "shooting stars" or "flavors of the month," as analysts call them.

Information Processing

The next step in the intelligence cycle is called processing, which involves the refinement of freshly gathered "raw"information into a form that is more easily studied by intelligence analysts. Coded data are "decrypted," foreign languages translated, and the focus of photographic material sharpened to provide maximum resolution of the imagery. Advances in technology have made a major contribution here too. State-of-the-art computer methods make foreign diplomatic codes more vulnerable to unraveling by cryptographers at the NSA and help sort out the elaborate calculations involved in converting radar images into digital data.

Here again technology rubs up against the human dimension of intelligence. The surveillance satellites—often described as gold-plated "vacuum cleaners" in the sky—yield far more data than the government has the resources to process. "The information coming down from these [satellites] is just going to choke you," laments the physicist Jerry Nelson. "You can't buy big enough computers to process it. You can't buy enough programmers to write the codes or to look at the results to interpret them. At some point you just get saturated."[38] Near the end of the Cold War the NSA reportedly processed only about 20 percent of the SIGINT it collected; recently another NSA official estimated that the figure has dropped to about 1 percent—although new techniques have improved (though by no means perfected) the NSA's ability to focus on the most important 1 percent.[39] Little wonder that a recent NSA director, Vice Admiral J. M. ("Mike") McConnell, was often heard declaiming, "I have three major problems: processing, processing, and processing."[40]

Another processing headache is language translation. The shortage of qualified linguists available to the secret agencies remains a serious deficiency, particularly with respect to the more exotic languages. Moreover, the technology to machine-read and translate texts reliably and quickly from foreign languages into English will not reach high levels of proficiency for decades—although it is reasonably good now for some limited tasks where the language is precise, such as translating Russian scientific texts.

Information Analysis

Technology has also aided the third crucial step in the intelligence cycle: analysis. At this stage the experts assess what the unevaluated intelligence actually means for the security of the United States. The objective is to produce fully interpreted intelligence based on a blend of covert collection products from all the secret agencies ("all-source intelligence") and open-source materials. The output of intelligence materials has been prodigious. In 1994, for example, the DI alone produced over thirty-five thousand intelligence reports of one kind or another, from oral briefings to encyclopedic studies.[41]

The written form of finished intelligence may be either an intelligence report or—the crown jewel of community-wide analysis—a full-blown National Intelligence Estimate (NIE). In both cases the focus may be on a single foreign country or a specific topic (say, Iraqi oil production).[42] In contrast, the intelligence product may also consist of short, up-to-the-minute reports known as "current intelligence." These can take the form of special intelligence reports (crisp, highly focused papers no longer than three pages), intelligence memoranda (five to seven pages), or, in sharply abbreviated form ("in-briefs"), one to several paragraphs in the prestigious *PDB* or one of several other intelligence "newspapers."

According to a recent unclassified CIA document, "hundreds of reports derived from SIGINT, imagery, and human sources are sent to consumers [policy officers] and other producers [fellow analysts] each day."[43] Interviews with intelligence managers conducted in 1994 indicate that a majority of the papers written by the DI are foreign leadership analyses, chiefly personality profiles of political and military elites.

For decisionmakers, the favorite product from among this extensive menu is no doubt current intelligence. "Research reports [like the lengthy NIEs] work their way from the in-box to the burn bag unread," concludes an INR analyst ruefully. Why? "Because consumers don't have time to read them," the analyst continues. "The demands today are for the quick report and the quick answer—'bumper sticker' or 'time-bite' intelligence."[44] This same analyst reports that at INR the number of extensive research papers has plummeted over the past decade from 250–300 to just fifteen a year.

Some policy officers prefer "reports" that are briefer still: the raw intelligence alone. "I would ask for some of the raw data which was behind the reports," Dean Rusk once recalled, "so I could make my own check."[45] At the NSC staff level a former senior aide has said, "When I wanted intelligence, I went straight to the Sit [Situation] Room and read the raw cable traffic coming in from overseas."[46]

Other policymakers prefer not to read any intelligence whatsoever, raw or evaluated; they rely instead on spoken communication. Commenting on the widespread use of oral intelligence briefings, Allen E. Goodman of Georgetown University wryly remarks that among policymakers, "some don't read, some won't read, and some can't read."[47] About one-third of the "products" created by DI analysts are oral briefings[48]—mainly presented to policy officers in the executive branch but increasingly to members of Congress as well. Now and then the briefings are delivered on the run down the corridors of power, as VIPs rush to the next meeting, or in the back seats of limousines on the way to Washington National Airport.

The oral briefing, despite its obvious shortcomings, plays a vital part in the intelligence cycle. "Estimation is more an oral than a written process," a chairman of the National Intelligence Council (NIC) has explained. "It starts with oral contacts between NIOs [National Intelligence Officers, senior analysts in the intelligence community assigned to the NIC] and policy makers, to find out what's on the policy maker's mind. Then it can take various written forms: an NIE, a two-page update on an earlier NIE, a short NIC memo of two or three pages. And it ends in an oral process, with the NIO briefing the policy maker on the key conclusions, because they're probably not going to have read the written report."[49]

Intelligence managers value the oral briefing highly—unlike many analysts, who prefer the opportunity to work on carefully nuanced written papers that display their expertise and allow them more room to hedge. "The situation we find the best," declares a former CIA manager, "is . . . when one of our substantive officers sees the president every day for a period, however brief, to get the intelligence [to the decisionmaker] and receive his reaction to it, including tasking for the next day."[50] This way the intelligence manager knows for certain that the product has reached the intended consumer instead of the circular file, and he or she can learn immediately what information the policymaker— ideally, the president—wants next.

Gerald R. Ford and, even more so, George Bush accepted this approach, for the most part. Some presidents, though, have refused oral briefings, preferring short written summations. Richard Nixon cut off DCI Richard Helms from the Oval Office after the director had enjoyed good access during the Johnson presidency; Helms remembers Nixon as "the ultimate loner."[51] Ronald Reagan, a former screen star, showed an enthusiasm for intelligence presented on videotape. Whether current intelligence, raw intelligence, oral briefings, or intelligence "movies," the declining emphasis on in-depth research holds a danger for the future. The intellectual resources stored by the secret agencies may simply dry up. "Long-term research is putting money into the bank," says former DCI Robert M. Gates; "current analysis is taking money out of the bank."[52]

By all accounts the secret agencies provide some of the best forums in the government for the analysis of international events. According to one experienced government official, "Intelligence analysts—essentially DI analysts—do 90 per cent of the analysis of the USG [United States Government] on foreign affairs."[53]

Further, regardless of all the help that machines have provided in manipulating data and crafting eye-catching graphic displays, the analytic process remains vitally dependent on the experience and intellectual abilities of the men and women preparing the written reports and delivering the oral briefings. Yet, does the analyst have the requisite skills to make accurate forecasts? Are the right experts available to give a full and timely response to the policymaker's request for an assessment of some foreign event? How deep-keeled is the analyst's knowledge of the country, or the circumstance, he or she is attempting to evaluate? Too few analysts have spent adequate recent time in the countries they are expected to understand. How many intelligence officers preparing reports for the NSC have lived in Somalia or Rwanda, Haiti or Iraq?

Moreover, the analytic process is replete with disputes over which of several competitive interpretations of "the facts" ought to be forwarded to the next level of the bureaucracy before going on to the White House. In the formal estimating process by which NIEs are produced, analysts have an opportunity (if their managers see fit) to register their dissent in the form of a footnote or, during the Clinton administration, in the text itself. Technology plays a role here too, as Lawrence Freedman shows. "As a profession, intelligence analysts are dedicated empiricists with a shared respect for certain types of 'hard' evidence, sufficient to force them to acknowledge it even if it contradicts strongly-held beliefs," he writes. "Such evidence is that which comes from technical collection programs, such as radar and satellites. Other evidence will have varying degrees of 'softness' and its reliability may be disputed. . . . The more estimators have to guess, speculate, infer, induce and conjecture in order to reach a conclusion, the greater the possibility of open disagreement."[54]

Most troubling is when the DCI or another manager decides to bury the work of an analyst because he finds his own interpretation of events more compelling, or because he hopes to curry favor with the White House by providing "intelligence to please." At times the DCI has been an ideologue who wants the intelligence community to shape its interpretations to match his own worldview. Robert Gates has testified that as deputy DCI he watched his boss, William J. Casey, "on issue after issue sit in meetings and present intelligence framed in terms of the policy he wanted pursued."[55]

For the most part, though, DCIs—like the analysts below them in the intelligence hierarchy—have exercised a professionalism that wards off temptations to distort intelligence. "Know the truth and the truth shall make you free" is the CIA's motto, and it is taken seriously by virtually all of the men and women who enter the analytic side of the profession. Thus, the recommendation of a well-regarded former DDCI is valid most of the time: "You have to have faith that the CIA's professionals are strong enough to make straight calls."[56]

Information Dissemination

Technology has had a major effect as well on the last phase of the intelligence cycle: the dissemination of information to the policy officer—the consumer of intelligence. Stewart A. Baker, a former intelligence official, is not alone in his conclusion that from Pearl Harbor on, "the intelligence failures that hurt the worst have not been those of collection but rather those of dissemination."[57]

To start with a positive case, Operation Desert Storm in 1991 provides a vivid example of swift and reliable intelligence support to the consumer. American surveillance satellites sensed the Iraqi anti-aircraft radar the moment it was activated and relayed that information rapidly to waiting fighter pilots and cruise-missile commanders. The word soon spread in Baghdad that it was suicidal to flip the "on" switch inside a radar facility, as moments later the person at the switch would be annihilated by American F-117 aircraft or self-propelled Tomahawk cruise missiles.

The "dissemination architecture" for intelligence during the Persian Gulf War was by no means flawless, however. In the field the military had fourteen different kinds of receiving devices for incoming intelligence, only two of which were compatible.[58] This lack of battlefield "connectivity" no doubt contributed to the frustrations later vented by General Schwarzkopf, who was unquestionably correct in this postmortem: "We just don't have an immediately responsive [imagery] intelligence capability that will give the theater commander near-real-time information that he personally needs to make a decision."[59]

In the aftermath of the Gulf War, General James R. Clapper, Jr., the talented DIA director, concentrated his attention on making improvements in the dissemination of battlefield intelligence. His objective was the "prompt delivery to all combat commanders, regardless of echelon, of the 'pictures, not reports' they tell us are essential to accomplishing their mission."[60] High-tech planners in the intelligence community foresee a time in the near future when all satellite and aircraft IMINT and SIGINT will be downlinked to vans in the backlines of the battlefield, where the processing and dissemination of data will be carried out close to the soldiers—not back in Washington. In General Clapper's vision, "the ultimate ideal is to have a constant God's-eye view of the battlefield. Anywhere, anytime, all the time."[61] One must wonder, however, about the practicality—not to mention the expense—of staring down on Earth as if one were God.

Whatever its shortcomings, the flow of information from sensor-to-soldier during Operation Desert Storm set a new benchmark for intelligence achievement in support of the fighting men and women. Indeed, the dissemination of information to distant battlefields has proven easier in some respects than across the few miles that separate the intelligence agencies from the White House and the National Security Council.

INFORMATION AND THE POINT OF DECISION

At some point a decision must be made. Until then, technology contributes mightily to the production of the richest stream of information, laced with secrets, ever enjoyed by a nation's leaders. At the moment of decision, however, statecraft becomes paramount, and all the sophisticated technology of a modern superpower is to little avail.

As officials prepare to deliberate on foreign policy, often they are too busy to absorb new information (let alone deep analysis); or their ideological lenses may distort the information that does reach them. Sometimes the problem is mutual ignorance: the intelligence officer is unsure what the decisionmaker really wants, and the decisionmaker is unaware of what the intelligence officer has to offer. As a former government official recalls, when he was on the NSC staff in 1989–90, he "did not read a single [National Intelligence] Estimate. Not one." He explains why: "DI analysts did not have the foggiest notion of what I did, and I did not have a clue as to what they could or should do."[62] Only years later, as a participant in arms control negotiations (a CIA forte), did he discover how a close working relationship with intelligence officers could prove beneficial.

Among the hazards found at the intersection between information dissemination and decision is the trap of intelligence to please—the politicization or "cooking" of intelligence, in which the facts are slanted to suit the political needs of the current administration. As DCI, Richard Helms reportedly changed an estimate on Soviet military intentions at the urging of a Nixon administration official. He is said to have gone along with the Pentagon's position on Soviet first-strike preparations, despite contrary views among analysts within the CIA, because "an assistant to [Secretary of Defense Melvin] Laird

Meanings and Methods

informed Helms that the [views of the CIA's analysts] contradicted the public position of the Secretary."[63]

As a result of intimidation, good information sometimes never even makes it to the table where decisions are made in Washington. "Nothing permeates the Cabinet Room more strongly than the smell of hierarchy," Peter Wyden remarks in his study of why DI analysts capitulated to the views of more senior government officials during deliberations over the proposed Bay of Pigs operation in 1961.[64] Policymakers in the Kennedy administration and their allies in the CIA's Operations Directorate (some of whom enjoyed the advantage of a Georgetown *bon vivant* relationship with the president) were so intent on toppling Castro that DI analysts convinced themselves that any discouraging prognostications—and they had more than a few—would not only have been fatuous but would also have been sharply resented and would have threatened their careers.

According to an expert on organizational behavior, this tendency to "*get along* with others and *go along* with the system is preferred [in all government bureaucracies]."[65] Steve Chan has discerned this conformist instinct inside the secret agencies. "Like other bureaucrats, intelligence analysts have to conform to the regime's basic views about the nature and morality of international relations if they wish to be treated as 'responsible' and 'serious,'" he writes. "Therefore, they refrain from asking the really 'tough' but crucial questions such as [during the Cold War] the aggressiveness of the Soviet Union, the morality of the Vietnam War, and the validity of the 'domino theory.'"[66]

The attempt to ensure that policy officers appreciate and understand information provided to them by the intelligence agencies, without misperceiving or otherwise distorting its meaning, presents another challenge. At times those in power will embrace intelligence only if it conveniently corresponds to their existing beliefs and ideologies, rejecting the rest. They quickly learn, observes a former INR director, "that intelligence can be used the way a drunk uses a lamppost . . . for support rather than illumination."[67]

The Eisenhower administration reportedly discouraged any assessments from the intelligence community "as to Soviet policy motivation that departed from the implicit stereotypical cold war consensus"—especially the hardline stance advocated by Secretary of State John Foster Dulles.[68] Former DDI Dr. Ray S. Cline has chronicled the unwillingness of the Johnson and Nixon administrations to accept the CIA's discouraging reports on the likelihood of an American victory in the Vietnam War.[69]

The rejection of objective intelligence became particularly controversial during the Reagan administration. The White House is said to have dismissed the conclusions of intelligence analysts who called into question the administration's views: that Syria was merely a puppet of the Soviet Union, or that Nicaragua aggressively exported arms to Marxist guerrillas throughout Central America; that a Soviet oil pipeline to Western Europe would significantly increase the vulnerability of U.S. allies to Soviet pressure; that the shooting down of a South Korean passenger airline in 1983 was an intentional murder of civilian passengers rather than a mistake made by a Soviet fighter pilot who thought it was a spyplane; and that the assassination plot against Pope John Paul II in 1984 had been concocted in Moscow.[70]

The danger of distortion by policymakers is thought to be greatest with political intelligence. On technical matters—military weapons and other "difficult" scientific or economic subjects—the policymaker is more inclined to accept the judgment of intelligence experts. "Hardware [weapons] estimates . . . have traditionally been first in acceptance and impact," reports an intelligence official.[71]

Wishful thinking is another form of self-delusion that can cause a policy officer to ignore or distort intelligence. A senior CIA officer likes to tell of the man who bought an expensive new barometer. He took it home only to discover the needle was stuck on "Hurricane," yet there had not been a hurricane for years in his part of the country, and it was perfectly sunny outside. He shook the barometer gingerly and tapped on the facing. No movement. The man sat down at his desk and wrote a scathing letter of rebuke to the manufacturer. Then he left home on a trip. When he returned, the barometer was gone. So was his house.

Ego defense further complicates the use of intelligence. James Thomson's reflections on decisionmaking during the Vietnam War emphasize "the central fact of *human ego investment*. Men who have participated in a decision develop a stake in that decision. As they participate in further, related decisions, their stake increases."[72] Fresh intelligence assessments that call into question their basic views are unlikely to be well received by individuals in leadership roles— especially when they may have already sent thousands of soldiers to an early grave to implement their policies. Yaacov Vertzberger's analysis of India's failure to anticipate a 1962 Chinese invasion concludes similarly: "The need to prove methodically, all through the period in question, that the policy pursued had been the right one, and that the level of aspirations had been realized, made it necessary [for Indian policymakers] to ignore any information that contradicted this."[73]

Even if no distortion of information occurs, have a nation's leaders sufficient time to evaluate carefully the implications of the reports placed before them by the intelligence agencies? A profile of Secretary of Defense Caspar W.

Weinberger, who served in the Reagan administration, reported him "swamped," "overwhelmed," "left with not enough time to think forward."[74] Another study of the highest decision echelons in America during the Vietnam War found widespread "executive fatigue," which had a deadening effect on "freshness of thought, imagination, a sense of possibility and perspective. . . . The tired policy maker becomes a prisoner of his own narrowed view of the world and his own cliched rhetoric."[75] Not exactly a hospitable environment for the absorption of fresh intelligence insights.

Time's winged chariot pulls leaders toward brief forms of current intelligence, as seen in a description of the intelligence cycle offered by a former head of the NIC. "[The analyst must] mine the great lode of outside material, compress it, add the clandestine nuggets, and put it in a form that is usable to policy makers. If you can't get it to them in three pages or three minutes, they're not going to get it."[76]

Perhaps nothing so underscores the importance of the human dimension in the making of foreign policy decisions as the fragile relationship between the producer and the consumer of intelligence. Dialogue, rapport, trust—here are the girders that attempt to bridge the gap between the technology-driven intelligence cycle and the deeply human point of decision. Ambassador Robert D. Blackwill advocates this widely endorsed prescription: "The key [to the success of intelligence] is getting close enough to the individual policy maker to find out what he needs."[77]

No doubt many a fine analytic report has died in the in-box simply because the requisite bonds of trust had never been established between the worlds of the intelligence officer and the policymaker. A balance between the two can be hard to achieve, though, because in establishing rapport the intelligence officer must at the same time avoid the trap of intelligence to please—the politicization of intelligence, the unforgivable sin.

Every nation—large or small, rich or poor—faces these intelligence/decision traps. What can be done to avoid them? The answer has roots in ancient philosophy: select leaders (and intelligence officers) imbued with wisdom and a love of truth—the human virtues, which continue to lag far behind our technological achievements.

The nation's secret agencies are but one source of information competing for the ear of the policy officer.[78] Friends and confidants, television news, radio talk shows, influential newspapers, lobbying groups, opinion polls, public and private pronouncements of foreign leaders, even at times astrologers—this information stream that feeds into the government is wide and deep.

Intelligence from the secret agencies can be a dominant current in this stream, notably on matters where they enjoy special access to covert information and can proffer a unique, synergistic mix of SIGINT, IMINT, MASINT, and HUMINT. With respect to weapons proliferation, terrorism, or events inside closed regimes, the clandestine services often have more reliable intelligence (based on covert sources inside an adversary's government) than the media or academe. On other occasions the reverse may be true. "Determining the situation in Rwanda [in 1994] was best ascertained from the people on the scene," writes a former NRO director. "Analyzing its significance and its relevance in that part of the world was best accomplished by scholars and others dedicated to understanding that society and that area, not members of the current intelligence community, which was developed to address quite different cultures."[79]

The secret agencies are likely to be considered by some policymakers a national asset of the highest order, but most think of them simply as one of many tributaries feeding the information stream—sometimes helpful, sometimes not. And for a few—usually those who have never taken the time to discover the value of intelligence—the secret government will be discounted altogether, as if its bed had run dry, leaving nothing to offer that could not be found in the nation's best newspapers.

CHAPTER 2

THE EVOLUTION OF THE INTELLIGENCE MISSIONS

In the aftermath of the Cold War some critics have called for a dismantling of the CIA; others have insisted that the world is more dangerous than ever and the United States must, if anything, strengthen its intelligence capabilities.[1] How have intelligence missions—long driven by an anti-Soviet raison d'être—changed since America's archnemesis vanished?

To measure changes, one must first establish a baseline of the essential features of the intelligence community during the Cold War. Among the most important features to consider are the Community's choice of missions, its structural permutations, its budgets and staffing, its relationship to supervisory bodies (accountability), and its ties to outside interest groups.

Gaining access to this information can be a daunting task. It becomes necessary to settle for a more qualitative methodology, and a lower level of precision, than one would prefer. Interviews with authoritative sources must be carefully cross-referenced, and the limited (but growing) documentary evidence on intelligence policy available in the public domain must be finely sifted. Despite the methodological difficulties, the importance of intelligence as an instrument of American foreign policy is substantial enough to seek an understanding of its activities as they have evolved since the Second World War. This inquiry begins with a look at the intelligence community's core missions during the Cold War.

The primary purpose behind the establishment of the Central Intelligence Agency was to improve the gathering, assessment, and coordination of information about foreign threats and opportunities facing the United States—the bedrock mission of collection and analysis. The CIA also immediately embraced a second mission, counterintelligence; and the National Security Council soon turned to the CIA to carry out covert actions as well—the most provocative mission.[2] What have been the intelligence community's priorities with respect to each of these primary missions during the Cold War years? The approximate trends are presented in figures 2.1 and 2.2.[3]

Collection and Analysis

A tracing of the collection-and-analysis mission during the Cold War requires four lines: two that track the emphasis placed on the collection of information (one for HUMINT and another for TECHINT), a third for analysis, and a fourth for the important managerial task of coordinating and disseminating the information to policymakers. For the most part the lines in the graph arc upward during the Cold War years, but at different rates.

Figure 2.1 Mission Priorities: Collection and Analysis

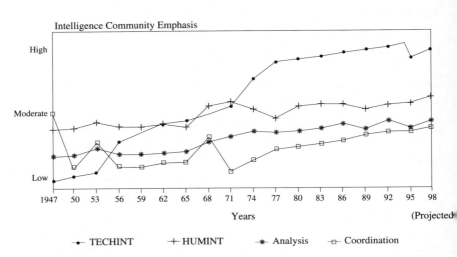

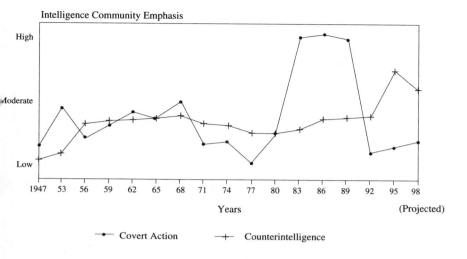

Figure 2.2 Mission Priorities: Counterintelligence and Covert Action

The collection task is captured in a fluctuating line of moderate emphasis for HUMINT and a rising slope for TECHINT, reflecting the intelligence community's technological breakthroughs with aerial reconnaissance and satellite surveillance in the mid-1950s and early 1960s. The TECHINT line steepens dramatically with additional technological innovations in the 1970s and 1980s.

The U-2 spy plane made its first flight over Soviet territory in 1956. Its valuable photography of Soviet missile sites came to a temporary end in 1960 with the shootdown of the plane piloted by Francis Gary Powers. In that same year, however, the United States placed its first reliable surveillance satellite in space, and by 1962 the KEYHOLE satellites had begun to provide vital imagery of targets formerly covered by the U-2.

Human espionage—less impressive to some intelligence managers than shiny, expensive machines and plagued by the risk of double agentry—lagged behind TECHINT during most of the Cold War. Exceptions include the intelligence community's earliest years, when TECHINT was in its infancy, and the brief tilting of resources toward HUMINT that occurred during the Vietnam War buildup and then under DCI William J. Casey, who throughout the Reagan years pursued his strong interest in classic espionage.

Thus, during the Cold War the intelligence community engaged in a steady expansion of its technical surveillance capabilities, accompanied by a more fitful allocation of resources to human agents.[4] As the number of nations increased because of the demise of colonial empires, so did the number of mechanical and sentient intelligence gatherers deployed by the secret agencies against them. When the United States found itself engaged in overt warfare abroad (in Korea and Vietnam), the collection of intelligence—both technical and human—intensified in the theaters of combat.[5] Technological innovations spawned an accelerated deployment of sophisticated hardware, especially for the purpose of achieving from a distant, more secure location in the stratosphere an accurate count of Soviet military units, rocketry, and warheads.

The emphasis on analysis has been similar to that on HUMINT, although analysis consistently trailed behind human collection (see figure 2.1).[6] And although the number of CIA analysts has grown at a steady rate, the progression has remained far behind the attention devoted to technical collection. As with HUMINT, it has been easier to sell budget officials on the stunning collection capabilities of satellites and spy planes than it has on the less glamorous job of analyzing what the stream of information actually means.

That human "assets" (an intelligence term of art for agents or spies) were granted much greater emphasis than analysts during most of the Cold War years reflects in part the dominant culture inside the intelligence community (and especially the CIA's influential Operations Directorate) that favors the clandestine side of the intelligence business—spying and aggressive covert actions abroad—over the office-bound writing of reports. "Ph.D. intelligence" was a favorite term of derision applied to CIA analysts privately by J. Edgar Hoover, the crusty director of the FBI from 1924 to 1972.[7] Even inside the CIA, several of its earliest leaders were drawn more to the brawny action officer overseas who recruited agents and (at least in the mythology) scaled walls at midnight with a dagger in his teeth. Action prevailed over erudition in the war against communism.

Moreover, HUMINT has proven itself over the years an indispensable contributor of vital information for policy officers. As reported by a senior staffer on the House Permanent Select Committee on Intelligence (HPSCI), a series of recent strategic intelligence reviews (still classified) indicate that with respect to 376 specific intelligence issues HUMINT made a "critical" contribution to 205.[8] Many of the intelligence consumers I interviewed professed a greater interest in raw intelligence than in finished reports, and they valued HUMINT, SIGINT, and IMINT about equally (though for some subjects—such as the economic activities of adversaries—imagery has only limited use).

Still, the Community's Ph.D.-toting interpreters of intelligence are considered extremely helpful by many policymakers, and their assessments have informed decisionmaking in such vital areas as trade policy and arms control. In 1991 Robert M. Gates became the first professional intelligence analyst selected for the position of director of central intelligence.

The coordination aspect of the collection-and-analysis mission began in 1947 with a fairly high level of commitment to improved intelligence management. Better coordination, after all, was a key reason for establishing a modern intelligence community headed by a *central* intelligence agency in the first place. One of the five functions assigned to the newborn CIA by the National Security Act of 1947 was (as Richard Snyder and Edgar Furniss put it) "to make recommendations to the [NSC] for the coordination of [intelligence] activities"; another was "to correlate and evaluate national security intelligence and to circulate the results"; and a third was "to perform services for existing agencies which are best done centrally."[9] This conception of a strong centralizing role for the CIA was, however, soon dashed on the shoals of interagency rivalry, as decentralization—fragmentation, critics would contend—became the hallmark of the intelligence community.

Following this jarring reality of bureaucratic turf protection, the best that the series of seventeen DCIs have been able to achieve from 1947 to 1995 is a slow movement toward greater centralization (see figure 2.1). Until near the end of the Cold War, coordination was a value that remained underemphasized by the DCI and the Community—largely because the military intelligence agencies and the FBI so firmly and skillfully resisted most proposals for increased centralization that emanated from the Office of the DCI through the years. Indeed, in 1995, the FBI threatened to establish its own empire of agents overseas to fight against international crime—the most blatant challenge to the DCI's authority over secret foreign operations since the beginning of the modern intelligence establishment.

Observers uniformly acknowledge this basic fact: American intelligence agencies have been plagued by internal and external dissension, a result not only of differences in bureaucratic cultures (the analyst "scholars" versus the covert-action "cowboys" inside the CIA, for example) but also of ambiguous chains of command throughout the Community. The DCI is supposedly in charge of all the intelligence agencies, though he soon discovers that the secretary of defense and the chairman of the Joint Chiefs of Staff can be muscular rivals on matters of military intelligence—some 80–95 percent of the overall intelligence budget (depending on how one counts some programs that straddle the strategic/tactical demarcation line).

Overcoming these centrifugal forces has been difficult for every DCI, despite responsibility for Community-wide leadership. The movement toward more centralized authority under the DCI advanced at glacial speed during the Cold War years, according to the interests and managerial skills of individual DCIs and the degree of resistance posed by powerful bureaucratic rivals like the secretary of defense and the FBI director. The trend toward coordination accelerated most rapidly in the last few years of the Cold War. The chiefs of the various intelligence agencies—the "program directors," as they are known in the Community—began to respond to looming budget constraints and criticism from Capitol Hill about excessive duplication by cooperating more with the DCI toward melding some Community-wide intelligence activities (such as sharing intelligence on counterterrorism).

Counterintelligence

In the early days of the intelligence community few officials paid much attention to the counterintelligence (CI) mission. It is an arcane chore devoid of glamour, relying on the tedious study of archival materials in search of clues to false defectors and moles inside the secret agencies. In contrast, the prospect of building and directing big-ticket collection platforms attracted some of the most ambitious talents in the Community. Within the CIA's Operations Directorate the chance to supervise ("handle") HUMINT collection agents and run covert actions promised travel, adventure, and rapid promotion.

In 1954, though, DCI Allen Dulles instantly gave stature to this lackluster mission by appointing James Angleton as the CIA's Chief of Counterintelligence.[10] Angleton was an experienced intelligence officer who had served in the OSS during World War Two. Just as important, he had attended the proper Ivy League schools and enjoyed close social ties with Washington's spymasters and foreign policy elites.

Yet despite the advantages that Angleton brought to the counterintelligence corps, under his leadership it became the victim of a paradox. His unassailable credentials initially elevated respect for the CI Staff throughout the CIA and beyond, and brought a greater commitment of resources to the CI mission at the highest levels. At the same time, however, Angleton's tight managerial control—not to say paranoia—over the security of "his" CI files led to a monastic sequestering of this mission within an isolated suite of offices at CIA headquarters. Until Angleton's dismissal from the Agency in 1974, the CI Staff remained a closed clique, criticized by insiders for its aloofness and excessive suspicion of Soviet penetrations inside the secret agencies.[11]

In the immediate post-Angleton phase of counterintelligence, the spy-catching mission underwent a devolution. Files and authority were dispersed across the geographical desks within the Operations Directorate. The new philosophy, advocated by DCI William E. Colby, was one of sharing counterintelligence data throughout the CIA and the larger intelligence community on a need-to-know basis. What good was it to have information about suspected moles if no one inside the secret agencies had access to it?

Along with a dismantling of Angleton's inner sanctum came an expansion of the counterintelligence corps. The CIA, for instance, trained a fresh cadre of CI officers for service in stations overseas, not just within the confines of the CI Staff at headquarters. From his forced retirement Angleton railed against this "disastrous breach of security."[12] For him, the idea of dispersing counterintelligence files outside the offices of the CI Staff seriously undermined the vaunted doctrine of compartmentation: sensitive information about suspected moles could fall into the wrong hands, perhaps tipping off the Soviet spies themselves before they were apprehended. Moreover, in his view, the typical case officer was ill-equipped to understand the intricacies of counterintelligence, for it took decades of study to master the minute telltale signs of treachery.

A rough graph of the commitment of the intelligence community leadership to the counterintelligence mission during the Cold War shows a line that rises slowly at first, as the CIA and its companion agencies organized themselves, then climbs sharply with Angleton's appointment (see figure 2.2). Commitment to the mission rises slowly during the Cold War as Angleton consolidates his position and expands his operations, then levels out and declines somewhat as his reclusive and often accusatory managerial style begins to alienate colleagues in other branches of the Agency and throughout the Community.

With Angleton's unceremonious ousting in 1974, counterintelligence experienced an overall decline in status and operational support (despite some new staff positions) as it underwent dilution and absorption into other CIA divisions. The post-Angleton phase of counterintelligence eventually climbed out of its trough, aided by the Reagan administration's attention to the CI mission. (The Reagan intelligence transition team included a number of Angleton devotees who consulted with the former CI chief on a regular basis.)[13] Under DCIs William J. Casey (1981–87) and William H. Webster (1987–91) the counterintelligence pendulum swung back toward the principle of centralization.

This movement accelerated in 1985—the so-called "Year of the Spy"—when America suffered a rash of espionage scandals (Pelton, Pollard, Howard, the Walker family) that indicated troubling weaknesses in U.S. counterintelligence.[14] In 1986 Casey created a Counterterrorism Center (CTC), and in 1987 Webster started up a Counternarcotics Center (CNC). In 1988 Webster took the additional step of establishing a Counterintelligence Center (CIC). The purpose of these new entities was to coordinate counterthreat responsibilities throughout the government, though without the black-hole concentration of CI files advocated by Angleton. Ironically, this increased attention to a more integrated defense against foreign threats began just three years before the Cold War ended.

Covert Action

Within the intelligence community, support for covert action (CA) during the era of U.S.-Soviet rivalry accelerated from the very beginning in 1947 to the height of the Vietnam War in 1968–71, then declined for a decade before a dramatic resurgence in prestige during the Reagan years (see figure 2.2). Within months of its creation the CIA became the instrument of choice for national security officials in search of a hidden means to influence the outcome of foreign events.[15] The war in Korea boosted the CA mission on the list of the government's priorities. As John Ranelagh reports, "because of the Korean War, covert operations [meaning "covert actions" in this instance] increased sixteenfold between January 1951 and January 1953," and the personnel assigned to the mission doubled.[16] Despite the fiasco at the Bay of Pigs in 1961, the DCI—and America's presidents—continued to be beguiled by the prospect of a secret quick fix to U.S. foreign policy headaches.[17]

The CIA could point to successes that offset the Bay of Pigs disaster, among them support for political parties and labor unions in Europe against Communist encroachment in the early days of the Cold War, along with successful coups in Iran (1953) and Guatemala (1954).[18] Moreover, for former OSS officers molded in the crucible of global warfare, covert action was the ultimate in anti-Communist escapades. Together with college recruits eager to save the world from Joseph Stalin, they rigged elections, blanketed the world with anti-Communist propaganda, staged labor strikes, blew up power plants, mined harbors, guided secret combat, and concocted assassination plots. Here was gallant duty.

Inside the Operations Directorate the budget of the covert action staff (CAS) soared as this mission attracted many of the CIA's most energetic officers. Covert action soon became the tail that wagged the intelligence dog.[19] Without mention in the intelligence community's founding legislation, covert action had by the late 1960s corralled most of the Community's interest, energy, and operational funds.[20] The clandestine officers and their native mercenaries waged a hidden World War Three against Communist forces—most notably the North Vietnamese and their allies in the National Liberation Front ("Viet Cong").

Then came a precipitous slide for the "quiet option," brought about chiefly by a souring of the war in Vietnam, government spending cuts instituted by the Nixon administration, tentative overtures of detente with the USSR, and a series of scandals that raised doubts about the propriety of America's involvement in secret "dirty tricks" abroad. Most conspicuous among the scandals that turned many members of Congress against covert action were the CIA's attempts to prevent the election and then undermine the presidency of Salvador Allende in Chile, as well as a series of assassination plots against of heads of state.[21]

One high-ranking intelligence official (now deceased) believed that the Ford administration was chiefly responsible for administering the coup de grâce to covert action in 1975. "The White House under Gerald Ford finally said [with respect to the investigating committee led by Senator Frank Church], 'Oh, well, let the Committee have what it wants so we can avoid a flap'" that might have accompanied a protracted fight with the Congress over access to the CIA's top-secret documents on assassination plots. "The effect was to bring covert action to a screeching halt."[22]

Interest in covert action as a policy option resumed late in the presidency of Jimmy Carter, after the Soviet invasion of Afghanistan in 1979. If the Soviets were going to behave like bullies, the thinking went, then the United States would have to fight back, though without engaging in overt warfare that might risk a world war.[23]

Attention to the quiet option expanded strikingly during the next administration as a means for carrying out the so-called Reagan Doctrine of opposing Communist-supported wars of liberation in the developing world.[24] William Casey shifted the attention of the intelligence community (and especially the CIA) toward defeating the Soviets in Afghanistan, the Sandinistas in Nicaragua, and other Communists (real and suspected) wherever they might appear—from El Salvador to Cambodia. When Congress balked at the zealotry of the covert actions in Nicaragua, the administration arranged for financial support of the contras outside the government, neatly bypassing the appropriations process and therefore the Constitution.

Although George Bush has acknowledged that he found covert action useful, its emphasis in the intelligence community went into a downward slide during the latter days of his presidency, leveling out at around 1 percent of the Community's total funding.[25] From its place of dominance in the anti-Communist crusade, covert action had declined to a level of near disregard by the end of the Cold War. Even though President Bush used covert action far less than his predecessor, it still played a greater role in foreign policy throughout most of his administration than it had during the early years of the Carter administration—the low point in emphasis since the very beginning of modern covert action in 1947. With President Bill Clinton covert action revived modestly as a means for aiding newly democratic regimes (Haiti, for instance) and making life difficult for weapons proliferators, terrorists, and drug dealers.

STRUCTURE

American intelligence facilities at home and abroad, as well as the internal organization of the secret agencies, make up the intelligence community's structure—the hierarchical wiring diagrams of Washington's secret government. Buildings and floor space provide one of the most tangible measures of growth for any organization. The CIA provides an illustration.

From its first headquarters in a stately neoclassical building atop a hill across the street from the State Department (with additional barracks-like offices along the Reflecting Pool) the CIA moved to an impressive new building in Langley in 1961—a manifestation of DCI Allen Dulles's clout in the Eisenhower administration (where his brother, John Foster Dulles, served as secretary of state). The number of CIA stations abroad housed in American embassies expanded rapidly under Dulles. This physical growth leveled off during the early 1960s, with some incremental expansion as the birth of a new nation somewhere in the world would lead to the opening of a new U.S. embassy sheltering a new CIA station.

The Langley headquarters changed little during the Cold War years, not only in physical capacity but also in terms of its internal structure—at least until near the end of the U.S.-Soviet standoff. The Agency's five basic units remained the Office of the DCI and four subordinate directorates: Science and Technology (DS&T), Operations (DO), Intelligence (DI), and Administration (DA).

The names of some CIA organizational units have changed, and fluctuations have occurred in their funding and status. But not until the tenures of DCIs Casey and Webster during the Reagan administration did the Agency significantly expand its physical facilities and begin to experiment with meaningful internal structural reforms. The physical expansion consisted of a sprawling new second headquarters building behind the original one—a modern edifice of steel and green-tinted glass completed in 1989, with a bronze tribute in the foyer celebrating its chief fundraiser, DCI Casey.

The primary internal reforms included a new—and, it would prove, short-lived—Directorate for Planning (1988–92), initiated by DCI Webster, and a series of interagency "fusion centers," at first for counterterrorism, counternarcotics, and counterintelligence, later for nonproliferation. (All were preceded by a centralizing prototype, though it was never called a "center": the DCI's Arms Control Intelligence Staff, established in 1985.) The new centers are housed at the CIA and a majority of their professional staffs are made up of Agency officers; nevertheless, they represent a good-faith effort by recent DCIs and the CIA to reach out to the government's other intelligence agencies in pursuit of better interagency coordination.

One of the more radical moves toward greater cohesion inside the CIA was the creation under DCI Woolsey of a "partnership" between DI analysts and DO operatives. These once-separate cultures—thinkers and doers—now have officers who sit together in the same suites of offices to focus on a specific country or region. Personnel from the two directorates used to shut one another out of their work spaces with special combination locks; now they confer side-by-side, sharing views on collection priorities and analysis. The analysts can now directly tell the HUMINT managers precisely what kinds of information they need, and the DO staff can contribute their extensive overseas experience to the writing of intelligence assessments.

The danger in this partnership is that the purity of the DI's tradition of objective reporting might be contaminated by the action-oriented DO officer with a stake in attracting policy support for operations overseas. Thus far this seems not to have happened, and the partnership idea has been successful enough to have managers thinking about including SIGINT and IMINT analysts on the teams.

The centers represent the most ambitious effort to achieve Community-wide intelligence fusion, at least on some topics. A glimpse inside the Nonproliferation Center (NPC) provides a sense of how they operate. The NPC, established initially in September 1991 and (after a stumbling start) given added authority in April 1992, sprang from a realization among policymakers in the wake of the Persian Gulf War that they needed better information on those like Iraq's Saddam Hussein who might threaten to produce nuclear weapons and other weapons of mass destruction. An added incentive was the belief held by DCI Robert M. Gates (1991–93) that the government agencies working on nonproliferation issues were far too fragmented. The political ethos of downsizing that swept Washington early in the Clinton administration also demanded elimination of inefficiencies through a pooling of resources across the Community.

The NPC is composed of a multidisciplinary corps of officers from the various intelligence agencies. The CIA's dominance, though, has led to criticism from some of the other elements of the Community—particularly from military intelligence, which wants the NPC to be more sensitive to its tactical battlefield needs, not just supplying information for American diplomats attending international conferences on arms control. Initially only 12 percent of NPC personnel came from outside the CIA. That figure rose to 25 percent in 1994, though, and the NPC's goal is to reach 40 percent non-CIA staff by 1997.

According to its director, Gordon Oehler (one of the government's top analysts), the NPC's primary usefulness lies in the strategic direction it can provide to the Community's nonproliferation activities. It also serves as a focal point for accountability over the government's operations in this policy domain.[26] Toward this end Oehler has established a comprehensive TECHINT and HUMINT targeting list and has brought closer coordination ("fusing") to all phases of the nonproliferation intelligence effort, from the collection of information through its analysis and dissemination. The NPC's major weakness is apparent in the final step: trying, without much authority, to coordinate the action phase of government operations designed to curb proliferation. Still, with NPC assistance the United States has been able to interdict weapons of mass destruction on three occasions recently, and in more than forty other instances additional proliferation-related materials have been intercepted.

Nonproliferation policy guidance to the intelligence agencies begins with top-secret presidential decision directives. President Clinton issued the most important of these in September 1993 (PDD 13 on Nonproliferation and Export Control). It presented fourteen guidelines that spelled out which agencies in the government were expected to do what in a range of clandestine operations against the spread of dangerous weapons. This directive has been supplemented by more detailed documents—National Security Council intelligence directives (NSCIDs, pronounced "en-skids")—that set forth explicit intelligence requirements.

Moreover, the NPC provides in-depth research reports on a range of proliferation issues and is responsible for planning and directing aggressive operations designed to make proliferation "expensive and embarrassing" for perpetrators.[27] This means various types of covert action. The president might order the CIA to feed propaganda to media outlets around the globe, revealing a nation's involvement in weapons proliferation activities (such as China's sale of M-11 missiles to Pakistan over the past few years) or persuading a country to reject proliferation—say, encouraging a country to concentrate on industrial technology instead of long-range rocketry.

The CIA might be directed (perhaps based on a recommendation which the Operations Directorate or the NPC might have proposed to the National Security Council through the DCI) to plant a virus in the computers at a weapons laboratory in a renegade nation or to provide the culpable nation with faulty equipment through "witting" (knowing) or unwitting suppliers (perhaps off-centered ball bearings). Of highest risk, the CIA might be asked to carry out paramilitary operations meant to set back or destroy weapons production programs, such as having an agent detonate a bomb in one of the underground caverns where North Korea hides its weapons facilities or at least sabotaging the 32-foot boring machines used to dig the catacombs.

Covert action holds a strong attraction to some policy officers who wish to avoid a public outcry, here and abroad, that might accompany an overt military strike against weapons laboratories, nuclear reactors, or weapons caches. The most notable recent examples of the overt approach to extreme nonproliferation measures include the Israeli destruction of French-built critical reactor cores before their shipment to Iraq in 1979, the Israeli bombing of an Iraqi nuclear facility at Osirak in 1981, and, as part of the wider war effort to force Saddam Hussein out of Kuwait, the U.S./U.N. coalition attack against a range of Iraqi proliferation targets in 1991—all noisy events compared to quick and silent sabotage.

MONEY AND PEOPLE

As with most new government entities, the budgets for America's secret agencies were initially modest and their staff limited. From humble beginnings, though, the intelligence community grew apace with Washington's fears of Soviet expansion. The intelligence agencies saw their budgets rise from approximately $3 million in 1947 to $5 billion in 1968.[28] The funding declined to $3 billion by 1973—the only backslide during the Cold War—largely at the insistence of the powerful House Appropriations Committee chairman George Mahon, who believed that the secret government had become too bloated during the Vietnam War.[29]

The budget then bounced back to roughly $5 billion in 1974, $6 billion in 1976, and, by the end of the Carter administration, $13 billion (in constant 1981 dollars). In the Reagan and Bush administrations the intelligence community joined the Pentagon in a spending spree: from $20 billion in 1981 to a record annual $30 billion during the last years of the Cold War (again in 1981 dollars).[30] Throughout the Cold War approximately 15 percent of the funding for the secret agencies went to national intelligence programs, led by the CIA, with most of the rest going into the coffers of the military intelligence agencies and the TECHINT hardware manufacturers and managers. Within these overall trends, spending on intelligence activities experienced spurts of growth fueled by a series of covert and overt wars conducted by the United States: the Korean War (1950–53), the CIA paramilitary (PM) operation in Laos (1963–73), the Vietnam War (1964–73), and the CIA's paramilitary operations in Nicaragua and Afghanistan (1980s).

A graph of personnel levels in the Community during the Cold War would track roughly the funding line: a hill during Vietnam, a valley, and another hill during the Reagan years. A more refined examination of staffing decisions, though, would disclose some important fluctuations. The number of scientists allotted to the CIA's Directorate for Science and Technology expanded rapidly after the Soviet launching of Sputnik (1957), for example, as did the number of economic analysts brought into the Community after the global recession of the 1950s, the U.S. balance-of-payments crisis in 1971, and the growing international trade competition with Germany and Japan in the 1980s.

ACCOUNTABILITY

The secret agencies have stood outside the traditional government framework of checks and balances—until recently. Members of Congress deferred to their expertise in the realm of esoteric intelligence activities, and preferred to avoid responsibility for errant operations like the Bay of Pigs invasion.[31] As a DCI from this era, James R. Schlesinger, remembers: "One time [in 1973] I went up to the Hill and said, 'Mr. Chairman [John Stennis of the Senate Armed Services Committee's subcommittee on intelligence oversight], I want to tell you about some of our programs.' To which the Senator replied quickly, 'No, no, my boy, don't tell me. Just go ahead and do it, but I don't want to know!'"[32]

With little scrutiny, the leaders of the House and Senate Armed Services committees quietly folded intelligence funding into the Defense Department's annual budget. Nor did the White House provide consistent supervision. Members of the NSC rarely saw the intelligence budget, and many of the CIA's aggressive ventures (including covert-action and counterintelligence operations) never received a thorough examination—or, in some cases, even formal approval—by the NSC.[33]

Reflecting this attitude of benign tolerance toward the secret agencies, the graph lines for commitment to intelligence accountability in the executive and, especially, the legislative branches remain relatively low from 1947 through 1974 (see figure 2.3). The few blips upward reflect occasional intelligence controversies, such as the U-2 incident (1960), the Bay of Pigs fiasco (1961), the

National Student Association exposé (1967), allegations of CIA involvement in the Watergate scandal (1973), and the growing concern for intelligence accountability displayed by Senate Majority Leader Mike Mansfield from 1969 to 1973.[34] In 1974 investigative journalism inexorably altered this relationship, propelling Congress deep into the hidden chambers of the intelligence agencies.

Correspondent Seymour M. Hersh of the *New York Times* reported in a series of articles in December 1974 that the CIA had spied on American citizens during the Vietnam War era (Operation CHAOS) and, further, had tried to topple the democratically elected president of Chile. While the revelations about covert action in Chile may have been shrugged off by Congress as so much Cold War politics as usual, spying on American citizens—voters back home— was an allegation too hot to ignore. Blazing newspaper headlines demanded an investigation.

Both houses of Congress—and, not to be caught in a posture of indifference to CIA domestic spying, the Ford administration—immediately launched major inquiries into the allegations.[35] Investigators triggered an avalanche of unsettling revelations from the vaults of the intelligence agencies: assassination plots against foreign leaders, widespread surveillance of American citizens by various intelligence units, drug experiments on unsuspecting victims, a storehouse of chemical-biological materials sequestered in violation of international treaty, and a host of other Orwellian nightmares. The stage was set for an infusion of genuine accountability into America's anemic system of intelligence supervision.

In 1975 the Ford administration created an Intelligence Oversight Board (IOB) and revived the President's Foreign Intelligence Advisory Board (PFIAB), both authorized to maintain a presidential eye on the secret agencies. The president also prohibited by executive order the use of assassination as an instrument of covert action, and he tightened NSC approval procedures for other aggressive CIA operations. By executive order President Carter additionally codified and strengthened the NSC's intelligence procedures.[36]

Attention to intelligence accountability went still further on Capitol Hill. In the waning hours of 1974 Congress passed a law (the Hughes-Ryan Act) that required presidential authorization for all important covert actions, along with timely reports to select committees of Congress. During the next year congressional investigative committees cross-examined—and sometimes humiliated in public hearings—intelligence officers for their overzealous operations at home and abroad.

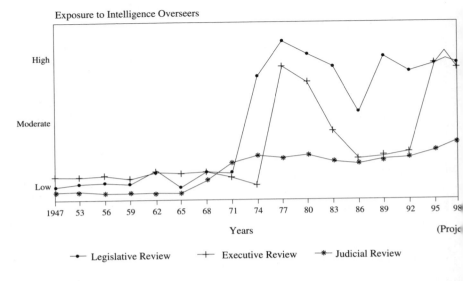

Figure 2.3 Accountability

Then, in 1976, senators took the major step of establishing a permanent Senate Select Committee on Intelligence (SSCI, pronounced "sissy") to monitor the annual budget requests and ongoing activities of the intelligence agencies. A year later the second chamber followed suit with the creation of the House Permanent Select Committee on Intelligence (HPSCI or "hip-see"). Throughout the Carter, Reagan, and Bush years the Congress enacted a series of laws to rein in the secret agencies. Even though these statutes were met with cries of "micromanagement" from some intelligence professionals, many—including almost all of the recent DCIs—liked the idea of sharing the burden of their responsibilities with members of Congress.[37] However reluctantly, the intelligence agencies had at last become a part of the government.[38]

The attention of legislators to intelligence oversight fluctuated during the period from 1975 to the end of the Cold War, depending on the attitudes toward clandestine operations held by individual overseers and, relatedly, whether or not the media had charged the secret agencies with wrongdoing. Oversight peaked near the end of the Cold War, in 1987, when it was discovered that Reagan administration officials had tried to bypass the new system of legislative accountability to supply arms to the Nicaraguan contras.

Despite these ups-and-downs, the overall trend for accountability was clear: intelligence policy had entered an era of partnership between Congress and the executive branch. The intelligence community would now have two masters— and sometimes a third, as the courts increasingly adjudicated intelligence-

Intelligence Missions

related litigation and regularly examined requests for electronic-surveillance warrants (as mandated by the Foreign Intelligence Surveillance Act of 1978).[39]

INTEREST GROUP POLITICS

Just as the intelligence agencies had stood apart from Congress for most of the Cold War, their effort to keep secrets from foreign adversaries (manifested most obviously in the barbed-wire fences and guardhouses around their perimeters) kept them insulated as well from the normal forces of pluralism in American society. Trend lines registering the presence of interest groups advocating specific intelligence policies, or the intelligence agencies lobbying on their own behalf (in the manner of the Pentagon), would run practically flat throughout the first thirty years of the Cold War—the FBI excepted, thanks to Director Hoover's political savvy. This all changed in 1975, when the secret agencies found themselves under siege by investigators.

In that "Year of the Intelligence Wars" a senior officer resigned from the CIA to form the Association of Former (now called Retired) Intelligence Officers (AFIO). Its purpose, embraced by the many former intelligence officials who quickly swelled AFIO's ranks, was to lobby Congress and the American people on behalf of the secret agencies, chiefly by issuing pro-intelligence literature and providing favorable witnesses for congressional hearings. Other pressure groups came into existence soon thereafter, some for and some against the clandestine world. In yet another way the intelligence agencies had become a part of the government and politics as usual. Still, compared to the extensive outreach and large war chests of most successful lobbying groups in the United States, those concerned with intelligence policy during the post-1975 era remained relatively small in number, modestly funded, and only marginally influential.

As for the intelligence community's own lobbying efforts (euphemistically known as "legislative liaison"), in the wake of the searing investigations of 1975 its managers had begun to understand a lesson already well learned by the Defense Department and the FBI, namely, the importance of selling one's programs on Capitol Hill. The number of attorneys in the CIA's Office of General Counsel mushroomed from two in 1974 to sixty-five at the end of the Cold War, and the Office of Congressional Affairs grew from two staffers to over a dozen during the same period. Forced out into the open to some extent by the scandals of 1975—a point not to be overstated, since the secret agencies remain largely closed to outside scrutiny when measured by normal government standards—the Community now tried to defend itself publicly in a manner similar to that of most government agencies.

This set of indicators—basic missions, structural developments, money and personnel, accountability, and exposure to pressure-group politics—provides a portrait of the intelligence agencies from 1947 to 1991. From the vantage point of missions it reveals a strong devotion to technical collection, a moderate commitment to human collection, a more modest attention to analysis, and a groping toward efforts at better Community-wide coordination; counterintelligence that went from drastic centralization to a dispersal of responsibilities, and then back again toward some centralization via counterthreat "fusion centers," in a search for some balance between these two management principles; covert action that became the CIA's major mission, only to plunge to a level of near insignificance during the early Carter years, then to rise once more near the end of the Cold War to its highest levels of emphasis as a central component of the anti-Communist crusade conducted by Ronald Reagan and William Casey.

It is a portrait of vast resources fed steadily into hardware; occasional spurts of growth in physical plant and relatively static internal structural configurations—until near the end of the Cold War, when DCIs sought to reduce the centrifugal forces that pulled apart the organizations comprising the intelligence community; ups and downs in funding and personnel, boosted by the Vietnam War and the Reagan-Bush years of national security buildup—the largest ever in time of peace. It is a portrait, too, of weak accountability and a conspicuous absence of pluralistic politics, until 1975—and even then, of only modest proportions throughout the remaining years of the Cold War.

POST–COLD WAR CHANGES IN U.S. INTELLIGENCE

With this set of benchmarks the changes that have occurred in the secret agencies since the demise of the USSR can be better understood. As the end lines in figures 2.1–2.3 show, the close of the Cold War has indeed brought changes to U.S. intelligence agencies. Several of the changes have been more incremental than abrupt, though, and a good many were already underway as a result of new directions pursued by DCIs during the mid-1980s—several years before the collapse of the Soviet Union.

Collection and Analysis

At the end of the Cold War one could have reasonably advanced two prominent hypotheses about the probable direction of intelligence collection and analysis. The first—the peace dividend hypothesis—might have argued that the intelligence agencies (along with the Pentagon) would suffer a general loss in resources, including funds for expensive collection platforms. The second—call it the snakes hypothesis—might have anticipated an increase in funding, if legislators embraced the argument of the first post–Cold War DCI, R. James Woolsey, that "we live now in a jungle filled with a bewildering variety of poisonous snakes."[40] According to this reasoning, one problem had been allayed (the Soviet Union), but several smaller—albeit still quite dangerous—ones remained (such as North Korea) that demanded the attention of the nation's intelligence agencies.

What in fact occurred from 1991 to 1995 was a mixture of the two hypotheses. Woolsey, a seasoned Pentagon bureaucrat before becoming DCI, at first aggressively sought an increase in funding for the intelligence agencies; and although the intelligence budget fell slightly (according to published reports) from its historical pinnacle of some $30 billion per annum in 1989–91, a precipitous decline may have been avoided as a result of the DCI's strenuous defense of a spending increase. In the process, though, Woolsey's strident style of advocacy managed to alienate many of his overseers on Capitol Hill.

Despite his choice of a colorful metaphor, Woolsey's argument rested less on the specter of poisonous snakes loosed on the land than it did on a persuasive management concept: the need for a short-term infusion of funds to allow long-term savings through the consolidation of intelligence community programs, especially satellite hardware. By 1997, for instance, Woolsey planned on a "50 per cent cut in numbers of satellites and much greater than that in the number of ground stations."[41] He foresaw a 26 percent reduction in DS&T personnel and a cut of 1,700 employees in other technical support services.[42]

Initially, the DCI advanced both the snakes hypothesis and the consolidation argument. Congress, though, was clearly in no mood for rising military or intelligence budgets; nor was the White House, at a time when politicians in both branches had adopted deficit trimming as a priority. Woolsey was forced to retreat from his broader brief on new dangers to settle mainly on a request for short-term relief during the period of program consolidation that followed the Cold War. A temporary surge in spending for management efficiencies, he argued, would soon reap savings—most notably in a reduced need for costly new satellites as older models were repositioned and given new duties.[43]

As for HUMINT and analysis, Woolsey envisioned a decrease in the number of case officers and analysts through 1997, accompanied by a shifting of HUMINT resources to spies and specialists with areas of expertise often overlooked by the Community when America was fixated on the Soviet Union. The Operations Directorate, home of the CIA's HUMINT case officers, would shrink by seven hundred people and the Intelligence Directorate by a thousand analysts, down to the personnel levels of 1977—a one-third reduction.[44]

The new espionage targeting priorities were to include a number of microstates that well might present a threat to the United States. (Near the end of the Cold War the Community had been unable to provide much useful information to policymakers on Grenada, Panama, Libya, North Korea, and Iraq, among other trouble spots.) Agencies were asked to provide more economic intelligence, a topic of increasing importance that absorbed 40 percent of the collection and analysis resources at the beginning of the post–Cold War era (compared to less than 10 percent before). The remainder of resources were to be devoted to a panoply of topics ranging from data on global health trends (the spread of AIDS, for example) and environmental threats (such as Russian dumping of radioactive materials in the Arctic Ocean) to refugee and narcotics flows and the growing problem of international organized crime.[45] Of greatest concern to intelligence managers was the specter of rampant weapons proliferation, including a suspected North Korean atomic bomb project and Chinese sales of advanced missilery to Pakistan and Iran.[46]

Overall, Woolsey froze hiring at the CIA and in 1993–94 cut back on personnel by 24 percent, twice the rate recommended by Vice President Al Gore's National Performance Review.[47] The Agency's personnel figures projected an additional 12 percent "glide path" downward for 1995–97.[48] "We must compensate for these reductions," the DCI emphasized, "with a structure that is flexible, and responsive."[49] Since some of the savings from program consolidation would be shifted toward new asset recruitments overseas (though with fewer case officers to carry out the recruiting), the post–Cold War trend lines for the collection and analysis mission under Woolsey moved downward for technical collection and analysis (see figure 2.1) but slightly upward for HUMINT.

Woolsey continued the efforts of his predecessors aimed at greater Community-wide coordination, including the fusion center experiments. Above all, he sought closer ties between the CIA and military intelligence, a relationship that had deteriorated over the years but would soon appear to carry itself to the opposite extreme under Woolsey and his successor, John Deutch. Woolsey established an associate deputy director for military affairs within his office and worked with the Department of Defense (not without tensions and under pressure from Congress)[50] to create and jointly manage a new National Imagery and Mapping Agency (NIMA) for improved dissemination of spy photography to the battlefield.[51]

The "militarization" of intelligence in the aftermath of the Persian Gulf War also increased cohesion among some elements of the Community, offsetting the FBI's bid for turf rights overseas. Woolsey had a Department of Defense background as a former undersecretary of the Navy, and he named an admiral as his deputy; but Woolsey's replacement, John M. Deutch, displayed even more conspicuous DOD credentials as a former undersecretary of defense—the number-two position in the Pentagon. Although he appointed a civilian as his deputy, the seventh-floor hallways of the CIA were soon awash with uniformed aides brought there by Deutch—even more plentiful than the "Navy mafia" that surged into the Agency with Admiral Stansfield Turner during the Carter administration. "Support for Military Operations!" and "Tactical Intelligence for the Warfighter!" became the battle cries of the new Deutch team. The CIA and the Pentagon had never been closer, joined at the top at any rate by Deutch's dual allegiances.

Below the seventh floor at Langley, though, CIA officers were less impressed by the cohesion the military connection promised for the intelligence community than they were fearful that this military takeover might mean the end of national strategic intelligence. The goal of a transparent battlefield, bloodless and free of body bags (at least on the American side), could lead to the demise of the CIA's traditional responsibility: providing the president with global intelligence on military, political, and economic matters that could prevent the outbreak of war. The stage was set for a bureaucratic showdown within the Community between the new warfighting team of tactical intelligence supporters fresh from Defense and the war-avoidance civilians in the CIA who supported a strategic intelligence perspective. With the DCI and the Pentagon lined up all on one side, oddsmakers in 1995 were placing their bets with the warfighters.

The decline in resources available to the government (a function mainly of domestic economic constraints and a perception that the international threat had diminished with the fall of the Soviet Union) encouraged both Woolsey and Deutch to search for ways of reducing redundancies and cooperating with one another. On Langley's seventh floor Deutch and his aides waxed enthusiastic about "'orchestrating the symphony' of the intelligence community's component parts."[52] One manifestation of the efforts toward greater Community harmony was some pooling of liaison resources across agencies for lobbying on Capitol Hill.

Counterintelligence

Paradoxically, attention to counterintelligence rose just as the Cold War wound down (see figure 2.2). The intelligence community had begun to focus on the subject through the creation of the counterthreat fusion centers for counterintelligence, counterterrorism, counternarcotics, and nonproliferation. Moreover, the Community came to realize that Russia's military intelligence service (the GRU) had actually stepped up espionage in the United States since 1989.[53] This reinforced a belief that the federal government would have to maintain, if not enhance, its counterspy capabilities. Further, American corporations complained that they had become the targets of intensive foreign espionage operations and requested help from the government's counterintelligence experts. While a long line of DCIs eschewed the rather controversial assignment of commercial espionage, they were prepared to assist companies in their efforts to block espionage operations directed against them by foreign intelligence services (see chapter 6).

The bombing of the World Trade Center in New York City in 1992 and the Federal Building in Oklahoma City in 1995 were chilling reminders that terrorism in the United States was alive and well. It was plain, too, that America was continuing to fail in its efforts to curb harmful narcotics from slipping across its borders. Counterintelligence, counterterrorism, and counternarcotics all became growth stocks in the intelligence community as the USSR (but not its intelligence services) disappeared.

The disclosure in 1994 that the trusted CIA insider Aldrich H. Ames was a Soviet spy—the highest-placed mole known to have penetrated the Agency—ensured even further attention to the counterintelligence mission, as executive-branch commissions and congressional investigators sought explanations for this incredible failure of Agency security.[54] Still, even the currently fashionable interest in counterintelligence is expected to suffer attrition through the end of the decade as officials turn their attention to less arcane topics. The counterintelligence mission, nevertheless, is likely to remain higher on the Community's agenda than in the past.

Covert Action

Support for covert action took a nosedive during the transition from the protracted period of superpower standoff to U.S. global preeminence in 1991 (see figure 2.2). Following a period of dramatic resurgence that lasted from 1979 until the end of the Cold War, spending for "special activities" leveled out at less than 1 percent of the intelligence budget at the end of the Bush administration. This percentage came close to matching the lowest ebb for covert action, reached in 1977–78 when a wary, moralistic President Carter drove this option gingerly, tapping the brakes—until the Soviet aggression in Afghanistan.

The main reason for the decline in the Community's emphasis on covert action was, of course, the disappearance of the USSR. In addition, though, the decline reflected the emergence of new avenues for supporting friendly governments and factions abroad, such as the National Endowment for Democracy, a U.S. government entity established during the Reagan administration for the public funding of democratic movements overseas. Covert actions once planned and implemented by the CIA have also to some extent been displaced onto the Pentagon, whose "special operations" units have become important to "democracy" and "nation-building" interventions like those carried out in Somalia and Haiti during the Clinton administration.

Despite the present low standing of covert action, one can readily envision its phoenix-like ascent in coming years—perhaps in support of the Community's top agenda item of nonproliferation or to assist the Clinton administration's foreign policy objectives in the Balkans. Increased propaganda aimed at stanching the hemorrhage of weapons from the former Soviet republics (among other places), along with covert actions of a political and economic character— or even paramilitary operations—wait in the wings for presidents and DCIs with a penchant for direct secret action by the CIA as a means for halting the flow of weapons to renegade nations.

Structure and Money

Although the intelligence community constructed most of its newest buildings before the end of the Cold War, some expansion has taken place since— most controversially, a new National Reconnaissance Office (NRO) headquarters near Dulles Airport which was roundly criticized for cost overruns hidden from legislators. The most significant structural developments, however, have been the establishment of the DO/DI partnership at the CIA, the fusion centers, the National Imagery and Mapping Agency (an imagery analog to the NSA), and Community-wide legislative liaison teams.

Following the demise of the Soviet Union, the U.S. intelligence budget began a downward slide to $29 billion in 1992 (according to newspaper reports) and $28 billion during DCI Woolsey's initial consolidation phase in 1993–94 (in nominal dollars, reflecting roughly a 10 percent erosion in real terms every four years). Some observers expect the Community's funding to continue in a downward slide, perhaps reaching as low as $20 billion by 1998; others—who are apt to be more correct—believe the solid pro-defense, pro-intelligence Republican majority now in control of both houses of Congress will halt the erosion, and intelligence expenditures will level out or even increase somewhat.[55]

In light of these budget alterations and other adjustments inside the Community, former DCI Gates rejects the notion that the intelligence agencies have resisted change since the end of the Cold War. "Bureaucrats are smarter than that," he maintains. "You won't survive in this day and age [if you resist change]; Congress will have your lunch." He points to a "massive reallocation of resources inside the CIA, because of the end of the Cold War. . . . [I]n 1993, [only] 13 percent of CIA's resources were directed against the former Soviet Union"—compared to some 50–60 percent during the Cold War. He notes, too, that the Agency has made "huge re-assignments of people. We took scores of scientists and engineers out of the old Office of Scientific and Weapons Research, took them off of Soviet weapons and programs and put them onto proliferation; and that kind of thing has happened throughout the Agency."[56]

Accountability

The new system of accountability is here to stay—despite its occasional feebleness, as during the Iran-contra affair, and the tendency toward deferential questioning of intelligence officials during oversight hearings (examined in chapter 4).

In 1993, for example, 1,512 meetings took place between legislators and the CIA legislative liaison staff, as well as 154 one-on-one or small-group meetings between legislators and the DCI; 26 congressional hearings with the DCI as a witness; 128 hearings with other CIA witnesses; 317 other contacts with legislators, and 887 meetings and contacts with legislative staff—a 29 percent increase over 1992. This does not even take into consideration liaison contacts between the other intelligence agencies and the Congress. In 1993 the CIA alone provided 4,976 classified documents to legislators, along with 4,668 unclassified documents and 233 responses to constituency inquiries.[57]

Another sign of a more serious effort to monitor the secret agencies and keep American citizens informed of at least some of their activities has been the spate of public congressional hearings that call intelligence officers as witnesses—a rarity during the Cold War years. DCI Woolsey testified in eight open hearings in 1993, whereas in previous years (even since the congressional investigations of 1975) DCIs often never appeared in public hearings during an entire session of Congress.

The degree of openness between the secret agencies and their legislative overseers—let alone the public—should not be overstated, though. That Congress was still kept in the dark on key aspects of intelligence policy was startlingly underscored in 1994 and 1995. In 1994 legislators learned only through a chance audit that the NRO had apparently incurred cost overruns amounting to some $150 million for its new headquarters. More unsettling still, in 1995 the Congress discovered that the CIA had failed to report that one of its Guatemalan assets may have been involved in the murder of an American citizen—the kind of questionable relationship that the intelligence agencies were now expected to report to their overseers without hesitation.

A rash of earlier scandals—especially the domestic spying charges against the CIA in 1974 and the Iran-contra affair of 1987—did more to open up America's hidden government to public scrutiny than anything related to the collapse of the Soviet Union (see figure 2.3).[58] In the wake of Iran-contra, for instance, came laws to tighten supervision over covert action, along with a statute to strengthen the CIA's Office of the Inspector General.

Throughout the Reagan years the intelligence community enjoyed an extremely close relationship with the White House, chiefly because DCI Casey was a personal friend of the president and had served as his national campaign manager in 1980. Moreover, Reagan was entirely supportive of aggressive covert-action initiatives against the Soviet empire, which in the middle of his tenure he labeled the "evil empire." Unfortunately, this free rein led to the Iran-contra scandal, the major foreign policy blemish on the Reagan presidency. Under President George Bush, a former DCI, the intelligence community had the luxury of a chief executive who understood and appreciated intelligence as well as any of his predecessors. He was largely sympathetic to the wishes of the Community—with the exception of free-wheeling covert actions, which Bush helped slow during his last two years in office.

The Clinton administration, by contrast, has displayed a relative inattentiveness to foreign policy and its underlying foundation of intelligence. (One of the reasons for DCI Woolsey's resignation in December 1994 was his sense of frustration over the president's aloofness from intelligence.) Significant intelligence snafus occurred during the administration's first foreign policy crisis, in Somalia. A failure to understand the intentions—or even the whereabouts—of the Somali tribal leader Mohamed Farah Aidid raised doubts among NSC officials about the competence of the intelligence agencies.[59]

In 1994, President Clinton decided to establish a presidential commission on the future roles and capabilities of the intelligence community. John Warner, of the Senate Select Committee on Intelligence, wanted an inquiry, too, and at first he pushed for a congressional commission instead. The two branches finally reached a compromise: the new commission would include legislators and private citizens, not just (as Clinton wished) members of the President's Foreign Intelligence Advisory Board. In October 1994 Congress established the commission by statute, with a membership of nine PFIAB members selected by the president and eight persons selected by Congress.

Clinton named former secretary of defense Les Aspin, the PFIAB chairman, to head the new commission, which was required by law to report by March 1, 1996. Aspin died of a stroke in May 1995, and the president turned to another former secretary of defense, Harold Brown, to replace him. The presence of a special intelligence commission was likely to ensure a higher-than-usual level of accountability over the secret agencies throughout 1995 and 1996.

The end of the Cold War also ushered pork barrel politics into the intelligence domain. As weapons contracts diminished after the disintegration of the Communist threat, industrial leaders cast an eye toward ongoing intelligence requirements for new TECHINT hardware. Members of Congress in districts with weapons plants—and jobs at risk—have been solicited for help in procuring collection platform contracts, just as they have been for Pentagon arms acquisitions and the forestalling of base closures.[60]

CONCLUSION

One might have expected the collapse of an imposing empire like the USSR to bring in its wake dramatic changes in other parts of the world as well, including the government of its archnemesis, the United States. This unexpected shift in the currents of history did in fact create several vectors of change for America's secret government.

Responding to the new era, the intelligence community planned to reduce its concentration on technical intelligence while upgrading its human spy networks. A large portion of both collection systems are now being radically reoriented toward formerly slighted targets in the developing world—especially unfriendly nations harboring military ambitions—and away from saturation coverage of the former Soviet republics (whose relative openness makes clandestine collection less necessary anyway). The intelligence community also began to focus more attention on improving its internal coordination, in part a cost-saving move in times of fiscal stress but also—some would say more so— a reflection of increasing control over strategic as well as tactical intelligence by Pentagon proponents in the Community.

The secret agencies gave more attention to counterintelligence after the Cold War because of ongoing (indeed, stepped-up) Russian spying in the United States, a resurgence of terrorist incidents, and, most important, serious security lapses at the CIA exposed by the Ames spy case. Facing less of a need to combat Soviet intelligence agencies in Third World liberation conflicts, the CIA began (at White House direction) to wind down its covert actions even before the dissolution of the Soviet system. This trend has continued through 1995, with covert action accounting for less than 1 percent of the CIA's annual budget—although rising frustration over the war in Bosnia and sundry outbreaks of violence elsewhere in the world have led key NSC officials to grumble about the dormancy of "special activities."

In addition to cutting back on costs for new satellites and reconnaissance airplanes (after a short-term funding infusion to consolidate existing systems), the intelligence agencies plan to shift spending toward the hiring of more analysts and spies while further phasing out covert-action specialists. Some observers projected a steady decline in the overall intelligence budget from 1994 to 1998, along with a 12 percent drop in personnel, to a restoration of 1981 spending levels at approximately $20 billion per annum (in constant, real 1980 dollars). Intelligence managers, though, continued to fight this trend, with strong allies in a new Republican Congress that looked upon intelligence as a "force multiplier" that warranted an increase in support, not a decrease, in times of Defense Department spending reductions.

Whatever the outcome of these budget battles, legislative and executive overseers seemed prepared to maintain a tighter rein over intelligence policy. Congress passed significant oversight statutes in 1991 and held a series of public hearings on intelligence policy in the immediate post–Cold War years—though it remained in the dark on NRO cost overruns and CIA ties with a suspected Guatemalan murderer. At the same time, in the ongoing Washington tug of war between saving and spending, some legislators joined with defense contractors to lobby on behalf of intelligence hardware acquisitions.

The demise of the Soviet Union, however, was hardly the only influence that brought about changes in American intelligence. Several of the course corrections for the secret agencies came in the very midst of the Cold War. Covert action, for example, underwent a serious, albeit temporary, decline in the 1970s.

Bureaucratic inertia cannot be overlooked either. James Woolsey, the first post–Cold War DCI, advocated budget increases at a time of economic retrenchment in part because that is the expected role of agency heads. For him to have done otherwise would have invited sagging morale in the Community—or outright rebellion, as a besieged DCI Turner discovered when he cut back DO personnel slots during the Carter years. Max Weber can provide greater insights into intelligence organizations than Ian Fleming.

Robert Gates's insistence that intelligence bureaucracies do respond to change does have some validity, though. Elements of both resistance and change can be seen in the response of the secret agencies to the "outside" world, both in Washington and beyond. In 1969 the House Appropriations Committee chairman Mahon told the intelligence community that it had better cut

$2 billion to reduce bureaucratic bloat accumulated during the Vietnam War era—or else. It quickly did. Two decades later, when Congress once again insisted on cutbacks, DCI Woolsey—having lost his "snakes" argument—began to comply with the prevailing cost-cutting sentiment on the congressional committees that authorized and appropriated the annual budgets for intelligence. What other choice was available, particularly when the president was unwilling to join the fight for increased intelligence spending?

This is not to say that DCIs have passively accepted direction from Congress. Even more than Casey, Gates had the advantage of a close relationship with a president. He had worked two or three hours a day with George Bush for three years as a national security aide in the White House before being appointed DCI in 1991. His close access to the president continued into his new job and, as he recalls, the relationship had an "extraordinary" effect on his ability to gain leverage over others with whom he had to negotiate in the government—including key legislative overseers. "My ability to do deals with [Senator David] Boren [the SSCI chairman] on intelligence legislation—particularly in cases where [Secretary of Defense Richard] Cheney didn't like it—was really phenomenal."[61]

As DCI during the key transition away from the Cold War, Gates also remembers using Capitol Hill to have his way in the intelligence community. "Boren and [HPSCI chairman David] McCurdy and I conspired a fair amount" in deciding what direction to take the secret agencies in the new era. "I was able to go back to these people in the Community and I'd say, 'You've got two choices: you can do it my way, in which you have a part in the say; or they [Boren and McCurdy] are going to tell you how to do it. They're going to go further in most of these things than I am, and they're probably not going to do it smart. We can do it smart, and we can do it radically enough that they will retreat on their legislation.'" As Gates recalls, that was "exactly what happened: both Boren and McCurdy essentially receded. Boren redrafted his [1991 intelligence reform] bill, in effect to write into law what I did; and McCurdy receded altogether. So I used the Hill against the Community, and that worked pretty well."[62]

Scandals, too, can play a significant role in organizational change. The Community's chilling involvement in domestic spying (disclosed in 1974) and the Iran-contra affair did more to rivet attention on the need for closer accountability than anything related to the end of the Cold War—although, of course, the events that led to the scandals were themselves offshoots of an overzealous pursuit of Cold War objectives. Finally, changes inside the intelligence community seem to have been affected by the state of the U.S. domestic economy as much as anything else—a condition influenced, to be sure, by a perception of declining external threat.

Has the end of the Cold War brought changes to the secret government? The answer is yes. But other circumstances have also had an effect—spy scandals and economic distress at home, a complicated interplay of institutional and group demands, the personal predilections of a range of individual actors from DCIs to presidents and legislative overseers. This rich mixture of influences gives to the study of American government its frustrations and its fascination.

CHAPTER 3

THE ETHICS OF COVERT OPERATIONS

"We must learn to subvert, sabotage and destroy our enemies by more clear, more sophisticated and more effective methods than those used against us," advised a secret annex to a presidential commission (the Doolittle Report to the Hoover Commission) in the 1950s. The United States would have to "fight in the back alleys of the world," concluded Secretary of State Dean Rusk a decade later. "Must the United States respond like a man in a barroom brawl who will fight only according to Marquis of Queensberry rules?" a retired senior intelligence officer rhetorically asked in the 1980s. Even when the Cold War had come to an end, a former intelligence official continued to emphasize the "ruthlessness that international espionage requires."[1]

Should one conclude from these perspectives that intelligence activities must be set apart from moral considerations? The first section of this chapter presents a "ladder of escalation" for covert operations, based on a rising level of intrusion abroad as policy officers climb upward from low-risk to high-risk activities. The second briefly surveys leading ethical, philosophical, and practical issues involved in trying to evaluate the effects of secret intelligence activities. The final section offers a set of guidelines for evaluating the propriety of proposed covert operations, from clandestine collection to counterintelligence and covert action. Despite a tendency for commentators on national security to overlook the subject of covert intervention abroad, the topic is important. For in contemporary global relations, secret acts of hostility between nations occur frequently.[2]

A LADDER OF ESCALATION FOR COVERT OPERATIONS

In 1965, the strategist Herman Kahn of the Hudson Institute published an influential volume in which he offered an "escalation-ladder metaphor" for understanding the coercive features of international affairs. Kahn described the ladder as a "convenient list of the many options facing the strategist in a two-sided confrontation."[3] It addressed primarily the overt manifestations of hostile acts carried out by one state against another, building from low-level expressions of enmity ("subcrisis maneuvering," which included political, economic, and diplomatic gestures, as well as—a step up—solemn and formal declarations of displeasure) and continuing ultimately to "spasm or insensate war"—Rung 44, a full-scale nuclear exchange.

Similarly, covert operations can be arrayed for heuristic purposes according to their degree of intrusiveness abroad, from nonforcible to forcible intervention (with all the accompanying caveats Kahn advanced regarding the limitations of a ladder metaphor).[4] In a ladder of escalation for covert operations (table 3.1), the underlying analytical dimension traveling upward is the extent to which most observers would view the options as increasingly serious violations of international law and national sovereignty, and, therefore, as intensified assaults on the international order.

Threshold One: Routine Intelligence Operations

At the lower end of the ladder for covert operations—Threshold One—are arrayed such relatively benign activities as routine sweeps of a nation's own embassy facilities overseas to detect possible electronic implantations and the giving of instruction and security equipment to enhance the personal safety of friendly foreign leaders against threats to their lives (Rung 1 counterintelligence/security measures). Also at this threshold is the assignment of intelligence officers to gather information from foreign officials in their normal daily rounds, say, at an embassy reception (a Rung 2 collection operation). At this threshold, too, low-level information is exchanged between friendly intelligence services by intelligence "liaison" officers (Rung 3)—a common arrangement among Western democracies.

Table 3.1   A Partial Ladder of Escalation for Intelligence Options
(C = collection of intelligence; S = security;
CE = counterespionage; P = covert propaganda;
POL = political covert action; E = economic covert action;
PM = paramilitary covert action)

Threshold Four: Extreme Options

38. Use of chemical-biological and other deadly agents (PM)
37. Major secret wars (PM)
36. Assassination plots (PM)
35. Small-scale coups d'état (PM)
34. Major economic dislocations; crop, livestock destruction (E)
33. Environmental alterations (PM/E)
32. Pinpointed retaliation against noncombatants (PM)
31. Torture (POL/C)
30. Hostage taking (POL/C)
29. Major hostage-rescue attempts (PM)
28. Theft of sophisticated weapons or arms-making materials (PM)
27. Sophisticated arms supplies (PM)

Threshold Three: High-Risk Options

26. Massive increases of funding in democracies (POL)
25. Small-scale hostage-rescue attempt (PM)
24. Training of foreign military forces for war (PM)
23. Limited arms supplies for offensive purposes (PM)
22. Limited arms supplies for balancing purposes (PM)
21. Economic disruption without loss of life (E)
20. Large increases of funding in democracies (POL)
19. Massive increases of funding in autocracies (POL)
18. Large increases of funding in autocracies (POL)
17. Sharing of sensitive intelligence (C)
16. Embassy break-ins (C/CE)
15. High-level, intrusive political surveillance (C)
14. High-level recruitment and penetrations (C/CE)
13. Disinformation against democratic regimes (P)
12. Disinformation against autocratic regimes (P)
11. Truthful but contentious information in democracies (P)
10. Truthful but contentious information in autocracies (P)

Threshold Two: Modest Intrusions

9. Low-level funding of friendly groups (POL)
8. Truthful, benign information in democracies (P)
7. Truthful, benign information in autocracies (P)

(*continued*)

Table 3.1   (*Continued*)

6. Stand-off TECHINT against target nation (C)
5. "Away" targeting of foreign intelligence officer (C/CE)
4. "Away" targeting of other personnel (C)

Threshold One: Routine Operations

3. Sharing of low-level intelligence (C)
2. Ordinary embassy-based observing and conversing (C)
1. Passive security measures; protection of allied leaders (S)

These activities represent little or no serious infringement of a nation's sovereignty and the widely held view that nations should not intervene blatantly in one another's internal affairs (the "noninterventionist norm"). They are widely practiced, with minimal international repercussions.[5] The first rung (counterintelligence/security measures) represents the least controversial of all the intelligence activities carried out between states, since every nation maintains some form of passive defense—most put in place within the defending nation's own territories with no intrusion against another nation, a basic shield against attack.

Threshold Two: Modest Intrusions

With Threshold Two, the degree of intrusiveness begins to escalate, and with it the risks involved in using the intelligence option. This category could include attempts to recruit, say, a foreign ministry clerk somewhere outside his or her homeland—in this sense "away" (Rung 4, collection); recruitment attempts against a low-level intelligence officer, still *outside* the target nation but more risky than the previous rung because an intelligence officer—someone with access to the target nation's deepest secrets—becomes the specific object of recruitment (Rung 5, counterespionage); and the use of distant (or "stand-off") technical intelligence (TECHINT) surveillance against the target nation—high-altitude reconnaissance satellites, for instance (Rung 6, collection).

This category would also include the insertion of truthful covert propaganda material on relatively noncontroversial themes (say, on the importance of preserving NATO) into the foreign media outlets of nondemocratic regimes as a means of reinforcing overt policy pronouncements (Rung 7, covert action); again propaganda, but this time targeted against democratic regimes with a free press (Rung 8, covert action); and the payment of modest sums to political, labor, intellectual, and other organizations and individuals abroad favorably disposed toward one's foreign policy objectives (Rung 9, covert action). All of these examples represent common and widely, if begrudgingly, accepted practices, even though they obviously infringe on a nation's sovereign rights. Even violations of a nation's airspace by satellites and reconnaissance airplanes—TECHINT collection methods once considered highly provocative—are now largely accepted (with existential resignation) as part and parcel of international affairs in the modern age of surveillance.

Still, the lines of demarcation between acceptable and unacceptable intervention can be fuzzy and controversial. Texts on the subject published by the United Nations General Assembly have elicited divided views from members. One illustration comes from the Special Committee on Friendly Relations, established by the General Assembly. In 1967 it reported the opinion of some committee members that covert propaganda and the secret financing of political parties represented "acts of lesser gravity than those directed towards the violent overthrow of the host government."[6] Other Assembly representatives, however, rejected this perspective—especially those who wished to avoid legitimizing covert operations that (in their view) had harmed their nations in the past. As a result of this divided opinion, the special committee equivocated, neither supporting nor prohibiting covert propaganda and secret political funding. A perspicacious student of the committee's work has concluded: "The texts that the General Assembly approved represent compromise formulations that are open to multiple interpretations."[7]

Threshold Three: High-Risk Operations

Threshold Three marks a series of steps toward dangerous covert activity that could trigger within the target nation a response damaging to international comity. Key features of this escalation zone include close-up, on-the-ground, direct operations against more sensitive targets, including activities within the target nation's own territory, as well as the use of methods and material that can lead to violence.

This third category consists of more intense covert actions. At Rungs 10 and 11, propaganda operations remain truthful and in accord with the overt policy statements of the sponsoring nation; but now they pump into the media of nondemocratic and democratic regimes more contentious themes—say, in the days before the end of the Cold War, attributing the prowess of the West European peace movement to financial and propaganda support from Soviet intelligence agencies.

At Rungs 12 and 13 (maintaining the distinction between nondemocratic and democratic regimes), propaganda activities take a nastier turn, employing deception and disinformation that run contrary to the aggressor nation's

Ethics of Covert Operations

avowed public policies—say, falsely blaming an adversary for an assassination attempt or falsifying documents to stain an adversary's reputation.[8] Even propaganda operations against nations without free media are of concern here (albeit less so than against democracies), because of the "blow back" or "replay" phenomenon by which information directed toward adversaries abroad can find its way home to deceive citizens in democratic regimes with free media.[9]

At Rung 14, an intelligence service "pitches" (that is, tries to recruit) a high-level potential agent or defector inside the target nation or attempts a high-level penetration into the opposition service—again on the adversary's own turf (counterespionage). The recruitment carries higher risks still if the potential agent is in the employment of a foreign intelligence service with a controversial record of real (or suspected) human rights abuse; or if the potential agent has been implicated in wrongdoing within his or her own country.

In 1995 it became public that Julio Roberto Alpirez, a colonel in the Guatemalan army charged with complicity in the murder of a leftist guerrilla and an American innkeeper in Guatemala, had served as a CIA agent. For months media stories in the United States pilloried the Agency for its unsavory ties in Guatemala and elsewhere, while "senior CIA officials" defended themselves as best they could by paraphrasing Henry Kissinger's famous remark that espionage should not be confused with missionary work.

If policymakers wanted to know what was going on in the world, argued defenders of the Alpirez relationship, the CIA and the American people would have to hold their noses and pay those foreign agents best able to provide the necessary information about their government's intentions, the whereabouts of narcotics dealers, and the entry of suspected terrorists into their country. "In cases of counterterrorism and counternarcotics," said John M. Deutch, DCI to President Clinton, "we are, of necessity, drawn into relationships with people of questionable character." The director made it clear, however, that there would be limits and ordered his general counsel to determine what the intelligence community should do about agents who "may have violated human rights or U.S. law."[10]

The Agency's inspector general, Frederick P. Hitz, offered this remedy in his still-classified seven-hundred-page report on the Alpirez case: fire any agent involved in narcotics, terrorism, human rights violations, or transgressions against any American law.[11] The Hitz report underlined another disturbing feature of the case: once again the CIA had failed to report an impropriety to its congressional oversight committees, as the law required.

At Rung 15, the aggressor undertakes intrusive surveillance operations (wiretaps, for instance) against prominent political leaders within their own native country. Or the aggressor may employ TECHINT or HUMINT "tradecraft"—the techniques or modus operandi of intelligence officers and their agents—against the target nation's highest decision councils (a collection operation); if discovered, a serious diplomatic rift could likely result.

At Rung 16, the covert aggressor attempts a break-in (a "second-story" or "black-bag" job) against a target nation's embassy, either in a foreign capital or in the aggressor's own capital (collection and counterespionage)—operations considered extremely risky and requiring high-level approval when resorted to by the government of the United States.[12] Rung 17 involves the sharing of intelligence with other secret services; but unlike Rung 3, in this case the information is highly sensitive—say, related to U.S. nuclear targeting plans, offered in an effort to gain greater attack coordination among NATO nations should war break out against the West. (A U.S.-French example is presented in table 3.2.)

Rungs 18 and 19 reflect first a large and then a massive increase in funding for covert political purposes in an autocratic regime—in a poor country a rise in secret expenditures of $1 million, then $5 million, or $10 million and then $20 million in a more affluent one. These large amounts of money can have a significant effect on elections, particularly within a small developing country. It is these sizable sums that no doubt most concerned those members of the General Assembly special committee who opposed permissive language that would condone nonforcible covert influence in the domestic politics of other nations.[13]

Again, as with propaganda, a distinction is made between nondemocratic target nations, at Rungs 18 and 19, and those which are democratic, at Rung 20. Interference in the internal affairs of democracies is considered a more serious step—all the more so if the operation is designed to rig a free election, in contrast, say, to building up a political party between elections (though the distinctions here can be fine). In a similar fashion, Damrosch argues that "a political system that denies basic political rights is in my view no longer a strictly internal affair," but rather one properly subject to international interventions.[14]

At Rung 21, the aggressor undertakes limited covert attacks against economic entities within the target nation. A power line is destroyed here, an oil storage depot contaminated there; perhaps labor strikes are encouraged inside the adversary's major cities—all carefully planned to remain within the limits of harassment operations, with a low probability that lives will be lost.

At Rung 22, a nation resorts to paramilitary operations (arms supplies) to counter weapons already introduced into a territory by an adversary. The

Ethics of Covert Operations

United States might provide a modest supply of unsophisticated but still deadly arms to a favored rebel faction (or factions) as a means of balancing the correlation of forces in a civil war. At Rung 23, the weapons are supplied to a friendly faction without prior intervention by an outside adversary; and Rung 24 involves the secret training of foreign armies or factions for combat (for an Israeli–Sri Lankan example, see table 3.2). Rung 25 envisages a hostage rescue attempt that could involve loss of life, but one carefully designed to be small in scale so as to limit the potential for losses—the Son Tay village raid in Vietnam in contrast to the more ambitious Iranian rescue attempt during the Carter administration.[15]

At Rung 26, massive expenditures are dedicated to improving the political fortunes of friendly factions within a democratic regime (around $20 million in a small democracy and $50 million or more in a larger one), in hopes of bringing them to power—tampering with electoral outcomes in free societies (political covert action). Attempts at covertly influencing truly democratic elections—those in which the rights of political dissent and opposition are honored—represent violations of the noninterventionist norm (and related rules of international law) and have no claim to legitimacy, in contrast to operations directed against self-interested autocratic regimes.

Threshold Four: Extreme Options

With Threshold Four, a nation enters an especially dangerous and controversial realm of intelligence activities—a covert "hot zone." Here is where the lives of innocent people may be placed in extreme jeopardy. At Rung 27, the types of weapons provided to a friendly faction are more potent than at earlier rungs. Rebellious factions inside the target nation (or within its theater of war) are secretly supplied with highly sophisticated weapons—say, Stinger and Blowpipe anti-aircraft missiles—that enable them to take the offensive, causing a drastic escalation in the fighting. The 1988–89 Afghanistan scenario, in which the CIA provided anti-Communist rebels with such weapons, is a good example. Rung 28 represents access to sophisticated weapons through theft, the most extreme case being the stealing of nuclear bombs—or the material for making them, as Israeli intelligence has been accused of doing (see table 3.2).

At Rung 29, hostage rescue operations present a nation with the prospect of extensive casualties—what President Bush referred to in 1989 as "collateral damage" (civilian deaths) in a public explanation of his rejection of this approach, for the time being, to freeing U.S. hostages held by terrorist groups in Lebanon.[16] At Rung 30, the taking of hostages, force is intended, carefully planned, and directed against specific individuals. Opposition intelligence personnel or foreign leaders are kidnapped ("arrested") for information (a collection operation), for instance, or as pawns in secret negotiations (political and paramilitary covert action). An illustration is the 1989 abduction by Israeli commandos of Sheik Abdul Karim Obeid, a leader of the Party of God, a pro-Iranian faction in Lebanon believed to have been holding three Israeli soldiers.

At Rung 31, hostages are tortured in a cruel attempt to coerce compliance in a hostage swap or some other deal (political covert action) or to obtain information (collection). At Rung 32, acts of brutality are directed against lower-level noncombatants in retaliation for hostile intelligence operations (counterespionage).

Beginning with Rung 33, intelligence activities escalate to include violence-laden economic covert actions as well as paramilitary operations against targets of wider scope—often affecting sizable numbers of noncombatants in the civilian population. The aggressor intelligence agency tries to bring about major environmental alterations, from the defoliation or burning of forests to the contamination of lakes and rivers, the creation of floods through the destruction of dams, and even operations (tried by the United States during the war in Vietnam) to control weather conditions through cloud seeding in hopes of ruining crops and bringing about mass starvation. At Rung 34, the aggressor attempts to wreak major economic dislocations within the target nation by counterfeiting currencies to fuel inflation and economic chaos (as the CIA has been reported to have done against Saddam Hussein in 1990–91), sabotaging industrial facilities, or perhaps destroying crops by introducing agricultural parasites into the fields or spreading hoof-and-mouth disease among livestock.

Rung 35 intimately involves the aggressor intelligence service in the overthrow of a foreign adversary—though at this rung with minimal intended bloodshed (such as in Guatemala in 1954). Rung 36 designates the assassination of specific foreign officials—murder of the highest order. Finally, at the top of the escalation ladder are two forms of secret warfare that inevitably affect large numbers of combatants and noncombatants: the launching of protracted, full-blown covert warfare against an inimical regime, with the sponsoring, combat-ready intelligence officers guiding indigenous rebel armies—comparable in scope to the CIA's lengthy "secret" war in Laos during the 1960s (Rung 37); and the possibility of spreading biological, chemical, or other toxic substances to bring about widespread death in the target nation (Rung 38).[17]

The examples of intelligence operations presented in this section have been drawn largely from the American experience. The various official investigations into the U.S. intelligence community conducted in 1975–76 and in 1987 provided a rich source of data on the activities of the American secret services since 1947. Further, the scholarly research on American intelligence stimulated by the new data is much more extensive than anything available about the secret agencies of other nations. Yet it must be emphasized that most developed nations in the West (and certainly the former USSR in the East) have vigorously engaged in most of the operations found on the ladder of escalation presented in table 3.1.[18] The public record on intelligence operations carried out by Western nations other than the United States is sparse because these nations have been more successful in concealing their "dark arts" from public scrutiny; nevertheless, table 3.2 presents some illustrations from other countries (as well as from the United States) to underscore the point that covert intelligence operations are a global phenomenon.

The primary usefulness of the ladder metaphor resides in the opportunity it affords for a visual inspection of covert options, roughly organized according to the growing risk and degree of violence involved in their implementation (and the rising moral qualms and legal controversies that attend them). Ladder construction is an opening exercise toward accomplishing the more difficult task of drawing a "bright line" separating acceptable intelligence operations from those that may be rejected as unacceptable.

INFLUENCES ON THE USE OF COVERT OPERATIONS

What, if anything, is beyond the pale of acceptability in the spectrum of strategic intelligence operations? Can—and should—a "bright line" be drawn, proscribing certain repugnant covert practices? A considerable amount of printer's ink has been devoted to these important questions.[19] The issues are complex and good people part company in response.[20] As with most complicated social topics, where one stands regarding the usefulness and legitimacy of intelligence options depends on one's education, socialization, evolving political and international perspectives ("operational codes"), and peer group influences, not to mention global circumstances and media reporting, among other influences on the formation of foreign policy beliefs.[21] Before attempting to answer the difficult bright-line question, it may be useful to consider at least briefly some key influences that shape a person's attitudes toward covert operations.

Ethical Perspectives

How one views the place of ethics in the conduct of international affairs provides an indication of how one will assess intelligence options. "Do no evil,

Table 3.2   Examples of Western Intelligence Operations since 1945,
Arrayed on the Ladder of Escalation

Threshold	Nation	Operation
Four	United States	Paramilitary action in Laos (1960s); assassination plots in Cuba and the Congo (1960s)
	United Kingdom	Paramilitary operations in Albania (1949), Iran (1953), and Oman (1960s)
	Chile	Assassination of Ambassador Orlando Letelier (1976)
	South Africa	Assassination plots in Zimbabwe (1980s)
	Israel	Assassination of PLO leader (1980) and other assassination plots, bombing of nuclear reactor storage sites in France (1979), paramilitary actions in Egypt (1950s), theft of uranium oxide (1968)
	France	Sinking of the *Rainbow Warrior* (1985); sabotage and various assassination plots

Sources: Threshold Four: Colby and Forbath, *Honorable Men* (on Laos); S. Rept. No. 465, 1975 (on assassination plots); Andrew, *Her Majesty's Secret Service*, 492–93 (on U.K. in Albania); Richelson, *Foreign Intelligence Organizations*, 26, and Roosevelt, *Countercoup* (on U.K. in Iran); David Charters, "The Role of Intelligence Services in the Direction of Covert Paramilitary Operations," in Maurer, Tunstall, and Keagle, eds., *Intelligence: Policy and Process*, 339 (on U.K. in Oman); G. Lardner, "Pinochet Linked to Murder Cover-Up," *Washington Post* (Feb. 5,1987), A1 (on Chile); S.Rule, "Trial in Zimbabwe Leads to Pretoria,"*New York Times* (June 18, 1988), A3 (on South Africa), Raviv and Melman, *Every Spy a Prince*, and Richelson, 203, 205–10 (on Israel); B. and M.-T. Danielson, *Poisoned Reign* (1986) (on the *Rainbow Warrior*); Richelson, 163, 167 (on France). Threshold Three: S. Rep. No. 216 and H. Rep. No. 433 (1987), Cohen and Mitchell, *Men*

though the world shall perish," admonished the eighteenth-century German philosopher Immanuel Kant. Taken to the extreme for intelligence operations, the Kantian school would reject every rung on the ladder of escalation beyond the first. This was the spirit in which Secretary of State James Stimson initially decided to close down his department's cryptographic division in 1929, politely explaining that "gentlemen do not read each other's mail."[22] One undersecretary of state suggested that the United States "ought to discourage the idea of fighting secret wars or even initiating most covert operations [because] when . . . we mine harbors in Nicaragua . . . we fuzz the difference between ourselves and the Soviet Union. We act out of character. . . . When we yield to what is, in my judgment, a childish temptation to fight the Russians on their own

Ethics of Covert Operations

Table 3.2   *(Continued)*

Threshold	Nation	Operation
		against leaders in Algeria and Egypt (1950s) and Libya (1980)
Three	Israel/U.S.	Covert weapons sales to Iran (1986)
	Israel	Training Sri Lanka security forces (1984)
	West Germany	Economic disruption in Guinea (1958)
	U.S./France	Sharing of sensitive nuclear intelligence (1970s–)
	United Kingdom	Propaganda in the Middle East (1950–1960s)
Two	United States	TECHINT surveillance worldwide
	France	Spying on U.S. officials in Paris (1964)
	United Kingdom	Worldwide intelligence collection
One	U.S./U.K.	Sharing of low-level intelligence
	United States	Assisting security of Egyptian leaders (1978), worldwide U.S. embassy security

of Zeal, 235, and Richelson, 204–5 (on Israeli arms sales to Iran); Raviv and Melman, "Killing of Wazir Ruthless and Inefficient," *Los Angeles Times* (Apr. 22, 1988), A1, and Richelson, 204 (on Israel) and 167 (on W. Germany); R.H. Ulmann, "The Covert French Connection," *Foreign Policy* 75 (Summer 1989), 3 (on U.S.-French intelligence sharing); Richelson, 26 (U.K.). Threshold Two: Bamford, *The Puzzle Palace*, and D. Kahn, "Big Ear or Big Brother?" *New York Times* (May 16, 1976), 13 (on U.S. TECHINT operations); Richelson, 160 (on France); Richelson and Ball, *Ties That Bind* (on U.K. espionage). Threshold One: Richelson and Ball, *Ties That Bind* (on U.S.-U.K. intelligence sharing); S.M. Hersh, "Congress Is Accused of Laxity," *New York Times* (June 1, 1978), A1 (on security equipment for Egypt); Johnson, *America's Secret Power*, 31–35 (on routine counterintelligence).

terms and in their own gutter, we make a major mistake and throw away one of our great assets."[23]

At the opposite ethical extreme is a point of view so nationalistic that virtually any use of secret intelligence agencies in defense of the nation-state becomes acceptable. The consequences of one's acts are more important, from this vantage point, than the intrinsic worthiness (or unworthiness) of the acts themselves. If the consequence is to help preserve the citizenry of a nation against a foreign threat, the act is justifiable. In light of the present anarchic and hostile world environment, a nation must defend itself in every possible way, including the use of all the dark arts available through the auspices of the secret services—thus the Doolittle Report, Rusk's war in the back alleys, and the rejection of Marquis of Queensberry rules. G. Gordon Liddy, a former CIA operative and Watergate conspirator, stated this point of view more colloquially on the campus lecture circuit: "The world isn't Beverly Hills; it's a bad neighborhood at two o'clock in the morning."[24] The CIA would have to act accordingly.

In between the poles of Kantian and consequentialist morality lies a vast expanse of intelligence options less pure in form than the two extremes of "Do no evil" and "Do anything." Even consequentialists like Gen. James Doolittle, Rusk, and Liddy would no doubt disagree on how far a nation ought to march down the road of "anything goes." Certainly Secretary Rusk had a more refined sense of moral limits than G. Gordon Liddy. In making moral judgments about covert options in this middle ground, most analysts would not blanch at the measures listed for Thresholds One and Two on the ladder of escalation. Ethical debate can grow quite heated, however, over the more intrusive interventions against national sovereignty envisaged at Thresholds Three and Four.

Yet even those ethicists who generally prefer nonintervention are prepared to acknowledge the existence of certain conditions in which the aggressive use of secret intelligence agencies abroad may be in order. Foremost among these conditions, for some analysts, is simple self-defense—a central stanchion in the traditional theory of the just war (though the term "self-defense" can be notoriously slippery).[25] High on the list too is the moral imperative to help people who face enslavement, wholesale brutality, or genocide—covert intervention on humanitarian grounds.[26]

Others would add to this list the need to assist oppressed friends of Western democratic values who ask for help (or, during the Cold War, at least those who were anti-Communists)—a considerable opening of the interventionist door.[27] Going a step further, some ethicists would defend the sovereign independence of any state, regardless of regime type; they prefer to honor above all the inviolability of national boundaries as a central postulate of contemporary international law. This was the main public defense of the U.S. insistence, supported by the United Nations in 1990, that Iraq remove its invasion force from neighboring Kuwait.[28] Some would use only the degree of force that was proportional to the perceived threat—another central postulate of the just-war theory.[29]

Still others would eschew most unilateral actions, seeking greater moral legitimacy in multilateral intervention.[30] Practical considerations are also essential to some analysts. They argue that to be acceptable, covert intervention must have a good chance of succeeding and should be in harmony with the overt policy positions of the sponsoring nation.[31]

Although these propositions (as with the wider literature they briefly sum-

Ethics of Covert Operations

marize) are clouded in ambiguities, the spires of four fundamental conclusions poke through the mist. The first, expressed by two intelligence officials, posits that "given the depravity of the world around us . . . free societies have no choice but to engage in intelligence activities if they are to remain free."[32] The underlying assumption here—one accepted by most contemporary scholars, government officials, and citizens—is an acceptance of the preeminence of the nation-state and the correctness of its defense. World order theorists have a different vision, perhaps ultimately a better one, in which global human needs gain ascendancy over state interests; but, for the present at least, their arguments remain quixotic.[33]

If one accepts the need for some intelligence activities, the next question becomes: which ones are acceptable? At this point the second major ethical conclusion emerges, namely, that this determination depends morally on the extent to which one is willing to accept loss of life and the physical destruction of property as a part of a covert intervention.[34] Here are the considerations that give pause to Threshold Four and lend it the name "Extreme Options."

A third major conclusion follows from the second: agreement on the moral acceptability of low-threshold intelligence activities is widespread, but the appropriateness of higher-threshold activities is a topic riven by dissension. As a former DCI properly notes, "There are few absolutes in the ethics of covert action."[35] Experts and laypersons alike are frequently of two minds on when—or even whether—covert violence ought to be part of a nation's foreign policy.

In light of this disagreement, the fourth conclusion—a procedural one that lies at the heart of this book and of my earlier studies on intelligence—is that no single authority ought to make this important decision. Rather, in a free society it is appropriate that decisions on contentious issues be made by a group of elected officials (though, for sensitive intelligence matters, one small in size and whose deliberations are conducted in secrecy). In a democracy the great moral issues of covert intervention warrant debate, even if it is confined to a more limited number of elected officers than normally participate in policy deliberations. These often far-reaching choices stand to benefit significantly from the advantages of a candid dialogue between the branches, from the airing of different points of view and the sharing of experience and insight—in a word, from democracy.

Difficult ethical issues may not be resolved in any definitive fashion by a group decision process, but pooling the moral judgments of leading officials gives a better chance at arriving at a worthy outcome than entrusting the results to one or two individuals deciding alone. This, at any rate, is the gamble that underpins the theory of constitutional government.

View of the Enemy

Just as ethical perspectives are important in determining the proper level of intrusiveness abroad, so too is one's perception of the adversary. For some, the adversary is so venal, so intractable, so dangerous—the devil incarnate—that the us-them relationship can only be thought of as a zero-sum game in which any gain for one side must mean a defeat for the other. Mixing realpolitik with Bible-thumping morality, a chairman of the U.S. House Committee on Armed Services once referred to the Cold War as "a battle between Jesus Christ and the hammer-and-sickle."[36] Extreme intelligence options designed to subdue the Soviet Satan became acceptable, even attractive.

Others hold a more hopeful outlook, viewing the adversary as someone with whom one might deal—cautiously, to be sure—in order to achieve positive gains for both sides. Attitudes toward an enemy can change—witness Ronald Reagan's transition from denouncing the Soviet Union as an "evil empire" to rejecting this bleak characterization a few years later—and as they do, harsh intelligence options directed against the foe may become unacceptable.[37]

Target Regime

The nature of the target regime can be another factor in assessing the ethics of covert operations. Some analysts believe that in selecting intelligence options, it makes a difference whether one has targeted free and open societies or closed totalitarian and authoritarian regimes. In targeting the former, they argue, one ought to be more circumspect and less intrusive. As regards the latter, restraints can be fewer—especially against the totalitarian regimes, which (the argument goes) represent a greater threat to Western civilization than authoritarian ones.[38]

Take covert propaganda. To interfere with the free press in a democracy—say, the *Times* of London or New York—is abhorrent to some, striking at the root of Western values. But since during the Cold War *Pravda* and *Isvestiia* were widely considered mere organs of the Soviet Communist party, their content was fair game.[39]

Leadership Personality

The personal characteristics of the DCI can move policy officers toward particular views on the efficacy and appropriateness of the various intelligence options. The Reagan administration's first DCI, William J. Casey—by reputation a hard-core, zero-sum, anti-Communist tough guy—seemed more prepared to climb rapidly up the ladder of escalation than some of his predecessors. For ex-

Ethics of Covert Operations

ample, William E. Colby, a Nixon appointee, was more of a pragmatist who acknowledged some moral restraints on covert operations and harbored some sense of the possibilities for detente with the Soviet Union.[40]

Funding for covert action declined precipitously under Colby and rose sharply under Casey (see chapter 2). Although the causes of covert-action budget trends extend far beyond the personalities of the DCIs, the directors' individual perspectives on the world certainly have played a role.

Imminent Threat

If information is the sine qua non of good decisionmaking, time keeps it close company.[41] An assessment of intelligence options depends on one's sense of imminent threat to the national security. If (to use an extreme scenario) a nation's leaders believe that a major city was about to be vaporized by a nuclear device stolen by terrorists, they would no doubt use every means available to avoid this calamity. Constitutional safeguards would be thrown out the window. Even the assassination of the suspected terrorists would be an option if the nation's leaders were persuaded that murder would prevent the nuclear annihilation of millions—a consequentialist's imperative. Given the luxury of more time (the normal circumstance), the ladder of escalation can be climbed more prudently and with greater deliberation.

Severity of the Threat

As the nuclear scenario implies, the perceived severity of the threat is also relevant. Terrorists armed with nuclear weapons demand a quick and highly intrusive response. In contrast, Greenpeace environmentalists in creaky old sailing ships protesting nuclear testing in the Pacific Ocean represent a much more modest threat to a nation's sovereignty, warranting at best a low-rung covert response (if any at all).

Clearly, the 1983 bombing of Greenpeace's *Rainbow Warrior* in Auckland harbor by two French intelligence officers, in which a Greenpeace photographer was killed, represents a response far out of proportion to the threat. The bombing was a provocative slap at New Zealand's sovereignty, not to mention an infringement of the civil liberties of the ship's owners and passengers. If the French had felt that their interests were so threatened by the *Rainbow Warrior* (a "bucket of bolts," according to a high-ranking New Zealand national security official), disabling the ship at sea with a low-charge explosion on the propeller shaft—or even with tangled wire—would have been enough covert action to deter its further passage.[42]

Prevailing conditions of war or peace are necessary considerations as well.

If one nation is involved in an overt military conflict with another nation, whether or not war has been formally declared, its leaders have decided that the threat to their national interests is sufficiently grave to warrant a major foreign policy response. In these conditions—and especially in circumstances of a formally declared war—covert operations are likely to be stepped up. Indeed, assassination plots against the adversary's leaders, along with other extreme measures, become standard—although even the rules of open warfare proscribe some activities, such as the use of chemical and biological agents against noncombatants. In times of overt warfare, *almost* anything goes when it comes to supportive intelligence options.

Short-Term and Long-Term Effects

Ideally, one would also like to know before judging the appropriateness of a covert operation what its effects will be on the future of the target nation, its people, and their relationship with the perpetrator of the covert operation. Such prognosticating is the most difficult task of all.

To what extent does the United States (or other nations using covert operations) have a confident sense of the historical forces their secret activities may unleash? Very little, especially over the long term. Certainly the United States was unable to anticipate how despised the shah of Iran would become within his own nation after the CIA (and British intelligence) helped him into power in 1953.[43]

The inherent difficulty of predicting long-range historical results has been exacerbated by the lack of knowledge the United States has sometimes exhibited concerning the circumstances within target nations. Ignorance of Fidel Castro's wide popularity in Cuba—a phenomenon well appreciated by CIA analysts in the Directorate of Information but not by paramilitary covert-action specialists in the Directorate of Operations, who had closer ties to the Kennedy administration—led White House officials to endorse the ill-fated Bay of Pigs operation. Can-do covert-action bureaucrats displaced the more scholarly intelligence analysts from the decision process, leaving policymakers with a one-sided view that Castro could easily be toppled.[44]

Though mistakes and misjudgments are inevitable, governments contemplating covert intervention ought at a minimum, as Charles Beitz has stressed, "to know enough about the culture and values of the target society to make informed judgments about its welfare, and enough about its politics and history to calculate the likely consequences of the kinds of intervention contemplated."[45] This level of understanding requires greater attention by decisionmakers to the recommendations of intelligence analysts and outside academic

Ethics of Covert Operations

experts. It is worth remembering, however, that covert-action specialists themselves can be insightful, and their views ought to be weighed. Operations Directorate case officers often have more direct knowledge and experience from having lived in the target country than anyone else in the American government.

A BRIGHT LINE ON THE LADDER OF ESCALATION

Where should the line be drawn against excessive covert operations? No single policy officer, not even a president, can settle the answer. Each covert operation requires inspection. A decision must draw on the substantive knowledge and ethical wisdom of a small number of well-informed individuals: elected officials in the executive and legislative branches (assisted by their top aides), who understand the theory and practice of intelligence, have studied the conditions in the target nation and its region, and, most significant in a democracy, are sensitive to the likely attitudes of the American people toward the proposed secret intervention.

The Importance of Process

Making ethical decisions about covert operations requires a thorough decisionmaking process. The process should involve elected officials with national security experience, assisted by well-trained intelligence and foreign policy specialists who understand the possibilities—as well as the dangers and limitations—of using clandestine agencies in support of democratic values.

Who should stand within this "witting circle" of intelligence decisionmakers? The model in use in the United States approaches a good balance between secrecy and accountability. Important initiatives are first scrutinized by intelligence professionals, then by top policy aides in the executive branch, followed by their principals (including, since 1975, formal presidential approval for covert actions); finally, operations are vetted by the House and Senate Intelligence Committees. In times of emergency, the number of legislative participants is limited to just the top eight leaders of Congress.[46]

Ambiguity and controversy have surrounded these procedures, especially over whether the congressional Intelligence Committees (or at least the Gang of Eight) should be notified prior to all important intelligence operations. Following passage of the 1980 Intelligence Oversight Act, which seemed to require prior notice (though the language contained ambiguities), the White House failed to honor this understanding in only a single known instance: the Iran-contra affair.[47]

The 1991 Intelligence Oversight Act clarified congressional expectations and at the same time yielded to the White House somewhat on the question of prior notice. The clarification came in the form of the first explicit statutory definition and authority for covert action, coupled with a reemphasis that prior notice was expected in most instances. But in times of emergency the president could delay his "finding" report to Congress for a few days. This proviso, inserted at the insistence of President Bush, overrode the understanding since the Hughes-Ryan Act in 1974 that reporting would occur within twenty-four hours.[48]

Most officials in the intelligence community, the White House, and the Congress have come to accept the "New Oversight" as an appropriate means for deciding on intelligence options while at the same time trying to keep the secret agencies within the bounds of American law and the prevailing sense of ethical propriety. The great tragedy of the Iran-contra episode was the disdainful attitude of high officials toward this delicate balance. Although according to one report "the intelligence scandals and institutional reforms of the 1970s remain living lessons in the secret world,"[49] obviously some individuals in the Reagan administration failed to get the message. Or, more likely perhaps, they understood but rejected the idea of legislative supervision of intelligence policy.[50] Gregory F. Treverton pinpoints the unfortunate implication: "Excluding Congress also excluded one more 'political scrub,' one more source of advice about what the range of American people would find acceptable."[51]

Why was Congress excluded? The administration's national security adviser, Vice Admiral John M. Poindexter, said he wished to avoid "any interference."[52] Nor did William J. Casey want legislators peering over his shoulder. According to testimony from Poindexter's assistant, Lieutenant Colonel Oliver L. North, the DCI sought nothing less than a secret entity (nicknamed "the Enterprise") "that was self-financing, independent of appropriated monies, and capable of conducting activities similar to the ones that we had conducted [during the Iran-contra operations]."[53] Investigators learned, moreover, that the Iran-contra conspirators had even excluded the president from their machinations, as a way of allowing the White House "plausible deniability"—a slippery doctrine bitingly criticized by the Church Committee a decade earlier.[54] In short, they excluded democracy.

The rejection of democratic procedures by NSC staffers during the Iran-contra affair points to another critical element of intelligence: the personal integrity of those holding positions of public responsibility. As the ancient Greeks well understood, the forms of government are but empty shells in themselves; they must be made to work by honest individuals who possess more than love for country. Leaders must also have a deep appreciation for the principles of democracy—a system of governing that, as a guard against the abuse of power, depends vitally on the kind of "interference" so disdainfully dismissed by Admiral Poindexter.[55] Military personnel are generally imbued with a strong sense of ethics and the importance of democratic procedure—above all, the idea of civilian supremacy in decisionmaking. The Iran-contra case, however, showed that this socialization sometimes fails to take.

Admiral Poindexter professes to have been the victim of a liberal attack aimed at the Reagan revolution.[56] How widely this view is shared is unknown, although some Republicans on the congressional Iran-contra investigating committees seemed prepared in their Minority Report to fully exonerate the admiral and his staff.[57] To many critics, however, the affair went much deeper than partisan politics, striking at the foundations of constitutional government by undermining the appropriations process, not to mention the sanctity of laws (the Boland Amendments limiting covert action in Nicaragua, among other statutes) and the established covert-action reporting requirements (the Hughes-Ryan Act and the 1980 Intelligence Oversight Act). During hearings and investigations into the affair, leading Republicans and Democrats—conservatives and liberals alike—spoke against the controversial operations of the NSC staff.[58]

Consequently, in speaking of process as vital to the selection of intelligence options, one must in the same breath add a caveat: in a democracy officeholders are expected to honor the laws and respect the rights and opinions of those to whom they owe their office—the people. In turn, the people in modern society are forced to rely chiefly on their elected surrogates in both Congress and the White House to monitor and assess the wisdom of secret foreign policy initiatives. When the surrogates are shut out, so are the people.

GUIDELINES FOR APPRAISING PROPOSED COVERT INTERVENTIONS

In a society where ethical standards can change, a case-by-case examination relying on a small bipartisan group of executive-legislative overseers is the most sensible approach to evaluating the acceptability of covert operations. This review process, however, need not begin anew each time; some widely accepted standards can provide at least general guidance to the deliberations.

Threshold Four

On the ladder of escalation (table 3.1) most observers would probably agree that the democracies can shun altogether the highest rung—the use of chemical-biological agents and other toxic substances. The other extreme options at this threshold (Rungs 27–37) should garner support in only the most extraordinary circumstances: when the survival of one's society is at stake (self-defense) or for humanitarian purposes when passivity might lead to enslavement, wholesale brutality, or genocide within a heinous regime.

One perplexing scenario at Threshold Four arises when an indigenous, democratically inclined faction asks for covert assistance to overthrow an autocratic regime or to repel foreign intruders. In such instances sophisticated arms supplies (Rung 27), small-scale coups (Rung 35), and even major "secret" wars—the classic oxymoron of an "overt-covert" intervention (Rung 37)—may be worth considering. First, however, the prudent policy officer will want to see whether the pro-democracy faction displays signs of legitimacy among the indigenous populace, whether it has a viable leadership and a credible organization—that is, some reasonable chance of succeeding—and whether less extreme responses might work instead. Among the latter is massive funding to the pro-democracy faction (Rung 17) or, better still, open activity, including economic inducements and punishments, diplomatic negotiations, moral suasion, and organizational support.[59]

Above all, those who propose secret intervention must remember the risks of being drawn into a swamp of protracted and costly warfare, with no victory in sight—indeed, with the possible decimation of the supported faction. The fate of the Kurds in Iraq and the Meos in Laos, abandoned by the CIA to sure defeat after they had been encouraged and armed to fight for their freedom, is a painful reminder of this unfortunate outcome.

The temptation can be strong to move quickly forward toward Threshold Four in an effort to rid the world of an evil dictator. After a few failed attempts at mounting a coup against Panama's General Manuel Antonio Noriega,[60] the United States finally chose to depose him in 1989 through an overt military operation. In retrospect, though, even some analysts who normally reject clandestine intervention have wondered whether more persistent covert efforts to topple Noriega might not have been the lesser of two evils. The appeal of a coup or assassination in this and similar cases lies partially in the more limited loss of life that may accompany a stealthier approach to foreign policy than open warfare. Several hundred Panamanian civilians died in the U.S. attack against Noriega; thousands of Iraqi civilians perished in 1991 during the attack against Saddam Hussein's armies in the Persian Gulf.

The avoidance of deaths among innocent noncombatants, a central tenet of the just-war tradition, is a principle that enjoys widespread support. Yet the promise of a quick coup or assassination—even though such tactics have the attraction of safeguarding innocent civilians—can draw a nation all too readily into unsavory remedies for its international grievances. Is it not better to renounce these dark and slippery options in favor of open military action (if all the other overt options have failed)—even if the cost in human lives may be higher than in a more narrowly focused paramilitary operation? If intervention had to be open and highly visible, with the possibility of considerable loss of life—civilian and military—policymakers might be inclined to think twice about the necessity for using force to influence affairs in other nations, and about the extent to which the American people would be likely to support the use of force.

More broadly, America's leaders might well consider whether it is really the responsibility of the United States to rid the world of its dictators and other assorted scoundrels. Does the United States have the resources—the blood, the treasure, the will—for this responsibility? Was Noriega—as revolting an individual as he was—a more heinous threat to U.S. interests than, say, the Colombian drug lords? Was his forced extradition to the United States as a drug dealer worth the lives of those people killed, American and Panamanian, during the invasion?

If force is to be used against a foreign dictator, a multilateral overt operation would be preferable to a U.S. paramilitary activity in all but a few extreme situations. Overt intervention itself, however, ought to be a matter of last resort, turned to only when American interests are directly and obviously assailed. For the most part, the sad problem of autocratic regimes must be combatted with diplomatic initiatives, trade sanctions (directed toward the adversary's rich, not the poor), and moral suasion by means of such tools as the increasingly strong force of worldwide media condemnation to make tyrants international pariahs. Above all, the United States must rely on the indigenous population itself to rise up against a cruel master, just as the American colonists did in 1776 and the courageous citizens of Eastern European nations and the Soviet republics did at the end of the Cold War. These democratic rebellions may warrant measured support, overt and covert, from the outside world—especially in places where political and other human rights have been suffocated.

There are two important exceptions where covert may be preferred to overt action: in self-defense against possible attack with weapons of mass destruction and for humanitarian purposes against autocrats with genocidal designs. If a dictator (or a renegade faction) is reliably believed to be on the verge of obtaining a capacity to use nuclear, biological, or chemical (NBC) weapons against other nations or groups, this threat must be dealt with before it is too late. In 1981 Israel chose an overt military air strike to destroy an Iraqi nuclear reactor near Baghdad thought to be used for making nuclear bombs; in 1991 the United States and its allies took advantage of the opportunity to seek the destruction of Saddam Hussein's NBC weapons capacities at the same time that they drove his troops out of Kuwait. In lieu of unilateral or multilateral actions of these kinds, a limited paramilitary strike (multinational, if possible) may be necessary in the future against an outlaw regime that threatens a chemical-biological or nuclear surprise attack.

Ideally, the covert action would involve a small force acting under the United Nations Security Council or other international authority, with the right of a U.S. veto *and with the most exacting supervision.* When diplomatic initiatives fail to curb the appetite of heinous regimes for weapons of mass destruction, this approach may serve as a better alternative—in the extreme instance of chemical-biological or nuclear threats—than a full-scale military invasion costing thousands of civilian lives.

The second exception is in response to a genocidal regime. Leaders who have engineered and encouraged mass murder invite arrest by a multinational paramilitary arm—again, ideally under the authority and supervision of the Security Council—followed by a fair trial before a respected international tribunal of jurists. The precedent for this exception was established after World War Two when Nazi leaders were put on trial at Nuremberg for crimes against humanity.

Threshold Three

The options of Threshold Three are similarly clouded by broad patches of gray. The best approach is to incline against their use, unless the reasons for accepting them are highly compelling. In the American system, during normal times, the president and the members of the congressional Intelligence Committees should be consulted; in times of emergency, the president and the "Gang of Eight." Moreover, policy officers should never turn to an option that would violate the laws of the United States, unless they believe—as did Lincoln in 1861—that the very survival of the nation is at stake if the law is honored. In such cases they must explain themselves thoroughly and be held accountable (through impeachment proceedings, if necessary) as soon as the danger subsides. For Thresholds Three and Four, those in power would do well to recall the prudent prescription tendered by John Quincy Adams in his inaugural address. America should be "the friend of all the liberties in the world, [but] the guardian of only her own."

Thoughtful critics have long emphasized the wisdom of reserving the more extreme covert options for only the most pressing circumstances. At congressional hearings in 1975 Cyrus Vance, soon to be named secretary of state by Jimmy Carter, thought they should be used only when "absolutely essential"; and Clark Clifford, a drafter of the National Security Act of 1947, testified that they should be undertaken only in circumstances that "truly affect our national security." In 1976 the Church Committee admonished that such measures should be contemplated only in response to "a grave, unforeseen threat"; more than ten years later the Majority Report of the Iran-contra Congressional Investigating Committees declared that they had to be "conducted in an accountable manner and in accordance with law."[61]

Thresholds One and Two

At the bottom of the escalation ladder, Thresholds One and Two will probably continue to be acceptable behavior in the eyes of most practitioners and observers. Perhaps even these options will be scaled back one day, if more nations embrace democracy and conduct their affairs in a more open fashion.

Spelling Out the Guidelines

The preceding discussion suggests eleven guidelines by which the merits of proposed covert operations may be judged by policymakers and their overseers.[62]

1. Whenever possible, policymakers should shun covert operations in favor of a diplomatic resolution of international disputes.

2. Covert operations should be kept in harmony with publicly stated policy objectives, except in the rarest of occasions when deception is deemed vital to the safety of the United States.

3. Only those covert operations should be conducted which, if exposed, would not unduly embarrass the United States.

4. Before proceeding, policymakers should consult extensively with intelligence analysts and other experts on a target nation, not just covert-action specialists.

5. Policymakers should never bypass established decision procedures, including congressional reporting requirements (which ought to honor the concept of prior notice—except in times of the most acute emergency).

6. In support of covert operations, policymakers should never violate the laws of the United States, short of the rare need to save the nation in a time of desperation.

7. Against fellow democracies policymakers should eschew all but the most routine, low-level covert operations—unless a democracy is engaged in activ-

ities inimical to the well-being of other democracies (such as abetting the illicit spread of weapons of mass destruction).

8. Even against nondemocratic regimes, policymakers should strive to remain at the lower, less intrusive end of the escalation ladder, applying the just-war rule of proportionality, and climb higher up the ladder only when all else fails.

9. Case officers should repeatedly warn foreign agents that their relationship with U.S. intelligence agencies will be terminated if they engage in acts of murder, terrorism, narcotics trafficking, human rights abuses, or violation of American law.

10. In almost all cases, policymakers should reject secret wars, coups d'état, and other extreme measures, for if American interests are so jeopardized as to require major forceful intervention, then properly authorized overt warfare—ideally multinational in nature and at the invitation of a legitimate government or faction—is a more appropriate and honorable option.

11. In considering covert operations, America's long-standing and widely admired tradition of fair play should not be forgotten.

The first guideline may seem obvious enough. All too often, though, policy officers are tempted to try a silent "quick fix" through the use of covert action rather than to employ trained diplomatic negotiators—who themselves may have to engage in secret discussion with adversaries, a more acceptable process than clandestine intelligence operations. An overly hasty dismissal of the diplomatic approach in favor of a paramilitary hostage-rescue attempt in Iran led Secretary of State Cyrus Vance to resign in protest from the Carter administration.[63]

The second guideline, if followed, would have stopped the Reagan administration's secret sale of arms to Iran (another paramilitary operation)—a policy in sharp contradiction to the overt U.S. stance against the sale of weapons to terrorist groups or their allies. Some thoughtful observers maintain that a two-track foreign policy may be necessary at times, with the open track going in one direction to fool adversaries and the secret track heading toward a nation's true objectives. In time of war, deceptive operations are obviously useful and will always be employed in combat situations; but, short of open warfare or acute emergencies, the existence of two diverging tracks leads only to a disjointed foreign policy and ought to be avoided. Seeking detente with the Soviet Union, for example, while carrying out aggressive covert actions against it rarely made sense.

The third guideline would make policy officers think twice about secret alliances with particularly unsavory people. The recruitment of Panama's General Noriega for intelligence collection, former Nazis like Klaus Barbie for counterintelligence, Saddam Hussein for covert action against Iran, and organized crime figures for assassination plots backfired.[64] This is not to suggest that the United States should deal only with angels (they are in short supply) but that even in the pursuit of national objectives, some limits ought to be recognized.

The fourth guideline seeks to avoid the trap of groupthink. Study after study of U.S. intelligence has revealed a tendency to drive analysts and other lower- and middle-level officials—precisely the people with a rich experience in foreign countries—out of decision forums in favor of covert-action specialists who may understand less about the history and culture of the target nation.[65] This does not mean that policymakers should go to the other extreme and discount the views of covert-action experts; the best of those in the Operations Directorate have genuine country expertise and a level-headed sense of what will work. A key objective of these consultations with specialists (including outside academicians) should be to calculate, to the extent possible, the likely side effects (short-term and long-term) of a proposed covert intervention.

Guidelines 5 and 6 stress the importance of honoring the established decision processes for covert operations—blatantly disregarded during the Iran-contra affair. Here the purpose, so vital in a democracy, is to maintain both dialogue and accountability, drawing on the collective judgment of Congress and the president. In circumstances of acute emergency the president retains the right to take those steps he or she considers necessary to save the nation—steps for which the president will be held accountable. Of the various prescriptions presented here, none is more cardinal than this emphasis on process: *never bypass established decision procedures.*

The remaining guidelines, 7 through 11, underscore the special place of democratic values in the world's political evolution.[66] The seventh, for example, acknowledges the value that Americans place in the global fellowship of democracies. The nurturing of free societies—perhaps never more promising than now in the nations of Eastern Europe and the former Soviet republics—is done great harm when America's leaders order harsh covert operations against fellow democracies.

The ninth guideline means rejecting some potentially useful intelligence sources, like Guatemala's Colonel Alpirez. Admittedly, though, if Alpirez were a colonel in the Russian intelligence service providing the United States with a direct espionage channel to military planning in the Kremlin unavailable through any other source, severing ties would be more problematic. But even in this hypothetical instance, if the Russian colonel were involved in the murder of an American citizen (as has been alleged in the Guatemalan case), that would go beyond the pale of acceptability.

This final set of guidelines recognizes that the higher rungs on the ladder of escalation are fraught with risk and clouded with ethical doubt. Indeed, in circumstances serious enough to warrant considering covert options above Rung 23, the use of overt force backed by a formal declaration of war (or at least given legitimacy through the provisions of the War Powers Resolution of 1973) would be in order. As for the exceptions—when a renegade regime with avowed hostile intentions approaches chemical-biological or nuclear weapons sufficiency, or when a mass murderer begins a campaign of genocide within his society—a paramilitary operation (as described earlier) can be justified.

Among the more controversial, and questionable, options on the escalation ladder is the assassination plot. Almost always, it remains an unworthy, illegal, and for that matter impractical approach to America's international problems.[67] Even if one places ethical considerations aside, assassination plots invite retaliation against U.S. leaders, who are highly vulnerable in an open society. Further, the execution of a foreign leader offers no assurance that the successor will be any more favorably disposed toward the United States. Such plots are also difficult to implement; Fidel Castro was able to elude the many CIA attempts against his life.[68]

The counterargument in favor of assassination in extraordinary circumstances usually raises the example of Adolf Hitler. What if the United States, France, or Britain had murdered Adolf Hitler before Germany invaded Poland? Is it not possible that his successor might have forgone exterminating millions of Jews and overrunning Europe? And even if Hitler's assassination had brought about a retaliation against President Franklin D. Roosevelt, would it not still have been worth trading two lives for the six million lost in the Holocaust?

The trouble with these and similar questions is that they are too speculative: Hitler's monstrous intentions were less clear before the war than they became later. Further, his underlings seem to have been as mad as he—perhaps even more insane in some instances. Should it be U.S. policy to assassinate all who are, or might become, venal tyrants—and their immediate staff and relatives, too, just to be on the safe side? And is the matter of retaliation unimportant?

In times of war, properly authorized by Congress, assassination takes on a different coloration. As former DCI Admiral Stansfield Turner has observed:

[Assassination] is tempting to me only in wartime. I would have approved assassinating Saddam Hussein after the 16th of January [1991, the date when Congress gave its authority to use military force against Iraq]. And that's exactly the reason: there's a big difference between a President—and, heaven help us, somebody below him—taking on him- or herself to say, "Noriega ought to die," and the Congress of the United States and the public of the United States saying, "We're going to war with Panama, and Noriega is just as much a target as Joe Jones, Private First-Class." And if you happen to target Noriega specifically—and surely we targeted Saddam Hussein, [but] it didn't work—I think that's all right.[69]

The eleventh guideline stands as a reminder that Americans take pride in the difference between their country and autocratic regimes. America's reputation for fair play—often stained by CIA excesses—has distinguished U.S. foreign policy from the approach of more brutal governments and has won respect and friendship for the United States in many parts of the world. In the interests of maintaining this vital difference between dictatorships and democracies, Roger Fisher (among others) has argued against using the coercive instruments of covert action. He urges, instead, greater reliance on "the most powerful weapons we have: idealism, morality, due process of law, and belief in the freedom to disagree, including the right of other countries to disagree with ours."[70]

In table 3.3, instances of failed U.S. covert operations are presented to suggest how they might have been avoided (or at any rate modified) by adherence to these eleven guidelines.

Table 3.3   Failed U.S. Intelligence Operations That Might Have Been Rejected or Modified If Filtered through the Recommended Guidelines

Guidelines	Operations
1.	Iran hostage rescue attempt (1980)
2.	Iran arms sale (1984)
3.	Funding of Christian Democratic Party in Italy (1979)
4.	Bay of Pigs invasion (1961)
5.	Diversion of arms to Nicaraguan contras (1985)
6.	Operation CHAOS (1967–74)
7.	Anti-Allende operations in Chile (1963–73)
8.	Escalation of covert actions in Nicaragua (1982–87)
9.	Ties with Panamanian dictator Noriega (1975–89)
10.	Anti-Diem activities in Vietnam (1963)
11.	Assassination plots in Cuba and the Congo (1960–65)

Can the United States and other democracies truly compete in the present international arena without resorting to extreme covert operations, when their adversaries have often seemed prepared to carry out the most ruthless measures against the open societies? I am persuaded that the democracies will win their ideological battle with the nondemocratic regimes mainly by virtue of their higher principles and more humane behavior, along with their more appealing economic systems. The people of the world care most about food and shelter, clean air and pure water, the education of their children, and their rights to political dissent, liberty, justice, and happiness. The democracies have much to offer here.

As a leading member of the U.S. House Committee on Foreign Affairs once said, "The best way to promote our interests is to promote our ideals."[71] In contrast, brutality, coercion, and violence—too often the specialties of nondemocratic regimes—are poor alternatives. Those who ply these wares have attracted no admiration, only fear.

The excessive use of highly intrusive intelligence options has done much to discredit the United States and other democracies, making their secret services seem at times little different from their erstwhile enemy during the Cold War, the Soviet KGB and GRU. By employing its secret agencies mainly for relatively nonintrusive collection operations, and by resorting to more aggressive operations—particularly covert actions—only with an abiding regard for the principles presented here, the United States can lay claim again to the high esteem it enjoyed throughout the world in the aftermath of World War Two.

CHAPTER 4

INTELLIGENCE ACCOUNTABILITY

The time: December 6, 1977. The setting: the first intelligence briefing on a presidential finding before the newly established U.S. House Permanent Select Committee on Intelligence (HPSCI), known informally by members of Congress as the Boland Committee, chaired by Edward P. Boland of Massachusetts.

Three years earlier, in December 1974, the Congress had passed the Hughes-Ryan Amendment to the 1947 National Security Act.[1] This law required the president to approve all important covert actions by way of a finding, usually a sentence or two—or at most a short paragraph—that endorsed the proposed operation. The law required the president further to report the finding (by way of the DCI) to the "appropriate committees" of Congress. In 1974 that meant the House and Senate committees on appropriations, armed services, and foreign relations—six panels altogether. With the creation of the Senate Select Committee on Intelligence (SSCI) in 1976 and its House counterpart a year later, the DCI began reporting mainly to the two new intelligence oversight committees on most activities (along with the defense subcommittees of the House and Senate appropriations committees on budgetary matters). In the case of a finding, he reported exclusively to these new oversight panels—a custom made into law by the 1980 Intelligence Oversight Act.

At this first important meeting of the House Intelligence Committee, Chairman Boland, a sixty-five-year-old bachelor, a former roommate and a close friend of Speaker Thomas "Tip" O'Neill, as well as the best baritone on Capitol Hill, welcomed Admiral Stansfield Turner, President Carter's DCI, to his maiden appearance before the committee. Silver-haired, stocky, ruggedly handsome, a former Rhodes scholar and middle guard on the Naval Academy football team, Turner smiled back confidently at the semicircle of legislators arrayed behind a thick mahogany bench to hear the initial House briefing on a presidential finding. After an exchange of pleasantries, the DCI read the short finding statement and sat there silently waiting for a response.

Only seven of the committee's thirteen members had bothered to attend the meeting, six Democrats and one lonely Republican. The crush of last-minute legislative duties on the more established committees—panels that controlled money for district projects—evidently held a greater attraction for them than this opportunity to be in on the panel's first top-secret covert-action briefing. After a full minute of silence, in which the admiral gazed around the bunker-like HPSCI hearing room with a bemused look, Roman Mazzoli, a feisty Democratic legislator from Kentucky, cleared his throat and launched into a serious criticism of the finding. Turner clenched his teeth, the muscles in his jaw flexing, then offered a spirited defense of the operation.

Mazzoli remained unimpressed by the rebuttal. To the admiral's surprise and obvious irritation, the congressman laid out a series of further objections. Soon Chairman Boland raised his hand to end the exchange. "I'd like to have a serious debate," he said, "but this is not the place."[2] The three staff aides in the room, seated behind the legislators, threw looks at each other: if this was not the place to have a debate with the DCI—in a closed meeting, guarded by Capitol Hill police, within the inner sanctum of HPSCI's suite of offices near the Capitol Dome—then where was?

"I don't want any adversary proceedings between this Committee and the intelligence agencies," said Boland flatly. Mazzoli sank back into his chair, a look of shock tinctured with annoyance registering on his face. A few of the other members turned toward Boland in dismay, but no one came to Mazzoli's rescue. Crossing swords with a committee chairman was unwise, especially during the first important meeting of the committee—and doubly so when the chairman was also the second-ranking member of the all-mighty Appropriations Committee as well as a close pal of the Speaker.

Within minutes the meeting was over. Admiral Turner and his aides left the room draped in smiles, pleased no doubt to have someone of Boland's stature as an ally on Capitol Hill.

Chairman Boland likely had the memory of the Pike Committee in mind when he muzzled Mazzoli. In 1975 Otis Pike of New York had headed the House inquiry into the secret agencies during the Intelligence Wars. Congressman Pike, a former Marine aviator, was an able and fair-minded person, but his committee ran amuck nonetheless, pulled in a dozen different directions by an ideologically diverse membership and an overzealous staff. The Pike Committee lost the support of the House membership, which refused to vote in favor of releasing its year-long investigative findings. The committee's report was subsequently leaked to the *Village Voice* in a blatant breach of security; the culprit (or culprits), whether on the Hill or in the secret agencies themselves, was never determined, despite a lengthy investigation by the FBI.

The experience with the Pike Committee's controversial skirmishes with the CIA and the NSA left a sour taste in the mouths of House members and delayed the creation of an intelligence oversight committee in that chamber for more than a year after the Senate established SSCI. Once HPSCI was established, Boland, as its new chairman, was determined to avoid following the confrontational route chosen by Otis Pike that had led to war with the DCI and disrepute in the House. There would be a new, cooperative relationship between the House and the intelligence community. Debates, if needed, would be conducted in the hidden recesses of the chairman's office; only Boland would confront Turner, if necessary—not the full committee.

Boland's approach was far different from the one adopted by Pike or even Frank Church, who led the 1975 Senate investigation. Pike and, more civilly, Church (a liberal Democrat from rock-ribbed conservative Idaho) were prepared for combat with the secret agencies, if that was what it took to set them straight. They were unhappy with flawed intelligence estimates and violations of law uncovered by their committees, and they were not at all shy about saying so in public hearings. These five-star generals in the Intelligence Wars preferred hot pursuit—Grant and Sherman, not McClellan and Meade. When the Intelligence Wars ended in 1976, Boland saw himself as a peacemaker; the time had come for comity instead of conflict.

The HPSCI chairman's view was understandable. It did no good to strain relations with the intelligence agencies to a breaking point. The tradition of separate institutions sharing power in the American system of government depended on goodwill between the branches. Nor would House members tolerate another Pike Committee; Boland had his marching orders from the Speaker himself. Yet a chummy relationship was unlikely to put the secret agencies on notice that henceforth they faced serious oversight on Capitol Hill.

Within weeks of his first House meeting, Admiral Turner returned with a second covert-action finding. Mazzoli, a small man but one not easily dissuaded, immediately displayed his unwillingness to embrace the posture of quiescence so sternly laid down by Chairman Boland. The congressman fired in Turner's direction a hail of pointed questions about the latest clandestine adventure approved by President Jimmy Carter. This time Les Aspin, a Democrat from Wisconsin who had missed the first meeting, joined in. A magna cum laude graduate of Yale University with a degree in history who went on to earn a doctorate in economics from MIT, Aspin possessed an incisive analytic mind. He was also a battle-scarred veteran of the Pike Committee accustomed to verbal fisticuffs with intelligence officers. He seemed to relish the opportunity to spar with the DCI—or, for that matter, anyone else who came along with an idea or a policy proposal worth debating.

For this second meeting on covert action, the committee's staff director had requested the presence of a transcriber in the room, called a "recorder," to keep a verbatim record of what was said by the DCI and his assistants, as well as by HPSCI members. Employed by the Congress for such purposes and carefully screened by the FBI in a rigorous security clearance (as were the staff aides on the House and Senate intelligence committees), the man repeated what was said into a mask that covered his face, his voice activating a tape recorder. As a backup, he typed every word in special shorthand.

After watching the recorder at work for a full two minutes, Admiral Turner abruptly stopped his briefing on the finding and told Boland that to keep a record of the proceedings would be a breach of security that could not be allowed. The room fell silent. Boland looked up from the bench and expressed his agreement with the DCI. A staff aide quickly jotted a note to Aspin and slipped it onto the benchtop in front of him. It read, "We *must* have a record of these briefings! How else are we going to have any memory of what the DCI said, and whether the CIA is living up to his assurances? It'll be his recollection against ours." In a politically risky move, Aspin spoke forcefully against the chairman's capitulation. With equal conviction, Mazzoli backed up Aspin.

First the chairman, with the grim look of a headmaster before disobedient school lads, then Turner tried to slough off the Aspin-Mazzoli position with assurances that a record was unnecessary; the committee, after all, would have a copy of the finding in its files. Yet Aspin insisted that the finding itself was insufficient; the DCI's dialogue with committee members, in which he explained in greater detail the goals and methods of the operation, was far more important. Glowering at Aspin, Boland repeated that he saw no reason for a transcribed record. He ordered the recorder to put down his mask.

Unbowed, Aspin thrust his head and shoulders across the green baize tabletop and stared along the curve of the bench toward Boland. "I call for a vote on this, Mr. Chairman," Aspin said coldly. Mazzoli followed with a crisp "second." His face darkening, Boland grimaced, pushed his chair back from the bench in disgust, and ordered the committee's clerk to call the roll.

It was gut-check time on the Boland Committee. The chairman was unlikely to forget who voted against him in this challenge to his authority. The clerk called out the names of those present: eleven of the thirteen. When the tally came to an end, Les Aspin—by a one-vote margin—had won the right for HPSCI to keep a verbatim record of the full DCI briefings on covert-action findings. By implication this meant that a recorder could be present for any other presentation by the DCI and his deputies deemed important enough for a permanent committee record. Boland was forced toward a more serious form of oversight that would allow legislators to monitor the ongoing performance of the secret agencies in light of promises made by their leaders during committee briefings.

Throughout the early days of the Boland Committee, the tug-of-war continued between the chairman and the more outspoken members of his panel— notably, along with Aspin and Mazzoli, the Democrats Wyche Fowler of Georgia and Morgan Murphy of Illinois. In opposition to these "upstarts," several members sided with Boland in favor of cordial tête-à-têtes between the chairman and the DCI whenever intelligence disputes arose. Sometimes Boland had a majority on his side; sometimes he did not.

Then came the Reagan administration and the beginning of a transformation in Chairman Boland's attitude toward intelligence oversight. President Reagan appointed an even more assertive DCI—the obstreperous William J. Casey—who by all accounts had never seen a covert action he didn't like. Relations between the CIA and the Boland Committee soon began to deteriorate, as Casey was unwilling to keep the committee well informed. More significantly, the Reagan administration elected to bypass Boland's efforts to limit covert action in Nicaragua through a series of six statutory prohibitions—each more stringent than the other—known collectively as the Boland Amendments.[3] This drew the HPSCI chairman belatedly to the view that the secret agencies did require close monitoring—and perhaps even sharp admonishment from time to time. The eruption of the Iran-contra scandal in 1987 propelled Chairman Boland away from his early comraderie with the CIA and Admiral

Turner to a deep and abiding distrust of Wild Bill Casey and the Operations Directorate.

The education of Eddie Boland provides only a glimpse into the state of affairs between the secret agencies and the congressional committees in the early days of the new intelligence oversight. This chapter offers a more systematic look at this relationship by exploring the commitment to meaningful intelligence oversight displayed by every legislator who served on the House or Senate Intelligence committee from 1975 to 1990, as evidenced in the questioning of CIA witnesses during public hearings.

LEGISLATIVE SUPERVISION

The supervision of executive activities by Congress takes place both formally and informally.[4] Full-blown investigations like the Pike and Church Committee inquiries can cost millions of dollars and last over a year, with elaborate public hearings conducted under the klieg lights of television cameras and a standing-room-only crowd of spectators. These are genuine media events with a national audience. Other means of formal oversight include less well publicized hearings that nonetheless subject officials in the executive branch to close—sometimes heated—interrogation; debates and colloquies in the chambers of Congress; explicit agency reporting requirements (covert action findings among them); inspections of an agency's facilities at home and abroad; and the publication of committee reports bearing on an agency's programs.

In this examination of intelligence accountability, even hearings on new legislative proposals affecting CIA programs are treated as a supervisory activity, since legislators are attempting to control the agency's policies and practices. For some, this perspective may seem to blur the traditional distinction between lawmaking and the supervision of existing programs. Yet legislators spend much of their time looking at federal agencies in order to understand not only how well existing statutes are working but what changes in the law (and executive regulations) may be desirable. These two concerns are part of a seamless web of legislative oversight. Where supervising ends and legislating begins (and vice versa) is often difficult to say. The distinction is artificial, anyway: both represent efforts to place—or sometimes to remove—controls on an executive agency.

On the informal side of legislative supervision stands another long list of activities, far less visible (and therefore knowable) but often of consequence in the daily affairs of government. Here are the winks and nods across committee room tables; the private dinners where tacit policy understandings are reached between agency directors and legislators; and the tennis matches, golf at the Congressional Country Club, and bourbon-soothed "socials" in the hideaway offices of the Capitol. Obviously, much of this side of legislative supervision lies beyond the purview of most researchers. Some former officials and aides have reported on these events; other investigators have gained access to the inner sanctums of government by developing a rapport with members of Congress and observing their behavior.[5]

FORMAL HEARINGS AS A MEASURE OF INTELLIGENCE ACCOUNTABILITY

From the wide range of supervisory activities engaged in by Congress, this chapter focuses on one of the most significant: participation in formal public hearings on the CIA, both investigative and routine. The differences between Congress's closed and open supervision of the CIA cannot be tested in any satisfying manner at the present time, since the overwhelming majority of executive-session hearings conducted by the intelligence committees remain classified. Despite the obvious importance of executive-session oversight, however, public hearings on the CIA provide a vital indicator of intelligence accountability.

As a former staff aide on the Senate and House intelligence committees, I have listened to hundreds of hours of closed-door testimony by CIA officials and questioning by legislators. The behavior of committee members showed little variation from the private to the public forum. Those who attended the public hearings were likely to attend the closed hearings; those who were energetic in public hearings were energetic in closed hearings; those who were deferential in public were deferential in private. Moreover, an examination of the four closed SSCI hearings that have been declassified reveals questioning patterns quite similar to those seen in open hearings.

Some observers have been highly critical of the executive session as a meaningful forum for legislative supervision of the CIA. Representative Pike put it this way, in frustration, after consenting to shut the door to the public during hearings on the CIA in 1975: "We went into executive session and the result could only be described as acutely disappointing. . . . [W]e went round and round for a while; and the fact of the matter is that we got absolutely nothing out of our executive session. . . . [t]he public thinks that [the CIA] has indeed been forthcoming in executive session. . . . But the fact of the matter is that we learn more in open session than we do in executive session."[6] In Pike's view, all his committee gained from executive session was that "the newspapers somehow get the appearance that we are learning things which in fact we are not learning."[7]

The thick volumes of open testimony gathered over the years by the congressional intelligence committees (and their ad hoc investigative surrogates) provide a rich chronicle for studying the role of Congress in the supervision of the secret agencies.[8] These documents disclose the attendance records of members at hearings and, of still more value, the thoroughness of their questions and remarks (Q & Rs).

Which members were in attendance is easily determined by reading the transcripts of the hearings. It is also simple to count the number of Q & Rs offered by each legislator.

The Frequency of CIA Hearings

From 1975 to 1990, the Congressional intelligence committees averaged only 1.6 public hearings a year. In some years—1976, 1985, and 1990—neither House nor Senate overseers met openly with CIA officials. The peak periods of open oversight took place in 1979 and 1980, when the House subcommittees on oversight and legislation, led by Les Aspin and Morgan Murphy, respectively, produced a series of thirteen public hearings with CIA officials— 54 percent of the House Intelligence Committee's total from 1975 to 1990. As veterans of the Pike Committee investigation, Aspin and Murphy knew more about the CIA than most legislators. Both men were ambitious, bright, skeptical—and the chairmen of subcommittees with authority to conduct their own hearings.

By 1979 Aspin and Murphy had reached full stride in their interest in and knowledge of intelligence issues, as had their self-confidence as subcommittee chairmen. With their departures from the Boland Committee in 1981 (Chairman Boland ratcheted up the pressure to "encourage" their departure), much of that panel's energy and dedication to CIA supervision went with them. The effect of their absence emphasizes the importance of individual personalities in the conduct of oversight responsibilities.[9]

Thus, the frequency of public hearings with CIA officials during this period (1975–90) was low. Yet the public hearings that were held demonstrated the feasibility of carrying out a meaningful discussion of intelligence issues in an open forum. Among the several good examples are the Aspin subcommittee's inquiry into the relationship between the CIA and the media (held in 1977 and 1978), the Senate committee's review of a wide range of CIA activities at home and abroad (1980), and the House committee's exploration of oversight procedures for that most sensitive of all intelligence missions, covert action (1983).[10]

Attendance Patterns

A rudimentary indicator of a legislator's commitment to intelligence accountability is his or her attendance at hearings on the CIA. During this period each of the intelligence committees held twenty-four open hearings at which current or former CIA officials testified. By far the highest participation rates for legislators occurred during times of formal investigation into alleged CIA abuses: a 100 percent attendance rate during the Church and Pike Committee investigations of 1975, and again 100 percent on the Senate side (75 percent on the House side) during investigative hearings into the Iran-contra affair in 1987 held by the joint Inouye-Hamilton Committees.

Only in about one-third of the public hearings (35 percent) did the intelligence committees muster a majority—a markedly low rate of turnout. The Senate committee passed this majority threshold much more often than the House committee (65 percent), despite a senator's greater number of committee assignments and more frenetic schedule. The Senate committee members also proved more regular in their attendance, averaging a 51 percent turnout per session compared to 39 percent for the House committee. These last two statistics are inflated by the high participation of legislators in investigative hearings; if one looks only at routine hearings, attendance rates drop to 47 percent for senators and 35 percent for representatives. The extent of member participation in routine hearings varied according to the level of the sponsoring unit, either committee or subcommittee. When the full committees convened, the turnout rates averaged 55 percent attendance in the House (though the House Intelligence Committee met only five times in this fashion) and 48 percent in the Senate (twenty-two meetings).

In the House, the high-water mark for full committee participation in a routine hearing was 69 percent (the Boland Committee in 1978, shortly after the creation of HPSCI), the low-water mark 39 percent (the Boland Committee in 1982). On the Senate side, the intelligence committee under Democratic chairman David Boren reached 93 percent attendance in 1986 and 1987 during confirmation proceedings for the DCI and his deputy director, held in a Washington atmosphere black with rumors of the Iran-contra machinations. The low mark of 7 percent came in 1983 under Senator Barry Goldwater, who as a member of the Church Committee investigation had opposed the creation of the very panel he now had come to chair in a Republican-controlled Senate. The Goldwater Committee averaged only a 38 percent turnout for its six public hearings.

When open hearings were held at the subcommittee level—typically the case in the House, for Boland himself continued to eschew any public pillorying of the Agency by his full committee until his run-in with the roguish national security officials of the Reagan administration—attendance rates fell significantly, to 32 percent in the Senate and 31 percent in the House. Usually only the members of the subcommittee attended these hearings, with one or two additional legislators from the full committee dropping in for a brief question or two.

For the intelligence committees in their public forums, then, two scandal-driven bursts of high activity (1975 and 1987) bracketed a profile of fluctuating but much lower participation during the intervening years of routine hearings. After the Iran-contra investigation of 1987 participation again fell off sharply. It took extraordinary circumstances—major scandals—to bring the members out in full force, drawn in part no doubt by the phototropic effect of television lights. More routine oversight, the glamourless job of weeding out abuse before it seeds, was a burden taken up by far fewer hands—almost always a minority of the members on the two intelligence committees. Woodrow Wilson once observed that "Congress in its committee-rooms is Congress at work."[11] Applying this celebrated adage to CIA public hearings, one can only draw the conclusion that a good many legislators failed to show up for work.[12]

Q & Rs

What did those committee members who did show up do? The frequency of questions and remarks proffered by legislators provides one useful measure. During the fifteen years of the New Oversight examined here (the last stages of the Cold War) the CIA received 10,196 Q & Rs from overseers on the two intelligence committees in public hearings. On the House side, members generated 4,677 questions. Of the fifty-nine legislators who served on this committee during these years, only thirteen posed more than a hundred questions. The mean rate of questioning was seventy-nine questions per overseer, with sixteen committee members remaining utterly mute. Senators, perhaps accustomed to their chamber's more lenient rules of speech, spoke more than House members, posing 5,519 questions—though no senator came close to Representative Aspin's herculean individual effort of 997. Walter "Dee" Huddleston, a Democratic veteran of the Church Committee, set the record in the Senate at 623. Only nineteen senators, out of fifty-five, asked more than a hundred questions. The mean rate of questioning for senators was one hundred questions per overseer, with five senators choosing complete silence.

Between the two committees, then, twenty-one overseers (18.4 percent of

Intelligence Accountability

the combined membership) never asked a single question of a CIA witness. Even among those who did, the Q & R rates were often extraordinarily low. Democratic representative Clement J. Zablocki, for instance, put in seven years of service on the House Intelligence Committee, averaging but one question a year in public hearings and rarely attending closed committee meetings.

On average, the CIA faced twenty-two questions annually in public from each of its House committee overseers and twenty-four from each of its Senate committee overseers—not exactly a withering barrage. The most intensive questioning came, as one might expect, from the members of investigative committees, especially the Pike and Church committees. The chairmen of these two panels pitched the largest number of Q & Rs at CIA witnesses in a single year: 154 and 110, respectively. So, each year the CIA faced relatively few questions in public from the vast majority of its overseers—though a few legislators hurled long innings.

Softball and Hardball at the Committee Level

More qualitative, and thus more difficult to measure, is the seriousness with which members approach their oversight responsibility. To what extent do legislators delve deeply into the inner workings of the CIA and its programs? For this aspect of oversight, one must turn to the methodology of content analysis.[13] To evaluate legislative participation in CIA hearings, I sort the utterances of overseers into four categories: deferential, factual, probing, and adversarial. This sequence reflects a rising intensity in the critique of the CIA's activities.

The Legislator as Pal

Deference describes the attitude implicit in questions and remarks of a warm and supportive nature—in some cases an obsequiousness toward CIA officials and their programs. At times the purpose of the deferential Q & R will be to build rapport with the witness. Occasionally the deferential approach seems aimed only at exhibiting unalloyed support for the Agency. In a farrago of sycophancy, the CIA witness is offered assurances that his (there have been no female CIA witnesses) organization is functioning flawlessly; indeed, if fault is to be found, it is with Congress itself.

The chief complaint of one leading deferential member of the House committee, for example, had nothing to do with any shortcomings of the CIA but instead with (unsubstantiated) "egregious leaks of information" from Capitol Hill. Another House Committee member opined that legislative guidelines had usually served only to "inhibit good intelligence."[14] From these vantage points, the less oversight the better—especially to prevent the unauthorized disclosure of information by Congress. "This place [Congress] has more leaks than the men's room at Anheuser-Busch," a deferential senator joked during a hearing with CIA witnesses.[15]

Much of what the CIA does is laudable and warrants praise from overseers, so a degree of deferential Q & R is to be expected. Few would deny that Congress ought to acknowledge the good work of bureaucrats, not just criticize work that is shoddy. Still, a legislator who displayed only deference could hardly be viewed as a hard-nosed overseer. Surely, quality oversight involves asking some demanding questions about an agency's performance—even, from time to time, sharp criticism of its failures.

The Legislator as Fact Finder

Some legislative overseers concentrate on marshaling basic information about an agency's activities. These legislators are content to ask routine factual questions about the CIA or about the witness's role in its operations: "How long have you served as chief of the Covert Action Staff?" "Which component of the Operations Directorate is responsible for coordinating the CIA's covert propaganda with the Department of State?" The line of questioning is free of normative content.

The Legislator as Interrogator

At the next level of questioning, the overseer shifts from basic fact-finding toward a more probing line of inquiry into past performance, anticipated operations, and even charges of malfeasance. The questioning can extend from well-researched and thoughtful explorations about how the CIA functions to a cross-examination of alleged policy failures, misuse of funds, or violations of the public trust.

The interrogator stops short, though, of rendering a value judgment against the Agency. For example, during a hearing with a former DCI, a member of the House Intelligence Committee probed into the hazard of propaganda "blowback": "If [the CIA] puts out a story [overseas] which is totally false propaganda, how do you protect [Americans] against the domestic feedback of the planted story?" "What is your understanding of the legality of the covert mail operation?" asked a Senate overseer while questioning the CIA's chief of counterintelligence during an investigation into charges of unlawful opening of domestic mail.[16]

The Legislator as Adversary

The final category of Q & Rs displays a more explicit skepticism, sometimes even hostility, toward the Agency's programs or witnesses. At this level, the legislator is no longer content to be impartial; he or she (only three women have served on an intelligence committee) becomes an adversary. The CIA is chided for inefficiency, lambasted for error, ridiculed for stupidity, excoriated for abusing power, or shamed for transgressions against the law, the Constitution, American traditions, or commonly accepted norms of propriety. As distinct from the earlier roles of booster, fact finder, or prober, the legislator is now a prosecutor.

"You do not want to inform [the President] in the first place, because he might say no. That is the truth of it," said a senator to a senior CIA official, concluding with disgust and heavy sarcasm, "And when [the President] did say no [to an illegal mail-opening program] you disregard it—and then you call him the Commander in Chief." Similarly, a member of the House sharply rebuked a CIA counsel for trying to control what information Congress could release: "The executive branch is not going to have this thing both ways with the legislative branch. . . . You come in here and bug our rooms, you throw us out for forty-five minutes and yet you feel free to go out and tell anybody and everybody you want whatever you choose. . . . I resent it."[17]

SOFTBALL VERSUS HARDBALL

In a democracy, some verbal sparring between executive and legislative officials is healthy as a means for informing the public about policy disagreements, failures, and violations. However, overheated confrontation between the branches—Edward Corwin's "invitation to struggle" run amok—would result in a tense and ultimately unworkable government.[18] Still, the opposite extreme of legislative fawning—overlook instead of oversight—represents a breakdown of auxiliary precautions, exposing the nation to concentrated, untended, and in this instance secret executive power.

The first two roles of the overseer, deferential and fact-finding, are from an agency's point of view relatively benign—at worst, a mildly intrusive intervention into its business. Probing and adversarial roles, however, constitute aggressive interventions that may threaten an agency's reputation and funding—perhaps even its raison d'être. Some legislators are satisfied to emphasize the first two roles—known in Washington as "playing softball." Legislators lob easy questions to witnesses, whose flattering answers are considered "home runs" for the Agency team. Others reject this approach (particularly deference) as a sign that the Congress has been co-opted by the executive branch. They prefer hardball—tough pitches, with many strikes.

The next focus is on the mix of lenient (softball) and challenging (hardball) questions directed toward CIA witnesses. The tendency in both chambers has been to toss mostly softballs. Yet despite the emphasis on fact-finding leavened with deference, both oversight panels have pitched a fair number of hardballs. Well over a third of the questions advanced by members of the Senate and House committees have been hardballs (39 percent and 36 percent, respectively), with about 10 percent for both panels posed in a heated, highly adversarial manner.

This year-by-year degree of hardball questioning is shown in figure 4.1. The highest levels of rigorous interrogation occurred in the Senate: 57 percent in 1975 (the Church Committee), 59 percent in 1987 (the Inouye Committee II investigation into Iran-contra, along with three related hearings), and 57 percent in 1989 (the Boren Committee, still provoked by the Iran-contra affair). These are the only instances in which Senate committees recorded a majority of hardball questions for CIA witnesses.

The most robust interrogations on the House side (though each time with a lower hardball quotient than the Senate) were 51 percent in 1975 (the Pike Committee) and 54 percent in 1983, when Representative Wyche Fowler led the Boland Committee (with Chairman Boland's begrudging acquiescence) through a sustained interrogation of Agency witnesses regarding their responsiveness to oversight procedures. These are the only two instances in which the House committee fired more hardball than softball questions. Thus, the oversight committees played hardball with the CIA chiefly during times of scandal (1975 and 1987), as one might anticipate, and when an individual member (Fowler in the House) chose to pursue a lengthy critical inquiry.

The level of intensity in oversight questioning has varied according to the topic of the hearing: investigations into alleged abuses, examinations of procedures (such as CIA censorship of works written by current and former officials or Agency use of the polygraph), proposed legislation, foreign intelligence (CIA operations abroad, a topic avoided altogether in Senate public hearings), and in the Senate (by constitutional prerogative) leadership confirmation. In the Church (1975), Pike (1975), Inouye II (1987), Hamilton II (1987), and Boren (1987–90) Committees, hardball questions outnumbered softball questions; and each committee was either involved in a formal investigation or, in the case of the Boren Committee, operated in the atmosphere of the Iran-contra scandal. Clearly, the oversight committees engaged in scandal-driven investigations behaved more aggressively toward witnesses than those conducting routine hearings.[19]

While investigative hearings elicited the most acrimonious questioning, confirmation hearings in the Senate stood a close second as an occasion for

Intelligence Accountability

Figure 4.1 The Percentage of Hardball Questions and Remarks Directed toward
CIA Witnesses in Public Hearings, U.S. House and Senate Intelligence
Committees, 1975–90

% Hardball

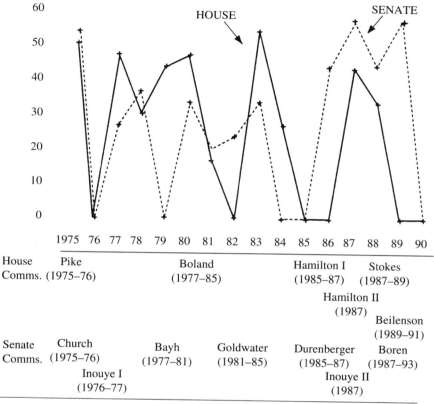

House Comms.	Pike (1975–76)	Boland (1977–85)	Hamilton I (1985–87) Hamilton II (1987)	Stokes (1987–89) Beilenson (1989–91)
Senate Comms.	Church (1975–76) Inouye I (1976–77)	Bayh (1977–81)	Goldwater (1981–85)	Durenberger (1985–87) Inouye II (1987) Boren (1987–93)

Source: Loch K. Johnson, "Playing Hardball with the CIA," in Paul E. Peterson, ed.,
The President, the Congress, and the Making of Foreign Policy (Norman: University
of Oklahoma Press, 1994), 58.

Note: The Senate intelligence committee held no public hearings with CIA witnesses in
1976, 1979, 1984, 1985, and 1990; nor did the House intelligence committee in 1976,
1985, 1986, 1989, and 1990. In 1982 the House committee held a hearing with Agency
witnesses but asked no hardball questions.

playing hardball (see table 4.1). The Senate Committee rejected two residential appointees for DCI, Theodore C. Sorensen in 1977 and Robert M. Gates in 1987.[20]

Next in order for hardball questioning were House hearings on CIA procedures, which often touched on civil liberties issues dear to liberal legislators (though procedures proved the topic that received the most lenient questioning in the Senate), on proposed legislation, and on foreign intelligence—often an exercise in Soviet bashing by conservative legislators during the Cold War, but now and then leading to a critical examination of the CIA's overseas operations. Hearings on legislation have sometimes ignited debates about the proper scope of congressional oversight; more frequently, though, they have served as forums for factual questioning about the likely effects of a proposed statute.

Most members of the intelligence committees offered a blend of questions from deferential to adversarial. A few, though, specialized in specific styles of interaction with CIA witnesses. In the Senate, Democrat Frank Church and Pennsylvania Republican Arlen Specter were clearly inclined toward hardball, while at the other extreme, GOP senators Goldwater and John Chafee of Rhode Island much preferred softball, with Chafee the record holder for easy pitches.

WHO PLAYS HARDBALL?

Ideology, party, seniority, and other influences on congressional behavior have shaped the style of supervision chosen by intelligence overseers. Those who were deeply involved in the public hearings with CIA witnesses, as indicated by high attendance records and lengthy questioning, were more apt to engage in hardball during their tenure on an intelligence committee (see table 4.2). Generally, the more time spent on the playing field and the more active the player, the more intense the play. For both committees, the total volume of questioning reveals the strongest correlation with hardball.

Ideology has proved to be a powerful correlate of voting behavior in the Congress,[21] and its importance is seen again in this analysis. The policy preferences of committee members reveal a definite correspondence with their readiness to ask difficult questions in public hearings. The index of ideology tabulated by the Americans for Democratic Action (ADA) is an especially significant predictor of hardball for House committee members. Those on the conservative end of the political spectrum were more inclined to express trust and support for the CIA; conversely, liberals expressed more skepticism. What most concerned the softball legislators (to quote from various hearings) was

Table 4.1 Rigor of CIA Oversight by Type of Hearing,
House and Senate Intelligence Committees, 1975–90

| | Intensity of Questioning | | | | |
| | Softball | | Hardball | | |
Hearing Type	Deference	Fact-finding	Probing	Adversary	Total
House					
Investigative	305	609	723	195	1,832
	(16.6)	(33.2)	(39.5)	(10.6)	(100)
		914		918	
		(49.9)		(50.1)	
Procedures	259	419	482	84	1,244
	(20.8)	(33.7)	(38.7)	(6.8)	(100)
		678		566	
		(54.5)		(45.5)	
Legislation	329	339	310	179	1,157
	(28.4)	(29.3)	(26.8)	(15.5)	(100)
		668		489	
		(57.7)		(42.3)	
Foreign Intelligence	29	265	106	44	444
	(6.5)	(59.7)	(23.9)	(9.9)	(100)
		294		150	
		(66.2)		(33.8)	
Senate					
Investigative	144	508	655	206	1,513
	(9.5)	(33.6)	(43.3)	(13.6)	(100)
		652		861	
		(43.1)		(56.9)	
Procedures	52	136	52	10	250
	(20.8)	(54.4)	(20.8)	(4.0)	(100)
		188		62	
		(75.2)		(24.8)	
Legislation	423	445	385	89	1,342
	(31.5)	(33.2)	(28.7)	(6.6)	(100)
		868		474	
		(64.7)		(35.3)	
Foreign Intelligence	—	—	—	—	—
Confirmation	367	862	962	223	2,414
	(15.2)	(35.7)	(39.9)	(9.2)	(100)
		1,229		1,185	
		(50.9)		(49.1)	

Source: Johnson, "Playing Hardball with the CIA," in Paul E. Peterson, ed., The President, the Congress, and the Making of Foreign Policy (Norman: University of Oklahoma Press, 1994), 60.
Note: Figures in parentheses are percentages.

the need for "better secrecy," "fewer restrictions" on the CIA, less "micro-management," "stopping leaks," and "improving CIA cover." In contrast, buzzwords for the hardballers included concern for "the rights of the American people," "a free society," "civil liberties," "access to information," and "prior notification" of Congress in the case of important Agency operations.

Republicans in Congress tend to be more conservative on interest-group ratings than Democrats; therefore, one would expect to find more hardballers among the Democratic overseers on the intelligence committees. The findings on party confirm this expectation (see table 4.2). In both chambers Democrats

Table 4.2   Multiple Regression of Hardball Questioning of CIA Witnesses in House and Senate Intelligence Committees, by Selected Influences on Legislative Behavior, 1975–90

| | *Hardball Regression Coefficients (β)* | |
| | *House Intelligence Committee* | *Senate Intelligence Committee* |
Independent Variables	*Total Number of Hardball Q and Rs*	
Involvement		
Attendance	.46**	.37**
Volume of Q & Rs	.96**	.93**
Ideology		
ADA	.86**	.43**
NSI	.41*	.18
Party	.79**	.51**
Seniority		
Chamber	−.16*	−.11*
Committee	−.11	−.14**
Divided government	.17*	−.29**
Periodical coverage	.56**	.43**
Superpower cooperation	.20**	.02
Constant	−110.22	1.18
R² (Adjusted)	.35	.35
No. of observations	4,677	5,519

*p ≤ .10. **p ≤ .05

Source: Johnson, "Playing Hardball with the CIA," in Peterson, *The President, the Congress, and the Making of Foreign Policy,* 61.

Note: National Security Index, with a score of 100 indicating a legislator unerringly in support of increased defense funding. See James M. Lindsay, "Parochialism, Policy, and Constituency Constraints: Congressional Voting on Strategic Weapons Systems," *American Journal of Political Science* 34 (1990), 36–60.

on the intelligence committees have been more inclined to engage in hardball questioning than Republicans. Party has been a more powerful predictor of hardball questioning in the House than in the Senate, though party in the Senate (unlike the House) demonstrates somewhat greater predictive strength than ideology.

Time in service proves a weak indicator of hardball questioning. First-termers and longtime incumbents are nearly alike in their willingness to ask searching questions, with a slight tendency toward hardball among newer members. Whether the hardball questioning by the new members mellows somewhat with the added insight and appreciation for the CIA's programs they may gain over the years, or whether legislators eventually are co-opted by skillful Agency lobbying, cannot be answered from these data. My own observations of the two committees suggest the presence of both phenomena from time to time for different members.

During the New Oversight the federal government was almost always divided between the two major parties. The exceptions were when a Democratic president (Carter) served with a Democratic Congress from 1977 to 1981, and when a Republican president (Reagan) enjoyed a partial respite with a GOP majority in the Senate from 1981 to 1986.

The relationship between divided government and hardball questioning is examined in detail in table 4.3. The proposition that Democratic Congresses are consistently tougher on GOP presidents than they are on Democratic presidents fails to hold up with respect to intelligence policy. It is true that the most rigorous series of questions were directed toward the CIA during the first six years of the Reagan administration by Democratic overseers on the House Committee, when they posed 94.9 percent of the hardball Q & Rs. Nevertheless, congressional Democrats as a whole were much harder on the CIA during the Carter presidency (84.9 percent, averaging both chambers) than they were during the combined Reagan-Bush presidencies (70.0 percent).

Democratic overseers were also tougher on the Carter CIA than were GOP overseers, by a wide margin; and the mildest Democratic questioning on both intelligence committees occurred during the latter years of the Reagan administration (1987–88). The Democrats on the Senate Intelligence Committee, for example, proved to be far more lenient in their questioning of the CIA during the Iran-contra travails than were some of the Republican overseers.[22]

While it is true that the Senate committee, when controlled by the GOP (1981–86), asked a small proportion of the hardball questions directed toward the Reagan CIA (24.4 percent), Republican overseers advanced an even lower proportion against the Carter CIA (13.7 percent). In every instance but one (the

Senate in 1987–88) the Democrats on the intelligence committees were far more rigorous in their questioning of the administration, regardless of the president's party, than were GOP legislators.

The years 1975 and 1987 saw some of the most intense hardball questioning on Capitol Hill—and the bleakest moments in the CIA's history since the Bay of Pigs fiasco. The scrutiny was brought on first by Operation CHAOS (domestic spying) and then by the Iran-contra affair. During these two years the CIA also endured its most widespread coverage in the print media.[23]

Whether the hearings spurred the coverage or vice versa is hard to determine. Most likely, the media allegations of CIA abuse (reported in the *New York Times* in 1974 and a Lebanese weekly, *Al-Shiraa*, in 1986) spurred Congress to hold investigative hearings. Media reporting on the hearings further encouraged legislators to participate in questioning—at least until the media executives calculated a declining public interest and pulled the plug on the television

Table 4.3 Percentage of Hardball Questioning on House and Senate Intelligence Committees, by Party and Administration, 1975–90

Party	Ford (1975–76) WH = R H = D S = D	Carter (1977–80) WH = D H = D S = D	Reagan I (1981–86) WH = R H = D S = R	Reagan II (1987–88) WH = R H = D S = D	Bush (1989–90) WH = R H = D S = D	Average
House						
Dem.	83.8	83.5	94.9	80.6	—	85.7
	(640)	(740)	(168)	(154)		(426)
GOP	16.2	16.5	5.1	19.4	—	14.3
	(124)	(146)	(9)	(37)		(79)
Senate						
Dem.	66.9	86.3	75.6	49.1	50.0	65.6
	(462)	(493)	(118)	(472)	(34)	(316)
GOP	33.1	13.7	24.4	50.9	50.0	34.4
	(229)	(78)	(38)	(489)	(34)	(174)

Source: Johnson, "Playing Hardball with the CIA," in Peterson, *The President, the Congress, and the Making of Foreign Policy*, 63.

Note: WH = White House, H = House, S = Senate, D = Democrat, R = Republican. So, in 1975–76, e.g., the Republican party controlled the White House, and the Democratic party controlled the House and the Senate. The percentages in the table represent the portion of hardball questions and remarks posed by each party as a fraction of the total numbers of hardball Q & Rs for the period. (The House held no public hearings with CIA witnesses in 1989–90.) Figures in parentheses are *N*s.

lights.[24] This much is speculation—though grounded in observation and interviews with legislators, staff, and CIA officers. What the coefficients in table 4.2 do indicate is a reasonably close correspondence between broad periodical coverage of the CIA and legislative hardball. Presumably both are influenced—in a complex, interactive manner—by allegations of wrongdoing in this subterranean tier of government.

Harry Ransom has argued that legislators are more likely to engage in serious oversight when superpower tensions are relaxed. Overseers may be reluctant to criticize the CIA as it faces a sharply hostile adversary abroad.[25] Table 4.2 indicates some support for this hypothesis during the House committee's public hearings; but on the Senate side, the year-by-year hardball questioning actually showed a decrease (though weak) during periods of detente. The measurements of U.S.-Soviet cooperation used here are crude, however, and these findings must be viewed as quite tentative.[26]

THE QUALITY OF INTELLIGENCE ACCOUNTABILITY

Since 1975 the supervision of intelligence by Congress has undergone a dramatic increase over the earlier years, when legislators had been largely content to rely on the president to guide the secret agencies. From among the wide range of new oversight activities, hearings—public and in executive session—have been the most important. When asked which forms of supervision he considered the most valuable, the response of a staff director of the Senate Intelligence Committee was typical. He motioned toward the committee's hearing room and replied emphatically, "Down there, with the members."[27]

Between the two types of hearings, public and private, most often the intelligence committees have chosen to meet behind closed doors. This allows members the freedom to explore any aspect of intelligence policy without fear of inadvertently revealing classified information. Nevertheless, public hearings provide a window into the content and quality of intelligence accountability. Members of Congress do not suddenly change their personalities, styles, and interests depending upon the openness of the forum wherein they find themselves. Those legislators who participate effectively in public tend to do so as well in private. Indeed, open hearings may in some ways improve oversight: the attendance of members tends to be much higher at public hearings that may be seen by voters back home, and legislators are likely to prepare themselves more thoroughly when on public view.

The hardball questioning by intelligence committee members in open hearings correlates well with the most significant instances of CIA transgressions and subsequent major congressional efforts at intelligence reform. Among the most conspicuous periods of hardball questioning highlighted in this chapter are 1975, 1977–78, 1980, and 1987—the years when the following important oversight efforts took place: investigations into Operation CHAOS and controversial covert actions (1975), the years of successful wiretap legislation (the Foreign Intelligence Surveillance Act of 1978) and a failed attempt to enact sweeping "grand charter" legislation for the intelligence community (1977–78); another, far more modest, and this time successful try at passing "mini-charter" legislation (the Intelligence Oversight Act of 1980); and the investigation into the Iran-contra scandal (1987).[28]

What does the evidence on public hearings suggest about the quality of the New Oversight? How has the congressional role been changing? Are legislators now playing a major role in the formation of intelligence policy? Is this leading to greater conflict with the executive branch? What are the policy consequences?

Judgments made on these vital questions depend to some extent on one's point of view. If the historical benchmark is the state of oversight before 1975, it can be concluded with confidence that the present level of congressional participation in this aspect of American foreign policy is markedly more robust and effective. Not everyone, however, believes that the activities of the CIA ought to be subjected to legislative guidance. A prominent school of thought, to which some members of the intelligence committees subscribe, maintains that, on the contrary, the best oversight is to strengthen the CIA's funding and let it proceed with the struggle against this nation's enemies in the back alleys of the world. For this school, congressional involvement merely impedes America's self-defense and its pursuit of global interests.

The Iran-Contra Affair Revisited

Even for those who believe in close congressional supervision and guidance for the CIA and find the comparison with the pre-1975 era heartening, the Iran-contra episode might well lead one to conclude that the New Oversight has failed.[29] In rebuttal, other observers argue that Iran-contra is an aberration—a distressing glitch in the intelligence partnership between Congress and the executive that, since 1975, officials have been hammering out on the anvil of experience. The failure of oversight during the Iran-contra affair is blamed on officials in the executive branch who lied to Congress and evaded the law in order to achieve their policy objectives in the Middle East and Central America. Under such circumstances, insist defenders of the New Oversight, no system of accountability would have succeeded.[30]

"Were it not for a fortuitous leak of the secret Iran arms-sale operation in a

Middle East magazine," concedes a senior staffer on the Senate Intelligence Committee, "the Iran-contra affair would probably not have been discovered through normal oversight activities."[31] A senior staffer on HPSCI adds, "When the nation's national security adviser [Robert C. McFarlane] and other top officials look you in the eye and tell you that the [Iran-contra] rumors are false, the inclination is to believe them."[32]

According to interviews with senior staffers on the intelligence committees, the chairman of the House panel, Lee Hamilton, went to the White House in 1986 and confronted McFarlane and Lieutenant Colonel North about the rumors. Sitting directly across a table from the two key NSC staffers, Hamilton— an experienced, wily legislator—asked them if they were involved in the operations in any way. McFarlane, who was graduated with high honors in his class at the Naval Academy, and North, a Naval Academy boxing champion and decorated Vietnam War veteran, stared back across the table and denied any culpability whatsoever. Hamilton accepted their word and, like his Senate counterpart (David Boren), failed to pursue the Iran-contra rumors further.

Presumably, in light of the Iran-contra experience, congressional overseers have again learned the importance of a healthy skepticism toward those in power. The continuing failure of the CIA to inform legislators of an agent's improper activities in Guatemala (Colonel Alpirez) has provided yet another tutorial. The newest DCI, John M. Deutch, has vowed to put an end to the "institutional predisposition" of the CIA's Operations Directorate to keep Congress in the dark about foreign operations.[33]

Feckless Accountability

The argument that Iran-contra was just an aberration is too flip for the critics of the New Oversight; they see more fundamental flaws. Certainly, most members of the intelligence committees have fallen far short of dutiful attendance at public hearings—and, even if present, have failed to ask weighty questions about CIA activities. The conclusion of several earlier researchers that congressional oversight has generally been uneven and episodic, relying on the dedication of a few legislators, is reinforced by the analysis of how Agency witnesses are questioned.[34]

The testimony of some former DCIs indicates that even the leaders of the intelligence community have found legislative guidance weak and ineffectual. Noting that "Congress is informed to the degree that Congress wants to be informed," William Colby places responsibility for many of the inadequacies of congressional accountability squarely on the shoulders of legislators, some of whom have not tried very hard to become informed.[35]

More direct, and more damning, is the testimony of Stansfield Turner. Admiral Turner, who came to the job from outside the ranks of intelligence professionals, can speak to the question of oversight with a detachment lacking in those former directors with career-long ties to the CIA. Appalled by the failure of legislative overseers to pursue Iran-contra leads more aggressively, Turner recollected in a statement before the House Intelligence Committee "being incensed at the time [in 1986, when rumors of possible scandal flitted around Washington] that nothing was being done in the media or in the Congress to stop this." Turner added, "I would say with all candor that in my four years when I think we had a very cooperative relationship, I believe the committees of Congress could have been more rigorous with me. . . . [I]t would be more helpful if you are probing and rigorous."[36] No one, though, recalls the admiral making this suggestion to Chairman Boland during the Carter years.

While the Colby-Turner view animates some activist overseers on Capitol Hill, a number of legislators still prefer to march under the banner of Justice Sutherland's opinion in *United States v. Curtiss-Wright* (1936). Some people have interpreted this opinion to mean that the president should be the sole authority for the nation in the conduct of its foreign affairs—a gross misreading of his commentary, according to most legal authorities.[37] Modern proponents of the expanded Sutherland view add a twist: the president should be the sole intelligence authority.

BONES OF CONTENTION

The debate over the proper role of Congress in supervising and providing direction for intelligence will continue, of course. The nation's founders were of many minds themselves on the proper division of foreign policy responsibilities among the branches of the federal government. With respect to the CIA, disagreements have been sharpest on several key issues: the reporting of covert actions, information security on Capitol Hill, micromanagement by Congress, and truthful reporting to overseers.

When should the president report to Congress on covert action findings—before or after their implementation? And if after, how long after? The present expectation in Congress, as stated in the Intelligence Oversight Act of 1991, is *before* in almost all cases. In extraordinary circumstances, however, the president may limit this reporting to selected leaders of Congress (the chairmen and ranking minority members of the Intelligence Committees, the Speaker and minority leader of the House, and the majority and minority leaders of the Senate—the so-called Gang of Eight). Or he may report to no member of Congress at all. In that case the president is required to explain "in a timely manner" why he failed to provide prior notice. The legislative history of the Oversight Act indicates that the reporting should be delayed by no more than "a few days."[38]

Yet those legislators with the most acute sense of congressional prerogatives continue to worry that the "extraordinary circumstances" phrase may prove to be a dangerous loophole. They would prefer advance notice, period—at least to the Gang of Eight. As Representative Aspin argued in an earlier legislative battle, over the 1980 Intelligence Oversight Act, by failing to embrace an explicit prior-notice standard, Congress opened a "statutory possibility that the Administration can, in effect, just waive the whole thing. . . . We had a chance in our bill here to make this very specific and to clear up once and for all that matter. We could not clear it up because there was an irrevocable difference as to what the Constitution allowed the President to do, how much freedom in this area does the Constitution give the President." Instead, Aspin concluded, they "still left it vague. I think that is unfortunate."[39]

Uneasiness continues, too, over how to distinguish covert actions carried out by the CIA under the findings process from secret diplomacy or secret military operations. Disputes over what is and is not covert action are ongoing. Some astute overseers have fretted in particular about the possibilities of unsupervised covert actions conducted by military personnel. The CIA may be closely watched now, but what about the "Special Ops" units of the Pentagon?[40]

Many government officials continue to worry about the discretion of congressional overseers. In their handling of secret intelligence, can legislators be trusted to protect classified information? It is still common for some intelligence officers to blame the Congress for leaking every secret that makes its way into the newspapers—even though studies of government leaks have found the executive branch infinitely more culpable.[41]

Has Congress created too many stifling regulations that only inhibit the CIA? Yes, say the Curtiss-Wrighters; no, say the civil libertarians and those wary of unsavory covert actions.

Will intelligence officers be sufficiently forthcoming with legislators to allow them a meaningful role as intelligence overseers? Here one detects the lingering odor of Iran-contra mendacity. The issue of misleading Congress still gnaws at the minds of foreign policy activists on Capitol Hill. In his attempt to explain why he deceived legislators during the Iran-contra affair, the CIA's chief of the Central American Task Force (C/CATF) argued that in his sworn testimony he had been "technically correct, [if] specifically evasive"[42]—a form of CIA gobbledygook that the Church and Pike committees encountered from time to time.

As so often in the past, legislative overseers during the Iran-contra probe were placed in the position of having to ask precisely the right question to have any chance of ascertaining the truth. In response to the C/CATF's limp defense, Senator William Cohen told him that "if Congress is satisfied that it is being told the truth and the whole truth, then the distrust of the Agency will evaporate and that is what has to happen."[43]

In the absence of forthright reporting by executive agencies to legislators on their activities, the opportunities for meaningful congressional involvement in intelligence policy will never be much more than a sandcastle washed away in the next flood tide of deceit. Here again is the C/CATF in post–Iran-contra testimony:

> I think that the final prerogative to make a decision and the man with his hand on the helm is the President and he [Ronald Reagan] wanted to do it [conduct covert action in Nicaragua to undermine the Sandinista regime]. . . . Congress passed a very awkward law [the Boland Amendments], put us in a terrible position. . . . I just couldn't understand it. There was a law. Why give us half a loaf, why give us something that we couldn't implement right? It was just ludicrous and it was partisan politics because the Congress didn't like [DCI William J.] Casey and the Congress didn't want CIA in because of the mining of the [Nicaraguan] harbor[s] and we couldn't get over our internecine warfare [between the two branches of government] and it shouldn't have been that way.[44]

In response, Senator George Mitchell offered a pertinent civics lesson. "I think it is simply preposterous to suggest that those who opposed contra aid did so because they didn't like Bill Casey," he said. "I would hope you would have a somewhat higher opinion of the motives of those who happen to disagree with you on an issue. . . . [E]very executive branch official has an obligation to obey and uphold the law, and not to select which laws will be obeyed or not."[45]

BRINGING INTELLIGENCE UNDER THE CONSTITUTION

What can one conclude about the state of intelligence accountability? First, the degree of participation by Congress in this policy domain has risen markedly since 1975, although it continues to remain relatively limited. The few public oversight hearings, the meager attendance of members at these sessions, and the often anemic quality of questioning all point to a lower level of legislative supervision than the record of errant intelligence operations in the past—domestic spying and the Iran-contra debacle—would seem to warrant.

Second, despite its uneven attention to public hearings on the CIA, other evidence indicates that Congress takes seriously some aspects of its intelligence supervision. Between 1986 and 1990, for example, the oversight committees received a vast amount of information through closed hearings and briefings from the CIA (not to mention the other secret agencies who also reported regularly to Congress). In 1986, Agency officers briefed SSCI and HPSCI on 1,040 different occasions; in 1987, 1,064; in 1988, 1,044; in 1989, 947; and in 1990, 1,012.[46] These sessions have given members and staff the opportunity to explore CIA programs. Moreover, the briefings have armed Congress with considerable ammunition in its struggles with the executive branch over the interpretation of world events and how best to react as a nation.

With its greater responsiveness to congressional requests for information, the CIA has helped to balance the power between the legislative and executive branches. The intelligence committees now have a definite role in shaping intelligence policy, and now and then they have forced the president to abandon some misguided secret operations. The Boland Amendments are the best-known examples of congressional involvement in intelligence decisions, but there have been other significant instances.[47]

Third, the rise of Congress as a player in the field of intelligence policy has sharpened conflict between the branches. This is not saying much, though, since before 1975 the executive branch had the field to itself. The extent of the new institutional conflict should not be exaggerated. The intelligence committees, the White House, and the secret agencies have agreed on well over 90 percent of all intelligence operations. Most of these activities have been sensible efforts to collect information about potential dangers to the United States, and even most of the more aggressive covert actions have been widely accepted by intelligence committee members as modest but useful attempts to shape international events in favor of United States interests. Only infrequently, as with the covert actions in Nicaragua during the 1980s, have strong disagreements erupted. On these occasions the American public itself has been sharply divided on appropriate policy, and this division—not surprisingly—has been reflected in congressional debates and voting.

Further, the vast majority of intelligence professionals have been law-abiding citizens sensitive to the nation's traditions of fair play and to the restrictions placed on them by Congress. The CIA and its companion agencies are probably no more rogue elephants than other organizations in the executive branch—though, to be sure, the secret agencies have strayed from the preserve at times.

When they do, their secretiveness and expertise at manipulation make them a threat that needs particularly close supervision.

Fourth, judging the overall policy consequences of the New Oversight is to some extent subjective. Those with an inflated Curtiss-Wright perspective will long for the abolition of the intelligence committees—a return to the days of full executive control over intelligence and an end to micromanagement. Those who are more sanguine about congressional activism point to the solid contribution legislators have made to intelligence: keeping the secret agencies on their toes, urging improved analysis, minding the budget, demanding more vigorous counterintelligence, and advocating HUMINT skills for regions of the world forgotten during the Cold War but now important. Their bottom line: secret operations benefit from a more collegial policy review involving the executive branch and the Congress—not unilateral decisions made by the White House or the DCI alone, with all the risks that attend concentrated power. (This congressional school also appreciates, though, the need for some degree of secrecy, which must at times confine oversight to the well-guarded inner sanctums of the intelligence committees.) The idea is to make intelligence policy more representative of the goals and ideals of the American people, as reflected in the judgments made by their elected surrogates in the White House *and* on Capitol Hill.

THE FUTURE OF INTELLIGENCE ACCOUNTABILITY

_ The most remarkable outcome of the American experiment in stronger legislative involvement in intelligence policy is that legislative and executive officials now acknowledge the value of congressional participation. In the view of one recent DCI, William H. Webster, "On balance, the oversight process has clearly been useful and helpful."[48] Similarly, William Colby concludes, "I think that supervision is absolutely essential. . . . We have to run American intelligence under the Constitution and under the law. I think it is the Congress's job to make sure that happens."[49] Admiral Turner concurs: "I am a strong supporter of Congressional oversight of intelligence, because unaccountable power is power that can be misused. That is not because the people using it are necessarily malicious, but because any of us, when faced with not being accountable, can be less judicious, less careful in making decisions. Therefore, the role of this [House Intelligence] Committee, and its counterpart in the Senate, is very important in terms of making the intelligence community recognize they will be held accountable for the decisions they make."[50]

These "modern" views stand out in bold relief from the philosophy and practice of the pre-1975 era. They are by no means uniformly shared. The controversial DCI William J. Casey expressed the opinion in 1984 that "the business of Congress is to stay out of my business."[51] Through evasiveness, Casey did his best to help Congress adopt his standard. Surely one objective of those who wish to see rigorous oversight succeed ought to be to ensure, during confirmation hearings, that would-be DCIs with Casey's extreme outlook on the role of Congress in intelligence policy are barred from this sensitive office.

Another DCI, Richard Helms (who served from 1968 to 1973), has expressed his dismay over the growth of congressional participation in intelligence matters.[52] He would be happier if, like a crab, intelligence oversight could go backward—though he is more or less resigned to the view that the earlier era of benign tolerance by legislators is unlikely to revisit Capitol Hill anytime soon.

Hearings, open or closed, are hardly the only means for providing a check on the potential abuse of power by the secret agencies. "The most important form of oversight goes unseen," a senior staffer on the Senate Intelligence Committee has commented. "The CIA worries that Congress is looking over its shoulder; therefore, it is less reckless. It makes them [intelligence officers] think twice before they act."[53] The media will also continue to provide a crucial check, as illustrated most vividly by the *New York Times*'s reporting on Operation CHAOS in 1974. "Don't forget the Freedom of Information Act," another intelligence committee staffer has suggested, pointing to the use of this statute by private citizens to unearth a recent case of improper FBI domestic surveillance (Operation CISPES). "It has been the best of all external overseers."[54] More frequent public hearings would be an added check on abuses. As DCI Turner appropriately stressed in his call for a more open discussion of intelligence policy, "A well-informed public is the greatest strength of our nation."[55]

From 1975 to 1990 the intelligence committees averaged less than two public hearings a year with CIA witnesses. Yet House subcommittee chairmen Aspin and Murphy and Senate committee chairmen Bayh, Boren, and Inouye have demonstrated that regular open sessions can be held on intelligence without jeopardizing security interests. Since the end of the Cold War, DCIs have been somewhat more willing to appear in public hearings. Robert M. Gates testified in public six times during his first five months in office (1992); his successor, R. James Woolsey, increased this frequency during his brief time in office (1993–94). DCI Deutch has promised to improve further the openness of the intelligence community and has appointed as his deputy a former SSCI staff director, George J. Tenet, and as his chief of staff Michael O'Neil, a past HPSCI chief counsel.

This is a promising direction—all the better to inform the public and their surrogate overseers about intelligence policy; all the better to keep Agency officials steadily aware of the congressional presence; all the better to deter, or at least discover, the next Iran-contra transgression before it gathers steam. These advances, coupled with increased member attendance and more hardball pitches, are likely to improve the quality of intelligence supervision on Capitol Hill.

CHAPTER 5

THE DISTINCTIVENESS OF AMERICAN INTELLIGENCE

Intelligence commonly encompasses two broad meanings. First, the secret agencies acquire and interpret information about threats and opportunities that confront the nation, in an imperfect attempt to reduce the gaps and ambiguities that plague open sources of knowledge about the world. A nation especially seeks secret information to help it prevail in times of war, with as few casualties as possible. Second, based on information derived from denied and open sources, policymakers call upon their intelligence agencies to shield the nation against harm (counterintelligence) while advancing its interests through the secret manipulation of foreign events and personalities (covert action). Intelligence thus involves both information and response. The support that the secret agencies provide to policy officers on these fronts can be crucial in a world dependent on fragile economic relationships and cursed by weapons of mass destruction.[1]

COMPARING NATIONAL INTELLIGENCE SERVICES

The modern American experience with intelligence has been unique in a number of respects. The central purpose of this chapter is to examine what is different about the American approach, what may be common to the secret services of democracies, and what features of intelligence virtually all nations may share regardless of regime type. The observations drawn here are but first steps into a region of study that has received insufficient attention. Little wonder: for the most part, the necessary maps have been kept carefully hidden by the national security establishments of every nation.[2]

Despite the difficulties of understanding the workings of secret agencies in other countries, a few propositions can be ventured with some assurance of accuracy. Every nation desires increased knowledge about dangers from abroad. America's intelligence apparatus is, in this sense, merely a variant of organizations found in sovereign states throughout the world.

Some intelligence agencies have been large and fearsome in their aggressive capabilities, like the Soviet Union's KGB during the Cold War. The KGB combined domestic and foreign intelligence duties all in one massive agency—a CIA and FBI wrapped into one package, with responsibilities for the security of nuclear warheads added to the basics of espionage and covert action ("active measures," in KGB terminology). During the Cold War, Soviet military intelligence (the GRU) loomed as another huge and pugnacious bureaucracy, and it remains so under Russian rule—a monolithic structure quite different from the American approach of dividing military intelligence into several loosely associated entities. In sharp contrast, intelligence organizations in small nations can be as rudimentary as the placement of an intelligence officer under embassy cover in a foreign capital, with instructions to gather whatever useful information is available.

Information is valued by all national leaders, no matter their level of sophistication and national wealth or the prominence of their countries in world affairs. Few nations are without enemies—real or imagined, present or potential. Thus, they all take steps to protect themselves. This instinct for self-preservation is most readily observable in the world's flourishing commerce in arms. Less apparent are the measures nations take covertly to protect themselves and to advance their worldwide (or, for smaller nations, regional) interests through the methods of strategic and tactical intelligence. But take them they do.

Intelligence, then, exists in every nation. And even though governments try to keep their clandestine organizations and activities largely invisible, it is possible to discern differences in the structures, skills, and objectives of the secret agencies in other countries. Intelligence establishments, whether comprising a few or many agencies, differ according to four cardinal measures: the size and scope of their activity (including technical prowess); the degree of their institutional cohesion (centralization versus fragmentation); the extent to which they are held accountable by internal and external overseers; and their adherence to, or rejection of, moral considerations in the conduct of covert operations. These differences may be summed up as scale, cohesion, accountability, and ethics.

Scale

Its unfavorable current trade balance and extravagant national debt notwithstanding, the United States continues to enjoy a robust economy. Its Gross National Product (GNP) remains the highest in the world, as it has since the end of World War Two. The revenue derived from this wealth allows U.S. officials to build a vast national security establishment, comprising (at the height of the Cold War) some ten thousand strategic nuclear warheads, along with more troops, military bases, and conventional weaponry distributed around the globe than any other nation.

Just as it is necessary for the maintenance of powerful, mobile armed forces, national wealth is vital for the development of a sophisticated and far-reaching intelligence apparatus. Indeed, the two go together, for intelligence is crucial to the effective use of armed force, as the Persian Gulf War underscored. In that conflict, imagery derived from satellites and unmanned aerial vehicles provided detailed maps and coordinates of Iraqi targets, thereby greatly increasing the accuracy of American "smart bombs"(although the 50 percent success rate was far less than the Pentagon had the public and the media believing).[3] An affluent nation—and certainly a superpower—will desire both a strong military and reliable information to guide it.

Suckled on an annual budget approaching $30 billion in the 1990s, the American intelligence agencies have grown large—indeed "bloated," in the estimation of more than one experienced former intelligence officer.[4] Their buildings sprawl around the Washington perimeter, with HUMINT and TECHINT tentacles reaching out to every corner of the globe. Nothing so distinguishes the American intelligence establishment from all others as its combination of size and technical capabilities—a function of its superpower interests, responsibilities, and wealth.

A nation must have deep pockets to recruit, train, and support thousands of intelligence officers and to construct modern and well-guarded buildings for their work. It must be able to nurture the growth of universities and laboratories where advanced technical skills, foreign-language proficiency, and expertise about other countries can be imparted to future analysts and case officers. A sizable resource capacity is necessary as well for the design and construction of long-range listening antennas, for swift spy planes with high-resolution cameras, and for elaborate, billion-dollar satellites. A primary indicator of the scope and prowess of an intelligence establishment, then, is likely to be the degree of affluence enjoyed by its host nation.

This is not to say that richer and larger is always better with respect to intelligence organizations. Israel's redoubtable intelligence service, Mossad, is comparatively small in size, but it has enjoyed much success as a result of an experienced and brainy leadership working with skillful, well-trained officers in the field. Its deft interception in 1986 of a suitcase bomb that terrorists intended to plant aboard a passenger plane of El Al, the Israeli national airline, is one of many operations that illustrate Mossad's prowess.[5]

Even the venerable British secret service, composed of three smallish agencies, is dwarfed by the global intelligence infrastructures ("the plumbing," in U.S. spyspeak) of the American and Russian intelligence services. The British counterpart of the CIA (the Strategic Intelligence Service, or SIS) is about one-fifth its size.[6] Her Majesty's Secret Service, nonetheless, has a long and worldly history to draw upon in the arts of espionage, counterintelligence, and covert action. Over the years this experience has yielded impressive intelligence successes where newer—and larger—services might have stumbled.[7] With an appreciation for the advantage that comes from experience, America's fledgling Office of Strategic Services (OSS, precursor to the CIA) relied heavily on British tutoring during World War Two.[8]

Great Britain has chosen to concentrate on selected aspects of intelligence without trying to compete with the United States as a "full-service" facility. British signals intelligence and cryptanalysis, for example, are in some respects as good as any nation's, although the vast sums of money the United States has poured into satellite photography and other forms of IMINT has led to a product superior even to British imagery. Another means for less affluent nations to economize in their intelligence budgets is through sharing arrangements with allies, commonly known as "intelligence liaison" or "burden sharing"—an increasingly attractive approach also for wealthy nations undergoing fiscal stress.[9] In 1948, for example, Australia, Britain, Canada, New Zealand, and the United States signed the UKUSA SIGINT agreement, promising cooperation in the gathering and sharing of signals intelligence—"the first global peacetime intelligence alliance."[10]

The United States has maintained and expanded its liaison relationships with nations of the British Commonwealth and has entered into more limited sharing agreements with other Western democracies (most extensively with Germany and Norway). Canada also provides a good example of economizing through liaison arrangements. The foremost trading partner of the United States has no agency whatsoever engaged in HUMINT foreign intelligence collection or even a centralizing agency like the CIA. It has concentrated instead on SIG-INT, shipping much of that product to the United States for analysis and relying on the DCI to return whatever finished intelligence might be relevant to Canada's interests.

This relationship has caused concern among some Canadians. "Countries like Canada which import finished intelligence products are buying a national perspective that is always to some degree foreign," observes the Canadian scholar Reg Whitaker. "The national interests of some states may overlap with others to a greater or lesser degree, but they are never identical. . . . To be efficient and effective, the Canadian security and intelligence system needs to be a great deal more present-minded, more autonomous and oriented to Canadian national interests, less tied down by ancient alliance obligations, and more capable of flexible response to changing challenges."[11]

This move toward greater intelligence self-sufficiency would cost money, however—lots of money. To what extent does a country like Canada wish to divert its current funding priorities toward a more full-service intelligence establishment or raise additional taxes on its citizens in order to achieve intelligence autarky?

Moreover, Whitaker's point may be somewhat overdrawn. After all, the American and Canadian intelligence services have had for the most part a mutually beneficial relationship. Nonetheless, it is certainly true that "friendship" among nations goes only so far. During World War Two, British and U.S. intelligence (such as it was) were joined together in mortal combat against the Nazi war machine. At the same time, however, the British were conducting a number of operations *against* the United States, including tapping the American transatlantic cable and forging German documents to convince President Roosevelt that Hitler intended to invade the Americas.[12]

While nations can choose to specialize, relying on liaison relationships to make up the intelligence slack, an independent capacity for global coverage provides an important advantage. Without its extensive inventory of satellites, reconnaissance airplanes, and listening posts, the United States would be unable to verify with confidence the location of an adversary's strategic arms, count its missiles and warheads, monitor troop movements, and observe other vital indicators of military strength and intentions. Take away these assurances and it is more likely that during the Cold War superpower confrontations between the United States and the Soviet Union might have led to a Third World War.

Yet wealth is only a necessary, not a sufficient, condition for an effective, modern intelligence apparatus. Japan is one of the wealthiest nations in the world, but its intelligence capabilities are limited compared to, say, the United States or Russia. The reason is that the Japanese state is less possessed by a sense of danger than are the great military powers. Modern Japan has benefited from the luxury of relying on America's military and intelligence shield; and the United States has been willing to protect the Japanese because it is in America's best interests to prevent Japan—with its imposing industrial capacity—from falling prey to hostile powers.

So, despite their undisputed resource base to create a vast, high-tech intelligence service, the Japanese have not done so. They do, however, gather economic information, mostly through open sources. Economic targets the Japanese take quite seriously: their livelihood as a nation and claim to a place among the world's leading nations stems from a remarkable manufacturing and marketing capability.

As Jean-Marie Bonthous points out, "Japan does not have an intelligence organization like the CIA in the United States or the DGSE in France. It does not need one." Instead, the Japanese focus their energies on business intelligence, relying heavily on information gathered by an alliance of governmental and (especially) private-sector organizations. These include MITI, a government economic planning group, and JETRO, Japan's external trade organization, along with the *sogo soshas,* large export trading companies. Bonthous notes another key business intelligence asset enjoyed by the Japanese—"hundreds of thousands of disciplined 'CIA citizens,'" traveling Japanese businesspeople prepared to watch for information helpful to Japan, "who willingly serve as the eyes and the ears of their country."[13]

In the Persian Gulf, tiny Kuwait—with the highest per capita income of any nation—has also been in a financial position to afford a more elaborate intelligence service than it possessed at the time of its forced annexation by Iraq in 1990. Instead, Kuwait officials chose to rely primarily on diplomatic maneuvering as a means for fending off external threats, as when they shrewdly convinced the Reagan administration to flag and escort Kuwaiti oil tankers through the Gulf. Diplomatic skill aside, though, more attention to intelligence gathering might have forewarned Kuwait of Iraq's dark intentions.

Richer still in oil deposits, Saudi Arabia boasts a greater GNP than Kuwait, yet its global interests remain limited. The Saudi intelligence apparatus has to be proficient mainly in the Middle East. In an age of expensive TECHINT hardware, however, wealth counts even when a nation has only limited regional objectives. Few regimes could afford the costly reconnaissance aircraft known as AWACS (Airborne Warning and Control System) purchased by the Saudis from the United States—over the strenuous objections of Israelis, who viewed a Saudi AWACS intelligence capability as a potential threat in future Arab-Israeli confrontations.

Israel presents a special case of intelligence: a small country with considerable wealth ($7 million a day in foreign aid from the United States alone) and technical acumen that since its birth has been surrounded by enemies. Not surprisingly, Israelis probably spend a higher proportion of their national wealth on intelligence than most other countries. Acutely sensitive eyes and ears, watching everywhere throughout the Middle East and to some extent beyond, have been mandatory to guard against a quick attack from one of several contiguous foes. Intelligence warning time in this region of the world is like the geographical distance between its various capitals: short—too short in the case of the 1973 Yom Kippur War, when an Egyptian invasion force took even Israel's highly alert intelligence apparatus by surprise.

Yet at least Israel is unburdened by the worldwide responsibilities shouldered by the United States. The Israelis have the luxury of concentrating their military and intelligence resources in defense against immediate regional vulnerabilities. The limited schedule of the national airline, El Al, for example, greatly simplifies Mossad's counterterrorist task of preventing skyjackings. Israel, though, has not altogether overlooked the advantages of having a covert action and counterespionage capability to strike at enemies operating inside and outside the region—reputedly with a high rate of success.[14]

Compared with other nations, then, the United States has a uniquely comprehensive intelligence establishment, as measured by total funding, the possession of advanced capabilities for information management and data processing, a large cadre of well-educated specialists, and a global network of TECHINT machines and HUMINT assets. The NSA, for instance, is considered "the largest and most expensive intelligence agency in the history of Western civilization."[15] Consider these features of the U.S. intelligence community: half the floor space at the CIA is covered with state-of-the-art computers; a U.S. spy plane is on the drawing boards that will be able to travel at incredible speeds—from Los Angeles to New York City in ten minutes; the CIA has access to modern weaponry for use in paramilitary operations (like the Stinger missiles provided to Jonas Savimbi in Angola and the Mujahideen in Afghanistan); the CIA alone—excluding U.S. military intelligence units—has thousands of agents in the field, mainly engaged in espionage, but in place for covert action and counterespionage operations as well. Yet what particularly puts the United States in a category by itself when it comes to the scale of modern intelligence is that its satellites and reconnaissance airplanes possess exceptional mobility and wide-span optics, producing high-resolution color imagery intelligence.[16] No nation can match the information synergism that results from America's blend of electro-optical, radar, and infrared collection from land, sea, and air.

The leaders of the United States have invested in this extensive intelligence capability for two major reasons. First, they can afford to—or at least they seem to think they can. Second, they feel widely threatened and therefore seek information from the far reaches of the planet to protect themselves—especially information about the spread of dangerous weaponry and the intentions of those who might use them against the United States or its allies. Nor has the intelligence community overlooked the fact that Russia remains strong in nuclear arms and vulnerable to takeover by neo-nationalist factions and criminal elements. Although the Kremlin is in the process of dismantling a high percentage of its long-range missiles, it continues to have a nuclear weapons capability that could decimate the United States within minutes. A perception of grave threat, immediate or potential, stirs every nation to defend itself as best it can, most obviously through soldiers and weapons, but also by way of an improved intelligence warning and reaction system. Preeminently, a nation's secret agencies serve as a shield against foreign threats, and this is why they tend to grow apace with overt military establishments, roughly at a rate of about 5-to-10 percent of what a nation is spending on its military defense.

Cohesion

Students of American intelligence are quick to point to its "pluralism," that is, the multiple centers of power that lie within its dominion—especially the rivalry over the military intelligence agencies that exists between the DCI and the secretary of defense. Although now more centralized than at the beginning of the Cold War, the intelligence community nonetheless continues to be a fragmented cluster of agencies.

The memoirs of Admiral Stansfield Turner, DCI from 1977 to 1981, testify to his frustration in trying to gain control over the scattered entities that comprise the Community—or, for that matter, even over his own agency, the CIA.[17] Turner found the NSA, which he refers to as "a loner organization," especially difficult to manage.[18] Earlier, another admiral, Rufus Taylor, concluded flatly after his tenure as DDCI (1966–69) that the Community was little more than a "tribal federation."[19]

Research on the organization of other national intelligence establishments brings a somewhat different light, however, to bear on this widely accepted notion of a badly fragmented American system. In comparison to other nations, the American approach to intelligence as organization is more cohesive than most. An appreciation of the differences requires a closer examination of organizational cohesion from three different vantage points: the degree of authority an intelligence director exercises over the government's secret agencies; the extent to which intelligence judgments are amalgamated into consensus documents ("estimates," in the American system) that draw together the views of a nation's secret agencies; and the extent to which a nation's intelligence agencies join together with decisionmakers in deliberations over policy options. These three dimensions may be thought of in terms of structural unity, analytic integration, and policy involvement.

Structural Unity As Michael Herman reports, the British model for the production of intelligence "assessments" (major intelligence studies for policy guidance to Her Britannic Majesty's Government—the equivalent of NIEs in the American system) emphasizes interdepartmental collegiality, with loose organizational ties between the policy departments and intelligence agencies. In contrast, the U.S. model leans toward a more centralized reliance on the CIA to guide the analytic process.[20] This British approach Herman refers to as "jointery": cooperation between the three British intelligence agencies and the policy departments through a system of committees. This use of committees to draw together intelligence analysts and policymakers in the production of assessments is, in Herman's view, "the greatest British contribution to intelligence assessment."[21] At its best, the British method resembles a university seminar, where policy officers and intelligence experts join together in the search for truth. The British even go to the trouble of directly inquiring into the views of their ambassadors before completing an assessment—obvious wellsprings of useful advice about a foreign country often ignored in the U.S. estimating process. Truth-seeking is the same objective pursued by the National Intelligence Council (NIC) in the American system. But a vital difference is that in the United States policymakers are left out of the drafting process, which is dominated by CIA analysts. (The NIC even has its offices at CIA headquarters in Langley.)

At the level of intelligence as organization, the American system begins to appear—in comparison to the British and other foreign intelligence services—less of a pluralistic and fragmented enterprise than commonly thought. As Herman perceptively notes, Langley is *primus inter pares* among the focal points in the American system, providing "a kind of central spine of the DCI, NIOs and CIA [that] holds the system together."[22] No such unifying structural entity exists in the British system.

Within the American system a plethora of interagency committees exist, too, in an effort to bridge the Community's "tribalism." But most of them are weak bonds, and the DCI, the NIC, and the CIA continue to be the essential adhesive that keeps the analytic pieces of the Community in contact. Still, while the degree of cohesion in the American system remains weak, with the separate agencies enjoying great autonomy, at least compared with other nations the American model *at the organizational level* is more cohesive than it is often regarded to be.

Analytic Integration This centralization must be thought of primarily in structural terms, though. From the point of view of the analytic process, the ongoing autonomy of the various U.S. intelligence agencies can be seen in the tradition of NIE dissents. The American agencies are allowed to offer their own separate views in Community intelligence estimates, by way of notations to NIE texts and, even more boldly (as an outcome of the tenure of Joseph S. Nye, Jr., as chair of the NIC during the Clinton administration), in the texts of estimates. This tradition of dissent stands as a clear acknowledgment of the analytic decentralization that exists in the American intelligence community—even if organizationally the CIA takes the lead in preparing estimates.

The DCI, the CIA, and the NIOs may be the strongest hands in shaping an estimate, but the various intelligence agencies in the United States are permitted a clear dissenting voice when they wish. In contrast, footnoting is disallowed in Britain; London favors the preparation of consensus analytic reports for senior officials—an intellectual fusing, even as the British intelligence agencies eschew a CIA-like centralizing organization. The British search for consensus leads, in the view of a former CIA officer closely acquainted with the process, to a "pitiful watering down of the intelligence product"[23]—although this criticism has been frequently leveled against NIEs, too, despite their occasional dissenting notes.

Most foreign intelligence establishments come down in favor of a pluralism of professional judgments and opinions from their secret agencies. They reject centralization or even collegiality in the British sense. This analytic discretion is a matter not simply of allowing dissent in intelligence reports but often of creating entirely separate "stovepipes" of intelligence that funnel information from each of the secret agencies straight up to the decisionmakers.

The stovepipe approach forfeits a formal interagency integration of estimates (in the CIA/NIC style, with dissents allowed in footnotes and text) or even committee sharing and brainstorming (in the British style, with no dissent). Stovepipe pluralism obviously can lead to duplication and competition.

Moreover, this tolerance for overlap is expensive. It does have the virtue, though, of escaping the filtering effect of a centralizing agency (like the CIA), as well as the "homogenizing" tendencies found in systems of collegiality (such as Britain's) where dissenters are expected, when all is said and done, to go along with the majority view—saving their breath to cool their porridge.

Policy Involvement At the intersection between policy and intelligence the British intelligence model suddenly takes on the attributes of a strongly centralized system. Decisionmakers and analysts join together at high echelons through a committee structure that allows a free interplay between the two worlds of policy and intelligence, but which requires consensus at the end of the day. The U.S. intelligence agencies are permitted to enter analytic dissents but are expected to stay out of the policy loop; participation in decisionmaking is considered anathema to the cherished norm of intelligence purity.[24]

The American end product is an *intelligence* estimate, while the British end product is a much broader assessment that blends the judgments of policy *and* intelligence officers. The culture of American intelligence is wary of commingling between the two, fearful that policy considerations might contaminate the crystal purity of intelligence judgments—the politicization of intelligence. In contrast, the British culture actually encourages commingling, in the belief that the best policy decisions are likely to result from a pooling of knowledge from among the country's international affairs experts. The British approach claims an additional advantage: policy officers brought into the analytic process are apt to view the finished intelligence products as more legitimate and acceptable since they have played an intimate role in their crafting.

Even the DCI, the intelligence official most apt to find himself at NSC powwows in the White House, is expected to remove himself from policy pronouncements. As the president goes around the long mahogany table in the Roosevelt Room soliciting policy advice, the DCI is there to offer facts and forecasts about what might happen in a certain part of the world—not policy recommendations.

A few intelligence directors, though, have conceded a willingness to enter the realm of policy deliberations if explicitly and privately asked by the president.[25] President Clinton's first DCI, R. James Woolsey, has explained his approach:

> The President told me when I took the job that, from time to time, he would ask [for my policy recommendations], but he wanted it to be a private matter; so, within an agency or interagency context, I do not normally express a view about what options ought to be followed or not. Sometimes I ask questions in such a way that

people might be able to divine what I think, I suppose. I've practiced law too long not to know that that's a possibility; and, often I try to make sure that all the implications of an option are understood. But when Tony [Anthony Lake, the national security adviser], or the President, goes around the table at one of these meetings, [asking] "What do you think we ought to do?" they skip me—and that's right.[26]

In previous administrations, however, John A. McCone advised President Kennedy to carry out a surprise air attack against Soviet missile sites in Cuba, and Ronald Reagan's intelligence director, William J. Casey, was never bashful about offering his own policy views. Casey had served as the president's political campaign manager and was the first DCI ever given membership in the Cabinet. (In 1995 DCI John M. Deutch also insisted on membership.)

These generalizations about the American and British approaches to the role of intelligence in policy decisions overstate the case. After all, even in the American system, intelligence officers on the NIC and elsewhere engage these days (more so than in the past) in widespread and intensive dialogues with policy officers, usually at the deputy assistant secretary (DAS) level. Nevertheless, the two systems do display distinct differences in their centers of gravity, with the Americans leaning toward policy neutrality by intelligence officers and the British toward policy involvement.

In diagrammatic form, a sampling of nations from the comparative intelligence literature can be arrayed along the three dimensions of structural unity, analytic integration, and policy involvement (figure 5.1). Nations exhibit a range of experiences along a centralization-decentralization continuum. With respect to organizational unity, most foreign intelligence communities lean toward decentralization because of the inherent difficulties of sharing responsibilities among civilian, diplomatic, and military intelligence agencies—with all their institutional jealousies and rites of turf protection. Analytic fusion in the British manner is unusual; and when it comes to policy deliberations, no foreign intelligence service appears to have tilted toward the extreme of antipolicy purity as much as the U.S. intelligence community. The British approach of commingling analysts with policymakers is the norm, including for the KGB during the Cold War and its replacement, the SVRR, today.[27]

Organizational decentralization can be considered a virtue from some vantage points. Competition within a community of intelligence agencies can lead to a wider array of separate collection operations, allowing the target country to be viewed from various angles and modi operandi. Further, "competitive analysis" can sharpen minds, keep analysts honest, provide policy officers with a better sense of their options, and, most important, safeguard against a con-

Figure 5.1 Intelligence Pluralism: A Comparative Perspective

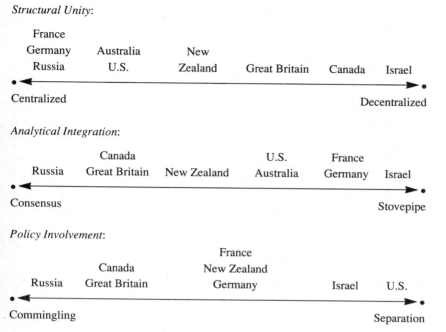

Structural Unity:

France
Germany   Australia   New
Russia   U.S.   Zealand   Great Britain   Canada   Israel

•◀───▶•
Centralized   Decentralized

Analytical Integration:

            Canada   U.S.   France
Russia   Great Britain New Zealand Australia Germany   Israel

•◀───▶•
Consensus   Stovepipe

Policy Involvement:

                          France
            Canada   New Zealand
Russia   Great Britain Germany   Israel   U.S.

•◀───▶•
Commingling   Separation

centration of power in a single, monolithic agency like the Cheka in the early years of the Soviet Union.

Decentralization can be a liability, though, when it produces needless duplication, poor coordination, bureaucratic in-fighting, and overzealous entrepreneurship among individual agencies—as during the Iran-contra affair, when the National Security Agency assisted Oliver North of the NSC staff with his communications needs without the knowledge of the DCI or of NSA's other boss, the secretary of defense.[28] It can be an impediment to effective government as well when the end result is bureaucratic game playing. During the Huston Plan episode of 1970, for instance, various intelligence agencies in the United States kept hidden from one another sensitive collection operations—as if their chief rivals were one another rather than the KGB and the GRU.[29]

Accountability

A third feature of America's intelligence establishment is distinctive: the degree of its internal and external accountability. The intelligence community is supervised from inside the secret agencies as well as from elsewhere in the executive branch, on Capitol Hill, in the courts, and in the public sector. "We're the most scrutinized intelligence agency in the world," a CIA officer has lamented.[30] "What we have is covert action by national consensus!" adds another, bemoaning the layers of decisionmaking now required for the approval of covert actions.[31]

In Britain, the Intelligence Services Act of 1994 created an Intelligence and Security Committee. The ISC consists of a small group of members of Parliament who report to the prime minister, who has the authority to decide what, if anything, shall be relayed to Parliament. This seems a rather weak system of accountability, at least compared to the opportunity in the U.S. Congress for legislators to question intelligence officers directly and to call for public hearings. The American approach emphasizes the Madisonian principle of checking power; the British approach, even with its new ISC, appears still to place the highest value on secrecy.

Only Canada's Security Intelligence Review Committee (SIRC) approaches the level of seriousness with which the United States monitors its secret agencies. The American system of review (oversight) is stronger overall, however, because unlike the SIRC the two congressional oversight committees in the United States have line-by-line authority for all intelligence budget approvals. Moreover, the SIRC is limited in its review to only a few of Canada's secret agencies, while U.S. overseers have responsibility for the entire intelligence community. The Canadian system nevertheless features a variety of rigorous review procedures, while the American system has often failed to function well. If intelligence documents are particularly sensitive (or if the U.S. secret agencies feel themselves under siege by outside critics), overseers in Congress can run into a stone wall in their dealings with intelligence officials. Legislators find that they must lobby or even issue subpoenas for access to documents, which they sometimes receive only after months of artful delays—or never at all.[32]

So, despite the relatively advanced state of intelligence oversight in the United States, the relationship between congressional overseers and intelligence officers remains uneasy. When legislators admonished DCI Deutch in 1995 that he had better punish those at the CIA responsible for the failure to report the Alperiz case to Congress, a retired intelligence senior officer viewed the remarks as simply another attempt at micromanagement from Capitol Hill. "It's his first real test . . . whether Deutch or the Congress runs the agency."[33]

The New Oversight ushered in with the intelligence investigations of 1975 has brought, nonetheless, an infinitely greater degree of interaction between the secret agencies and the Congress than in earlier times. Few foresee a return to the "good old days" when the intelligence community charted its own course, with only the broadest of guidelines from the White House and mostly quiescence from Capitol Hill.

Certainly the sheer number of intelligence overseers in the United States is remarkable. Before 1975 no one outside the Community kept close tabs on its activities. During the Kennedy and Johnson administrations NSC principals evidently never even saw the CIA's annual budgets.[34] Inside the CIA the Directorate of Operations enjoyed wide discretionary powers; and the counterintelligence staff, under its famous first chief, James Angleton, often ran aggressive operations overseas without the knowledge of the DO or the local U.S. ambassador.[35]

Now, in dramatic contrast, the Congress is very much in the "witting circle" (or what the British refer to as the "ring of secrecy") of those kept informed of current intelligence operations. Moreover, within the agencies a host of checks and balances have evolved—a response to White House (notably under the Ford and Carter administrations) and congressional insistence on reform in the wake of a variety of intelligence abuses and scandals.

Covert action offers an illustration of the new (and, critics insist, cumbersome) safeguards. Since 1975, all important covert-action proposals have had to run a daunting decision gauntlet.[36] Before an operation receives a green light, it has to be reviewed by a series of individuals and entities: CIA field personnel (the major checkpoint at this level is the Agency's chief of station, or COS; the ambassador is usually consulted, too—if the COS trusts the ambassador); the Special Activities (SA) division and, in the case of paramilitary operations, the Special Operations Group (SOG), both within the Operations Directorate at CIA Headquarters; the Department of State (for propaganda themes); the Intelligence Directorate; the comptroller; the Office of the General Counsel; the Office of Congressional Affairs; and the DCI.

The proposal then has to pass muster before an NSC interagency review group (comprised of deputies to the principal members) before it goes back to the DCI for another review and then on to the NSC itself. At the NSC the president and the three other statutory members of that panel (the vice president and the secretaries of state and defense) have an opportunity to take a close look, as does the president's national security adviser, the chairman of the Joint Chiefs of Staff, and other officials the president may ask to attend. If the president approves the covert action, it is reported as a finding to the legislative oversight committees, then returned to the CIA for implementation.

Along the way, strong criticism can lead to the modification or abandonment of a proposal. The stage of NSC deputy review has become a notorious graveyard for dubious covert-action initiatives. During the Carter and Reagan administrations over 50 percent reportedly perished at this stage. Moreover, the NSC deputies modified most of the successful proposals in one way or another. Subsequently another 15 percent or so met their demise at the hands of the two presidents themselves. Every now and then legislative overseers have also demurred—most visibly with the series of Boland Amendments in the 1980s, enacted to curb covert actions in Nicaragua.[37]

A few significant exceptions to this involvement of Congress in the review of covert actions have occurred. The Carter administration delayed reporting to legislators until after its attempted operations to rescue Americans in Iran had run their course, for fear that a leak might jeopardize the plans. President Carter ordered the reporting delay at the request of the Canadian government, whose embassy in Tehran offered to assist in some aspects of these operations—but only if this stipulation were honored. It is worth noting that the operations took place before passage of the 1980 Intelligence Oversight Act, with its statutory insistence on *prior* congressional notification of all important covert actions.[38]

Then, in a more notorious exception to established procedures—and one that took place after the passage of the 1980 Oversight Act—the Reagan administration chose during the Iran-contra affair to bypass most of the checkpoints inside the CIA and all of them on Capitol Hill. Administration officials raised millions of dollars privately from conservative benefactors within the United States (the Colorado beer magnate Joseph Coors, for one) and wealthy potentates abroad, including the sultan of Brunei and King Fahd of Saudi Arabia. The objective was to finance an "off-the-shelf, self-sustaining, stand-alone" covert-action capability secretly guided by the NSC staff and DCI Casey—free from the inconvenience of the constitutional requirement, in Article I, that government funds be appropriated by Congress.[39] This "privatization" of special activities dealt a sharp blow to constitutional government in the United States.[40] The NSC perpetrators of this extraconstitutional scheming were indicted in 1987; two years later a jury found the first to be tried, Oliver North, guilty of improper conduct. North's conviction was subsequently overturned by a District of Columbia appellate court, on a technicality, by a two-to-one vote—with two Reagan-appointed judges voting in North's favor and a Carter-appointed judge against. President George Bush, a former DCI who had been vice president at the time of the Iran-contra activities, conveniently pardoned the other co-conspirators, whose courtroom testimony might have implicated him. Also among the pardoned was John M. Poindexter, President Reagan's national security adviser (following Robert C. McFarlane).

The Iran-contra scandal serves as a reminder that even strict controls can be evaded by officials determined to have their own way, regardless of established laws and procedures. As always in government, the attitudes of men and women in office—especially their respect for the law—will be of overriding importance in any system of accountability. In the overwhelming majority of instances, however, the new oversight laws and reporting procedures have been honored by the NSC and intelligence officers.

A tight grip on the purse strings by congressional overseers can be a powerful influence on the behavior of America's intelligence agencies. As former DCI William Colby observes, "In order to persuade the CIA to abandon a proposed covert action, an [Intelligence] Committee chairman needs only to say to the DCI at the end of the briefing [on a presidential finding]: 'Write down in your notebook $100 million, because—if you go ahead—that is what is coming out of your CIA budget next year.'"[41]

Beyond the official instruments of oversight within the government, the American media have played a stronger role in monitoring the secret agencies than their counterparts in other nations. It was a series of *New York Times* exposés in December 1974 that triggered the official inquiries into CIA abuses and introduced the new era of intelligence accountability. In Britain, by contrast, a reporter still ventures out on thin ice when writing about intelligence matters. The Official Secrets Act carries stiff penalties against the disclosure of state secrets by correspondents—reputedly even the contents of the menu in the House of Lords dining room—casting a chill over serious media coverage of the British Secret Service.

The movement toward closer supervision of the American intelligence community has drawn mixed reviews by inside professionals and outside observers. Some critics of the New Oversight complain bitterly about dilettante legislators who insist on inserting their clumsy fingers in the small, delicate wheels of secret intelligence operations. They decry, too, alleged delays in the approval of operations, along with a new timidity among intelligence officers—supposedly a by-product of the hordes of nervous supervisors waving executive orders, committee reports, and statutes. Exasperated with the culture of delay and caution, one former CIA official declared, "The intelligence agencies need *horsepower*!"[42]

Yet others—both inside and outside the intelligence fraternity—welcome the idea of an executive-legislative partnership in place of the ambiguous boundaries of propriety in earlier days. "With today's supervision, and with the command structure trying to keep things straight, the people in CIA know what they should do and what they should not do—as distinct from the 1950s, in which there were no particular rules," William Colby has remarked. "If CIA people today are told to violate their limits, or if they are tempted to violate those limits, one of the junior officers will surely raise that question and tell the command structure, and, if not satisfied there, he will tell the press, and that is the way you control it."[43]

In a similar vein, DCI Stansfield Turner informed his senior staff and Agency stations around the world in 1978, "Oversight can be a bureaucratic impediment and a risk to security. It can also be a tremendous strength and benefit to us. It shares our responsibilities." The admiral further noted, "It ensures against our becoming separated from the legal and ethical standards of our society. It prevents disharmony between our foreign policy and intelligence efforts. It helps build a solid foundation for the future of our intelligence operations."[44]

These expressions of support for oversight differ dramatically from the avoid-Congress philosophy that permeated the intelligence community from 1947 to 1975. It was reinforced at the time by an attitude on Capitol Hill that intelligence professionals were "honorable men" (the title of Colby's memoirs) who could be trusted to carry out their duties without infringing on American laws or civil liberties.[45] The confidence in the new philosophy expressed by DCIs Colby and Turner, though no doubt sincerely held, comes across as somewhat glib in light of the Iran-contra scandal. Whatever the benefits of the New Oversight and however many the new safeguards, clearly they failed during the Reagan years.

Iran-contra serves as a reminder that the American experiment in intelligence accountability remains in its early, tentative stages, having seriously begun only in 1976 with the creation of the Senate Intelligence Committee. (The House of Representatives established a companion panel the next year.) These past two decades—the years of infancy and adolescence for intelligence accountability—have been marked by distress. Despite Jimmy Carter's ardor for intelligence reform while running for the presidency, his administration successfully rebuffed attempts to legislate an omnibus intelligence reform bill.[46] Moreover, the Reagan administration—with its cavalier operations in Iran and Nicaragua and the venomous anti-Congress views of DCI Casey—wavered between mild disdain and outright contempt for legislative overseers. Congress was to be kept in the dark, not treated as a partner. According to a well-regarded member of the House Intelligence Committee, "Casey wouldn't tell you that your coat was on fire unless you asked him."[47]

The Iran-contra scandal eventually "fractured" the increasingly brittle oversight relationship between Casey and Congress.[48] In the aftermath an atmosphere of wariness toward the secret agencies lingered on Capitol Hill. Upon

Casey's death in 1987 from a brain tumor, his immediate replacement, former FBI director William H. Webster (1987–91) proved much more adept in dealing with legislative overseers[49]—however maligned his managerial style. (He was widely thought to prefer afternoon tennis over the consideration of dry intelligence cables from around the world.) After a rocky beginning, the next DCI, Robert M. Gates, also enjoyed reasonably good relations on Capitol Hill and high marks for administrative skill during his tenure from 1991 to 1994.

The first DCI during the Clinton administration, R. James Woolsey, ran into trouble with the Senate Intelligence Committee almost from the start. He came across to the committee's chairman, Dennis DeConcini, as aloof and overly protective of the CIA—even though Woolsey was more willing than any of his predecessors to appear in public hearings. Relations quickly soured between the two. Between Congress and the intelligence community as a whole, however, business continued to be conducted fairly cordially—a far cry from the deep trough of acrimony into which Casey and the free-wheeling NSC staff of the Reagan administration had carried Community and legislative relations just a few years earlier.

As the Clinton administration stumbled forward into the uncertainty of the post–Cold War era, the search continued on Capitol Hill for a proper balance between an effective intelligence service and democratic accountability—both vital to the freedom of American citizens. Woolsey resigned in December 1994, and the new anti-Clinton GOP majorities on Capitol Hill augured poorly for smooth relations between Congress and the executive branch. Clinton's second DCI, Deutch, promised that he was "completely committed to keeping Congress fully informed;"[50] yet his bluff manner, along with questions about how adeptly he had handled the Alperiz flap, raised red flags about future relations between legislators and the secret agencies.

Ethics

Coupling *ethics* and *intelligence* in the same sentence may sound ludicrous to some, but in the United States moral considerations sometimes do enter into the clandestine realm. In most nations this linkage seems at best extraneous—indeed, virtually all nations are prepared to set morality aside in the conduct of some covert operations. Franklin Roosevelt's secretary of state, Henry Stimson, once remarked that "gentlemen don't read other people's mail"; one suspects that this injunction is now universally dismissed as a quaint but naive view of world affairs. Even in the United States the question of the morality of secret operations got scant (if any) attention during the Cold War—until the watershed year 1975.

Before the Year of Intelligence, the prevailing point of view echoed a now well-known (but then top-secret) passage from the Doolittle Report, presented to President Dwight D. Eisenhower in 1954:

It is now clear that we are facing an implacable enemy [the USSR] whose avowed objective is world domination by whatever means and at whatever cost. There are no rules in such a game. Hitherto acceptable norms of human conduct do not apply. If the U.S. is to survive, long-standing American concepts of "fair play" must be reconsidered. We must develop effective espionage and counter-espionage services. We must learn to subvert, sabotage and destroy our enemies by more clear, more sophisticated and more effective methods than those used against us. It may become necessary that the American people will be made acquainted with, understand and support this fundamentally repugnant philosophy.[51]

If a British or French intelligence professional had been able to read this document in 1954, one can imagine the response: "Welcome to the real world, America!"

An official change in the ethical standards for America's secret agencies did not occur until fully two decades after the Doolittle Report—in 1974, with the *New York Times* exposés and the subsequent congressional disclosures of intelligence abuses. Evidence that the CIA, the NSA, and the FBI had spied on American citizens, and that the CIA had tried to overthrow the freely elected leader of Chile, Salvador Allende, and had planned to assassinate foreign leaders, led to widespread calls for reform.[52] Coming on top of the Watergate scandal, U.S. Army domestic spying, and the high-level mendacity that infused policy pronouncements during the Vietnam War, these latest revelations of wrongdoing brought forth a strong public reaction.

At the end of a year's investigation, President Ford signed an executive order in 1976 prohibiting the assassination of foreign leaders as an instrument of American foreign policy. The order remains in effect except in times of war—as during Operation Desert Storm in 1991, when military and intelligence units were authorized to dispatch Saddam Hussein of Iraq if they could locate him (which they could not).[53] Also in 1975, former top officials recommended dramatic cutbacks in the use of covert action, and reform-minded legislators lambasted the unsavory practices of the secret agencies and moved to institute closer supervision over them.[54]

The New Morality, as some referred (often sarcastically) to this sudden interest in ethical introspection, had its limits. Efforts to enact an anti-assassination law—not just an executive order—failed in Congress during 1976; and a litany of reforms proposed in the Omnibus Intelligence Act of 1978 (including prohibitions against the covert spread of diseases, the creation of water shortages or floods in enemy nations, and the secret use of chemical and biological weapons) drew quick criticism from "realists" for locking the intelligence agencies in moral handcuffs while America's hard-fisted opponents swung freely. The proposed statute, over two hundred pages long, attempted to stretch the new ethical boundaries—and failed.[55]

One realist asked at the time: "Must the United States respond like a man in a barroom brawl who will fight only according to Marquis of Queensberry rules?" To which a leading proponent of morality in American foreign policy retorted with equal fervor: Must the United States "fuzz the difference between ourselves and the Soviet Union . . . [yielding to] a childish temptation to fight the Russians on their own terms and in their own gutter . . . and throw away one of our great assets?"[56]

As with the tug-of-war between micromanagement and accountability, the debate continues between realists and moralists over the proper balance between protecting the nation's interests abroad and maintaining its virtue. The merits of both schools aside, the debate is in itself unique: no other nation has devoted so much attention to the question of ethics and intelligence. Almost everywhere else, the moralist's argument has been roundly dismissed as quixotic.

Yet the influence of the moralist perspective in the United States should not be overestimated. Of late, American policy officers have been more squeamish than in the past about ordering aggressive covert operations; and assassination plots have been banned in peacetime. Nonetheless, high officials in the Clinton administration, frustrated by the war in Bosnia and other irritants, have expressed a strong interest in a more vigorous use of covert action.[57] A comparative perspective is again important, though, in evaluating the moral limits on intelligence. Moral compared with whom? The KGB in the Middle East is reported to have kidnapped the relative of a terrorist leader, castrated him, stuffed his testicles in his mouth, and, for good measure, shot him in the head—all in revenge for hostage taking. French intelligence blew up a Greenpeace ship in the harbor of Auckland, New Zealand, killing a crew member. These operations are inconceivable for the U.S. intelligence agencies.[58]

Still, the moral ground beneath foreign policy decisions can be notoriously slippery. While secret intervention abroad may lead to excesses, it may also be the only available course at times and might help an oppressed people find freedom. This was part of the motivation behind American support for the mujahideen in Afghanistan during the Carter and Reagan administrations, which moralists as well as realists supported. This same objective, however, was also a strong motivation for U.S. involvement in Vietnam during the 1960s, which most moralists ultimately opposed. Who is doing the dying—American soldiers or "merely" the CIA's surrogate mercenaries—has also entered into moral assessments of covert intervention.

While considerations of what is good and bad about secret interventions will continue to be difficult and contentious, one conclusion seems reasonable: questions of morality ought to be tied more closely to formal methods of accountability. Just as more individuals than the president and the DCI should be engaged in the supervision of the secret agencies, so should more than just a few officials in the executive branch decide the difficult ethical questions associated with their activities. Elected representatives in the Congress—or, at any rate, those serving on the two intelligence committees and in the Gang of Eight—should be consulted, in advance and in executive (closed) session, not just about the practicality but also about the morality of covert operations. Legislators who have served on the congressional intelligence committees—thoughtful people like Les Aspin, David L. Boren, William Cohen, Norman Dicks, Wyche Fowler, Porter Goss, Henry Hyde, Sam Nunn, and John Warner, among many others—have brought much wisdom to these judgments.

THE COMMONALITIES OF INTELLIGENCE

Just as national intelligence establishments have their distinctive differences, so too they have commonalities. Three ways in which the American intelligence experience has paralleled that of other nations are explored next, one for each of the primary intelligence missions: collection and analysis, covert action, and counterintelligence.

The Information and Understanding Gaps

Among the many features of intelligence shared by all nations, one stands out most conspicuously: no nation has the capacity to acquire all the secrets of the world, let alone understand all the mysteries. Moreover, policymakers and intelligence officers alike are fallible and are not omniscient. As a result, we will be forever vulnerable to intelligence "failures."[59]

In 1989 most countries seemed to have been astonished by the student rebellion at Tiananmen Square in Beijing and the harsh crackdown by the Chinese regime. Most were surprised, too, by the Khomeini revolution in Iran—including, apparently, Khomeini himself.[60] Even when one knows a country well, mistakes can occur. Just before the 1994 congressional elections, a group of American political scientists gathered in Atlanta to offer their predictions on how many seats in the House of Representatives the Democrats would lose. Most of the experts forecast anywhere from fifteen to twenty-five; one renowned specialist in the mathematical modeling of elections ventured that four was the right number. A few days later, the GOP swept in as the House majority with fifty-three new seats.

A seasoned NIO has observed that the CIA's intelligence forecasts should not be confused with prophecy. "We are a non-prophet institution," he remarked.[61] While no one can predict the future with confidence, the purpose of intelligence estimates is to reduce the number of surprises in so far as possible—especially those that can truly harm the nation—and to provide means for checking on the veracity and fullness of information gained from open sources. The elimination of surprise altogether will always lie outside mortal hands.

Some intelligence officers have responded to the risk of being caught unawares by forecasting danger everywhere. Dean Rusk remembers when he served as secretary of state in the 1960s, "The CIA predicted eight out of the last three crises!"[62] Others have adopted a converse strategy. Thomas L. Hughes, a former director of the State Department's Bureau of Intelligence and Research, tells the story of the analyst in the British government who served from 1903 to 1950 and in retirement reputedly confided, "Year after year worriers and fretters would come to me with awful predictions of the outbreak of war. I denied it each time. I was only wrong twice." With this methodology, Hughes observes, the analyst "can curl up in the luxury of a freebooting negativism. No reputation is staked, no career endangered."[63]

Some information that one would like to have is simply too inaccessible, such as the activities of small and elusive terrorist factions like the Abu Nidal or Hamas cells in the Middle East. Their recruitment methods are so tightly closeted that the chances of planting a spy on the inside are remote. The CIA was never able to pinpoint the exact location of American hostages held in the Middle East during the 1980s, some of whom had been held for years.

Then comes the added problem of ensuring that the secret agencies provide unadulterated information. To curry favor with those in high office, intelligence officers—in every country—may be tempted to provide intelligence to please. Another challenge is to make sure that policymakers appreciate and understand information supplied to them by the intelligence agencies without misperceiving or otherwise distorting its meaning. Sometimes decisionmakers will embrace only that intelligence which conveniently corresponds to their existing beliefs and ideologies, rejecting the rest (see chapter 1).

The Beguiling Quiet Option

Those nations that have developed a capacity for covert action—"disruption operations," in the more candid British phrase—frequently find it an almost irresistible alternative to the more overt instruments of foreign policy, such as dropping bombs on people or engaging in tedious negotiations. Open warfare is always noisy abroad and stirs controversy at home, and diplomacy is often too slow and frustrating. The "quiet option," in contrast, holds out the temptation of a behind-the-scenes quick fix. But it rarely lives up to its promise, for the currents of history resist the feeble efforts of politicians and spies to change its course. In democracies, some policymakers also find covert action attractive because it avoids debate with legislators. Recall Admiral Poindexter's candid confession: "I didn't want any interference."[64]

As practiced by the government of the United States, covert action seems to take on a life of its own, irrespective of existing overt policies. This occurs for two major reasons. First, officials in the intelligence agencies may sometimes have their own policy agenda which they seek to carry out, whether or not it conforms to the president's publicly stated goals. At the extreme, this behavior conjures the image of a "rogue elephant on a rampage," as Senator Frank Church put it during his committee's investigation into CIA assassination plots.[65] Second—and more likely in most instances—the White House has tended to conduct a two-track foreign policy: one overt, another covert. Paradoxically, the latter may pursue objectives (spelled out in top-secret Presidential Decision Directives) that run counter to the former. During the Cold War the subterranean struggle between the intelligence community and the KGB often continued unabated, even when the United States sought more peaceful relations with the USSR by negotiations during the period of detente.

The Security Gap

In the domain of counterintelligence, few nations felt secure during the Cold War and few feel secure today. Clearly, no nation can boast of perfect counterintelligence. Each is vulnerable to the Abu Nidals or Aldrich Ameses of the world. Despite the best efforts of security personnel, a Semtex-filled Toshiba boombox CD player may lie ticking in the baggage compartment of a national airline or in a bread truck parked outside an embassy. Further, every intelligence service will suffer defections, provocations, and penetrations.

The more technologically advanced states have the advantage of sophisticated capabilities for conducting embassy break-ins and remote surveillance. On this conflict-riven globe, however, the counterintelligence task (including counterterrorism, counternarcotics, and internal subversion) will remain a difficult assignment for all nations, as the recent unmasking of Ames and the bombings of the World Trade Center in New York City (1994) and the Federal Building in Oklahoma City (1995) have painfully reminded Americans.

Further, one suspects that every nation wrestles like the United States with the proper organizational approach to counterintelligence. Should one develop a tightly centralized cadre of specialists, as practiced in the CIA by James Angleton, with its risks of isolation and its advantages of security? Or should one embrace a more decentralized management principle that makes counterintelligence a part of every intelligence officer's responsibilities, with its risks of penetration and its advantages of broader coverage? This perplexing administrative conundrum is likely to remain an important part of the internal counterintelligence debate in all countries.

SOME IMPLICATIONS OF THE AMERICAN EXPERIENCE

America's intelligence agencies are distinctive in several ways. They are large and technically advanced, dispersed in their organization and management, watched closely by overseers (compared to earlier times and as against most other nations), and guided by at least some moral signposts. They also share common traits with their counterparts abroad, among them an inability to foresee and collect all the information that policy officers may need, the periodic distortion of information by analysts and decisionmakers, a beguiling attraction to covert action at times (even when these operations may run counter to publicly stated diplomatic initiatives) and persistent failures of counterintelligence.

These characterizations point to a number of prescriptions. Most centrally, the ongoing development of intelligence services warrants support, if closely supervised and directed chiefly toward intelligence collection and analysis. The more that nations can reduce uncertainty about the capabilities and intentions of their adversaries, the more likely that they will be able to avoid conflicts resulting from a fear of surprise attack or from other misperceptions and miscalculations. As former DCI William Colby has properly underscored, good intelligence can replace "ignorance, fear and suspicion [with] knowledge and confidence."[66] Intelligence can have a stabilizing effect on world affairs.

The organizational pluralism in the U.S. intelligence community remains excessive. Within limits, the authority of the DCI ought to be augmented—especially over the appointment of intelligence agency heads, budget allocations, and collection tasking. Given that the secretary of defense is a mighty figure in the government and clearly has a legitimate interest in the uses of intelligence, the DCI will have to work in tandem with the secretary in the making of these policy choices, just as throughout the government bargaining and persuasion—not command—is the time-honored approach to public policy in the United

States. As it stands now, though, the defense secretary is so dominant that the DCI has less leverage than he requires and deserves for policy negotiations.

Although consumer-producer dialogues are important, especially to improve the relevance of collection and analysis to the information needs of policymakers, the current distance at which U.S. intelligence officers place themselves from involvement in policy decisions is prudent. In the balancing act between relevance and avoidance of politicization, the latter must prevail. Proper, too, is the tradition of allowing full analytic dissent in the text and footnotes of intelligence estimates.

The system of intelligence accountability in America remains in a state of flux. More dedication to this responsibility is necessary by individual members of Congress. And, as congressional investigators urged after their Iran-contra inquiry, an improved "spirit of good faith with Congress" must be more forthcoming in the executive branch. Evidently this lesson has fallen on deaf ears within at least some of the intelligence agencies, in light of NRO cost overruns and hoarding of funds that were insufficiently reported to congressional overseers, DCI Woolsey's verbal contretemps with key members of the SSCI (especially its chairman), and the "batten down the hatches" attitude of some intelligence officers in 1995 toward congressional criticism of the Guatemalan "rogue agent" Colonel Alperiz.

The intelligence missions also need greater moral definition, particularly in sorting out "acceptable" covert actions. The defeated Omnibus Intelligence Act of 1978 doubtless went too far in this direction; but currently the CIA has too little policy guidance. (So do the military units involved in "special operations"—Pentagon vernacular for activities that often look suspiciously like covert action but evade the findings process.[67]) The abandoned ethical provisions of the Charter deserve another look, for some of the ideas had merit, such as the proposed prohibition against clandestine crop destruction.

As for the common problems of intelligence that touch all nations, leaders should begin to consider more seriously the possibilities of openly extending intelligence liaison relationships with their foreign counterparts and with international organizations. While some nations already share intelligence to some extent (as with the UK-USA SIGINT agreement), a greater pooling of information—say, in searches for mineral resources and responses to natural disasters, not just military and political threats—would help to build bridges of international cooperation. Despite opposition from senior intelligence officers, both the Bush and Clinton administrations have aided world peace by providing useful intelligence to U.N. peacekeepers with respect to Bosnia, Iraq, North Korea, and Somalia.

Moreover, in spite of a lingering reluctance within their intelligence establishments, the world's leading countries should begin to work toward establishing a U.N. Environmental Intelligence Agency equipped with state-of-the-art satellite capabilities for tracking ecological conditions. As the world community begins to acknowledge that global environmental degradation affects every country, it may recognize the value of a shared response through the United Nations—from data gathering on pollution to the use of spy satellites to monitor arms control and cease-fire agreements.[68]

Developing a strong U.N. intelligence capability for environmental and peacekeeping tasks will take years. In the meantime, the United States and other nations should share more generously with international organizations, as well as with ecologists in the private sector, their intelligence gained from aerial and satellite surveillance.[69] The sharing of intelligence among NATO units in Bosnia in 1996 demonstrates how successful this approach can be.

Further, just as treaties are signed on arms control arrangements, so nations should begin to prohibit by treaty at least some aspects of covert action, collectively resisting its strong tug. Covert action is unlikely to be banished by international convention any time soon; but efforts at better international supervision are warranted, including prohibitions against the use of special activities that directly contradict overt diplomatic initiatives and understandings—in essence, driving with the brake on.

Even the murky world of counterintelligence lends itself to some forms of international cooperation, most obviously in joint combat against terrorism, the rising drug epidemic, and international crime. Here, in fact, may be three of the most promising starting points for nations to work together toward solving common problems through intelligence liaison.[70] Although a few national leaders actually profit from the drug trade and other criminal activities, and, therefore, will have no interest in cooperation (or are too intimidated by indigenous terrorists and underworld figures), most would like to save their children from the scourge of drugs and lawlessness.

CHAPTER 6

INTELLIGENCE AND ECONOMIC SECURITY

As in the early days of the Republic, the world remains a decidedly danger-ous place for the United States. British men-of-war and marauding Barbary pi-rates have given way to nuclear-tipped ICBMs, terrorist bombings, and illicit narcotics. In his "bottom-up" review of the major threats facing the United States, Secretary of Defense Les Aspin pointed to the presence of outlaw states, with Cuba, Iran, Iraq, and North Korea high on the list; the proliferation of nu-clear, biological, and chemical weapons; the possibility that democratic reform of former totalitarian regimes might fail, especially in Russia; and America's global economic decline.[1]

The question of economic competitiveness served as a centerpiece in the 1992 presidential campaign of Bill Clinton. On the eve of assuming the presi-dency, he vowed to "make the economic security of our nation a primary goal of our foreign policy."[2] Coupled with his abiding attention to domestic eco-nomic issues, foreign economic policy became one of the president's foremost concerns during the first years of his administration. Early in office he created a National Economic Council (NEC), touted as equal in status to the National Security Council. Long a maid in waiting to defense issues, matters of trade and aid had risen high on the national security agenda. "It's the economy, stu-pid!" had been the mantra among Clinton's campaign strategists in 1992; now, within the government's community of national security planners, the slogan seemed to be, "It's economic security, stupid!"

Even before presidential candidate Clinton began to focus on the subject, his two Republican predecessors in the White House had started a shift in the gov-ernment's agenda toward questions of international economics. A 1991 review of intelligence priorities, initiated by President Bush, led to a dramatic reallo-cation of resources away from old Cold War concerns toward new economic tar-gets, as the world marketplace became an ever more important battlefield for America.[3] This chapter concentrates on a specific "transnational issue" fol-lowed by the secret agencies: economic intelligence. Its various meanings are first examined, then its manifestations during and after the Cold War, and finally its appropriateness as an ongoing responsibility for the intelligence community.

DEFINING ECONOMIC INTELLIGENCE

The terms *business intelligence, industrial espionage, economic espionage, commercial intelligence,* and *economic intelligence* are often used inter-changeably, leading to confusion. *Business intelligence* refers to the practice of one business gathering information about another, a common occurrence.[4] If this collection of information is carried out covertly (by spying), the gener-ally accepted term is *industrial espionage.*[5]

Beyond the collection of information about competitors, businesses employ a range of operations to protect and advance their international commercial in-terests, including security measures against foreign spying (private-sector counterintelligence). Business intelligence can also include the use of "dirty tricks" to disrupt the functioning of foreign competitors, such as supplying them with poor-quality construction materials for their factories—a private-sector covert action. The main distinction is that business intelligence does not involve the government; it is strictly a matter of business against business.[6]

In contrast, *economic intelligence* does involve the government. This catch-all phrase has two dimensions. In the first—variously called *microeconomic intelligence, microeconomic espionage, commercial intelligence,* or, loosely, *industrial espionage* (a misappropriation of the term for business-against-busi-ness spying)—the government engages in the collection of information on be-half of a society's business sector, thus constituting a business-government partnership in competition against rival foreign companies. The nation's secret agencies are called upon to provide faltering home industries with a competitive edge by acquiring information about international trade deals and the negotiating strategies of specific international competitors.

Also at the micro level, the federal government can help thwart foreign espionage against U.S. corporations (a form of government counterintelligence) or intervene abroad secretly to disrupt the activities of competitive corporations—sabotaging industrial plants, for instance (covert action). The hallmark of microeconomic intelligence is the presence of a secret government agency endeavoring to aid a compatriot firm for the latter's commercial gain in the international marketplace.

The second dimension of economic intelligence, which we may refer to as *macroeconomic intelligence* or *macroeconomic espionage,* similarly involves the use of secret government agencies. In this instance, however, the activities lie outside the realm of spying on specific overseas business competitors strictly for the purpose of accruing commercial advantages for American firms. Nor does macroeconomic intelligence involve the targeting of counterintelligence or covert-action operations against specific corporations abroad on the behalf of U.S. businesses. What delineates macroeconomic from microeconomic intelligence is the former's broader concentration on global economic information and activities designed to service the *nation's* strategic interests.[7] A paper written in 1984 in the CIA's Office of Global Issues, entitled "Future Newly Industrializing Countries: More Competition?" is an example of intelligence reporting at the macro level.[8]

The collection of macroeconomic intelligence can be based on open sources or on the clandestine acquisition of information (macroeconomic espionage). Regardless of the sources and methods used, here the government's secret agencies seek access to information on global economic trends, international financial and trade issues, likely negotiating strategies at government-sponsored multinational conferences, and worldwide technological developments.

So the collection and analysis of intelligence at the macroeconomic level, it bears stressing, has a primary objective: support of the *government* in a range of economic activities that are meant to help the United States and its business community. This support includes:

- developing knowledge about how foreign nations make economic decisions and what their commercial aims may be
- analyzing the patterns of international trade and searching for opportunities for the United States in specific markets overseas
- watching for unfair trade practices by foreign nations and companies (such as bribing and kickbacks)

- providing intelligence to U.S. negotiators attending international economic conferences, including—if possible—insights into the likely negotiating strategies of participants and their bottom lines
- verifying the compliance of foreign nations with their economic treaty obligations
- monitoring technological developments abroad
- designing and monitoring economic sanctions
- monitoring attempts to evade U.S. export controls
- assessing the spending priorities of other nations, especially their military expenditures and international arms transfers
- tracing illicit money flows from drug-trafficking, terrorism, and other forms of criminal activity.[9]

This partial listing underlines the broad character of the intelligence community's involvement in macroeconomic activities. "The greatest concentration of analytical experts on international economic issues in the federal government resides not in any of the executive departments but in the Central Intelligence Agency," writes Philip Zelikow. "It is even possible that the ranks of CIA analysts contain about as much economic expertise on international problems as can be found in all the executive departments of the government put together. Within the Agency, therefore, the economic mission looms large: about one-third of its analytical talent concerns itself with economic issues of one kind or another."[10]

Macroeconomic intelligence would also include counterintelligence and covert-action operations. These activities would be broad-gauged—not directed against individual companies overseas, but (in the case of counterintelligence) against the entire front of hostile economic operations perpetrated by foreign intelligence services and (in the case of covert action) against the economic underpinnings of an adversary government. Figure 6.1 summarizes the definitions.

MICROECONOMIC INTELLIGENCE

Business intelligence was a crucial part of global commercial intercourse throughout the Cold War. It continues so into the present as American firms react to growing competition abroad. What is of primary concern in this chapter, however, are economic intelligence operations that involve the government in one form or another—first at the microeconomic level.

In the United States microeconomic intelligence has for the most part been

Figure 6.1 Business and Economic Intelligence

SECTOR

Private	Private-Government	Government
Business Intelligence (overt)	Economic Intelligence	
Industrial Espionage (covert)	Microeconomic Intelligence (covert)	Macroeconomic Intelligence (overt/covert)

eschewed as government policy. This distancing between the government and a program of systematic spying against specific foreign companies remains the official policy today. "CIA does not conduct economic espionage against foreign firms for the benefit of U.S. companies," states an Agency official flatly. "That is, we do not seek to acquire foreign companies' industrial or commercial secrets or proprietary data for passage to U.S. firms. Former DCI Woolsey noted that doing so would risk putting CIA in the position of favoring some U.S. companies over others."[11]

The literature is replete with additional reasons why this policy has strong advocates, inside and outside the government.[12] In the first place, America's secret agencies are not well practiced at microeconomic intelligence and are therefore unlikely to excel at the job. "The companies are simply much better at commercial espionage than the CIA," concedes a former senior intelligence official.[13]

American companies themselves by and large reject this form of help, apparently more confident in their own collection, counterintelligence (CI), and covert-action (CA) capabilities. In part, the business community does not require help from the secret agencies because U.S. firms have already recruited former CIA and other intelligence officers to exercise their tradecraft against rival foreign companies on behalf of their new private-sector employers.[14] Moreover, just how secret government information would be distributed to the private sector and still protect sensitive sources and methods remains a significant problem. And of course if a secret operation became public—as some invariably do—the revelation could significantly harm relations between the United States and the host nation of the targeted industry.

Even the basics of how the "take" from microeconomic espionage would be disseminated can be recondite. Before the federal government could share secret information with an American corporation, officials would have to be assured that the company was indeed a creature of the United States. Yet determining the national identity of a corporation can be perplexing in this era of multinationals, with their global directors and stockholders. "What the hell is a U.S. firm?" asks a senior CIA economic analyst.[15] A study group at the Harvard University Intelligence Policy Seminar, composed of U.S. intelligence officers (on leave) and Harvard students, concluded in 1991, "It is difficult if not impossible to identify any corporation which is sufficiently 'American' to qualify for sustained classified intelligence support."[16]

A Pentagon analyst poses a companion question, one with obvious legal ramifications. Should the CIA spy on a foreign-based division of the Ford Motor Company?[17] Intelligence officials point to further legal problems associated with microeconomic espionage. A number of executive orders and federal laws, not to mention treaties, conventions, and copyright agreements, could be invoked. A CIA attorney notes, for example, that "the defense of sovereign immunity, which nations traditionally assert in foreign courts to shield themselves from local lawsuits, is generally not available when the lawsuit involves commercial matters." Therefore, he warns, through its conduct of microeconomic espionage the United States could be liable in foreign courts for the taking of private property without giving just compensation.[18]

The question of fairness, underscored by DCI Woolsey, lies at the center of the reluctance to adopt a systematic program of microeconomic intelligence. If America's secret agencies helped one U.S. firm, might this not disadvantage another? The dissemination of intelligence to Boeing on the activities of its European competitor, Airbus, could jeopardize an American company, General Electric, which manufactures jet engines for Airbus.

Beyond their own self-reliance in the arts of espionage, U.S. companies often prefer an arms-length distance from the secret agencies to avoid the stigma that might arise if such ties became known. American firms are wary, further, of what they may have to provide the secret agencies in return for their intelligence. The government may insist that a business receiving intelligence provide in return shelter ("cover") overseas for CIA officers and agents or the use of company employees for the government's espionage activities. Some American businesses are willing to offer such assistance (many out of pure patriotism, without remuneration); others are leery of losing their good reputations— and perhaps the lives of their employees who might be caught spying. This wariness apparently runs both ways. DCI Robert M. Gates has observed,

"Some years ago, one of our clandestine service officers overseas said to me: 'You know, I'm prepared to give my life for my country but not for a company.' That case officer was absolutely right."[19]

An American economist with the World Bank argues a broader point. "The world is concerned enough already about the American colossus—the one remaining superpower, with the most powerful intelligence-gathering apparatus ever known. If we use this intelligence capability to muscle our way to the top of international trade deals, our relations with the world—even our allies—may deteriorate."[20] Such considerations led DCI Gates to declare in 1992 that the intelligence community "does not, should not, and will not" practice microeconomic espionage.[21] His successor, R. James Woolsey, proved equally unwilling to adopt this "account" on behalf of American business.[22]

This does not mean that every intelligence expert endorses a "clean-hands" policy against microeconomic espionage. Former DCI Stansfield Turner has publicly recommended microeconomic spying as a means for evening up the international competition. He points out that America "would have no compunction about stealing military secrets to help it manufacture better weapons. If economic strength should now be recognized as a vital component of national security, parallel with military power, why should America be concerned about stealing and employing economic secrets?"[23]

Certainly a number of industrial powers have wholeheartedly embraced this use of their secret services. "All of America's major foreign competitors [have] the full weight of their governments' diplomatic and intelligence resources thrown behind their nation's companies or consortia," wrote one of the CIA's most respected officers, the late George A. Carver, Jr.[24] Media reports, as well as the business and academic literature, are filled with anecdotes about escalating industrial and microeconomic espionage directed against the United States by Russia and a host of other nations—including some long-standing allies like France.[25] Examples from the open literature are given in table 6.1.

According to interviews with American intelligence officers and policymakers in 1994, even the United States has been less pure with respect to intelligence gathering against foreign business firms than its public pronouncements would suggest. The line separating micro from macro suddenly vanishes when the foreign business is a defense contractor or telecommunications company whose activities are of vital interest to the U.S. government's strategic concerns. Moreover, many foreign companies are government owned and operated—another vanishing line.

Further, if in the course of their normal operations America's secret agencies *inadvertently* obtain microeconomic intelligence of probable value to an

Table 6.1   Examples of Microeconomic Intelligence Operations
Cited in the Open Literature

Canada	SIGINT used to discover U.S. bid on wheat sale to China[1]
France	DGSE penetration of IBM France, Texas Instruments, and Corning Glass on behalf of Compagnie des Machines Bull[2]
Germany	Spying on Western competitors in the international arms trade[3]
Israel	Targeted Recon/Optical in Illinois, for spy camera technology[4]
Japan	Targeted Silicon Valley in the early 1980s[5]
Romania	Targeted Mercedes Benz in Stuttgart[6]
South Africa	General targeting of foreign commercial competitors[7]
USSR	SIGINT used to gain favorable terms for purchasing U.S. wheat in early 1970s[8]

[1] Mike Frost and Michael Gratton, *Spyworld: Inside the Canadian and American Intelligence Establishments,* Toronto, 1994, pp. 224–27.

[2] American Institute for Business Research, *Protecting Corporate America's Secrets in the Global Economy,* 1992, p. 41.

[3] Craig Whitney, "German Finds that Spies Are Still Doing Business," *New York Times,* September 9, 1993, p. 1.

[4] AIBR, op cit., p. 45.

[5] Ibid., pp. 50–51.

[6] "Romanian Engineer Arrested for Spying," *Romania Libera,* July 15, 1994.

[7] "White Paper on Intelligence," South African Government, October 21, 1994, p. 2, cited in Samuel D. Porteous, "Economic/Commercial Interests and Intelligence Services," Centre for Trade Policy and Law, April 1995, p. 44, n. 12.

[8] Randall M. Fort, "Economic Espionage: Problems and Prospects," *Consortium for the Study of Intelligence,* 1993, p. 3.

American company, they pass it along to the Department of Commerce or other relevant department or agency. The responsible policy officer must then decide whether to relay this intelligence to the affected company or companies.

Here is the nub of the matter, stated succinctly by an Associated Press writer: "The debate over [the CIA's] economic intelligence role is not whether it should be stealing economic secrets but whether it should start passing them to U.S. companies."[26] A former State Department official offers an equally pithy answer: "If you are paying informants to provide this information, then sending it some place like the Commerce Department, it is surely going to end up in the hands of business."[27]

Yet "tilting the playing field" through a systematic program of microeconomic espionage remains beyond the pale of accepted practice. If a department decides to pass along the intelligence, it is careful to disguise all sources and methods; no documents or cables are ever disseminated. Circumlocution is the order of the day, with the department offering only generic advice.

This wink-and-nod intelligence dissemination is apparently rare. It is also rarely that helpful, because in most instances the firms already have all the information they need about a pending deal overseas, having tracked its development closely and often for a long period of time. "There are not too many surprises as far as what the other side is thinking in a trade negotiation," remarks the former United States trade representative Clayton Yeutter.[28]

Nonetheless, some policy officers regularly and enthusiastically make use of macroeconomic intelligence. Mickey Kantor, the trade representative in the Clinton administration, has reportedly found substantial merit in the ability of the intelligence agencies to ferret out the bargaining positions of various American rivals in international trade talks. (In contrast, President Bush's trade representative, Carla Hills, is said to have seldom relied on the CIA's economic reporting.)[29] In 1993 the intelligence agencies are said to have learned from agents in the European Union the bottom lines of various members during the Uruguay round of international trade negotiations—valuable information that helped guide U.S. diplomats in setting their own bargaining positions during the final stages of the talks. In 1995 information obtained by the intelligence community evidently provided useful ammunition during the confrontation with the Japanese over automobile trade.[30]

Especially prized by Kantor, as well as by the late Secretary of Commerce Ron Brown and the NEC, are efforts by the intelligence community to spot anticompetitive trading practices by foreign rivals. In 1994 the Community discovered an attempt by French intelligence to bribe Brazilian officials to favor a bid by Thomson, the huge French communications company. The U.S. government complained to Brazil, and Raytheon, the American company, ended up winning the $1.4 billion contract.[31]

The Community claims to have uncovered bribes affecting $30 billion in foreign contracts from 1992 to 1995 alone, helping to "level the playing field" for American businesses.[32] Former DCI James Woolsey has commented at length on this use of the secret agencies:

> We collect intelligence on those efforts to bribe foreign companies and foreign governments into, for example, awarding an airport contract to a European firm rather than an American firm. . . . And when we find out about those, and we do a fair amount of the time, we go not to the American corporation that's competing, but the Secretary of State, and he sends an American ambassador to see a president or a king, and that ambassador says, "Mr. President" or "Your Majesty," your minister in charge of construction is on the take, and you have a lot going on with the

United States, and we don't really take kindly to your operating that way . . . frequently, but not always, the contract is rebid and the American firm gets a share of it . . . sometimes the whole thing is done right, sometimes not.[33]

So America's rejection of systematic microeconomic intelligence operations has by no means meant quiescence across the clandestine economic front. Indeed throughout and following the Cold War, macroeconomic intelligence has been a lively concern of the U.S. secret agencies.

MACROECONOMIC INTELLIGENCE

Although during the Cold War the intelligence community dwelt primarily on military and political developments in the world (and especially inside the USSR), international economic issues gradually gained in importance over the years—even as early as the mid-1950s when the United States reeled from the effects of global recession.[34] Moreover, the secret agencies have always enjoyed a close connection to segments of the American business community. Their extensive involvement in matters related to economics—"since [the] inception" of modern U.S. intelligence, according to DCI Woolsey[35]—falls into several categories of activity: collection, cover, analysis, counterintelligence, and covert action.

Collection

While the intelligence agencies have avoided spying on behalf of U.S. companies, they have devoted considerable attention to the worldwide gathering of information about economic matters that might affect the broader interests of the United States. Former DCI Turner recalled shortly before the demise of the Soviet Union one of many reasons why macroeconomic intelligence grew in importance for the United States during the Cold War: "In 1974, we were taken by the Soviets. We didn't know much about the international grain market and the Soviets tricked us into a bad deal on U.S. grain sales. We got taken. Now the CIA collects on this subject. We know more about Soviet grain production than they do."[36]

In two separate listings of intelligence collection priorities made public by the CIA in 1975 and 1986, macroeconomic targets displayed a strong presence, including the pricing strategies of the Organization of Petroleum Exporting Countries (OPEC); the size of the annual Soviet agricultural harvest; the quality of Soviet computers and the resultant considerations for U.S. export controls; debt financing in the developing countries; international energy shortages; global food supplies; and worldwide developments in science and technology.[37]

In the aftermath of the Cold War and the accelerated shift of resources toward economic collection (now accounting for an estimated 40 percent of total collection),[38] the intelligence agencies have given their attention to such topics as the Uruguay round of the General Agreement Tariffs and Trade (GATT), the North American Free Trade Agreement (NAFTA), and a host of specific international trade negotiations.

Six main clusters of topics have attracted the intelligence community's resources.[39] First, the Community has tried to answer these questions: Are foreign governments playing fairly in their economic relations with the United States? Is a foreign government involved in a bribing situation? Has it tried to rig contracts? To what extent are foreign governments lobbying—or counter-lobbying—in the United States on behalf of their economic self-interests? A central focus is the large business deals pursued by foreign government-backed firms or by the governments themselves, as the Community watches for signs of inappropriate ("sharp") business practices.

The modus operandi used by the intelligence agencies for economic targeting (as with most collection operations) is initially to scan the open-source literature in search of major business transactions involving foreign governments. This step usually discloses knowledge gaps about the prospective deal making, which the secret agencies then attempt to fill through clandestine means. On the technical side, the National Intelligence Council has a national intelligence officer (NIO) for science and technology. "During the Cold War, that person would have spent much more of his time on Soviet military technology," a recent NIC chairman has stated, "but now [he spends] more time on broader types of technology that are in the commercial and economic area."[40] The goal is to uncover macroeconomic intelligence (without engaging in microeconomic spying) that might make America more competitive internationally.

Another technique—and another linkage between intelligence spooks and blue suits—is the CIA practice of debriefing (questioning) selected American businesspeople on their return from trips abroad, especially if they have been to relatively closed areas of the globe (Sudan, for example).[41] The CIA may also task selected businesspeople (if they are amenable) *before* they travel overseas, asking them to keep an eye out for specific intelligence requirements. This amounts to the recruitment of private citizens to spy for the United States as they carry out their own business transactions abroad. The public record includes some examples of close CIA-business cooperation in gathering information on foreign events and conditions, such as the assistance from the Hughes Aircraft Corporation in recovering a sunken Soviet submarine.[42]

Second, the intelligence community spends a large chunk of time preparing studies for officials representing the United States at international trade conferences. These include compiling regional matrixes indicating who is apt to be aligned with whom on key votes, and what configuration of alliances is likely to coalesce around what deals. Among other assignments, the secret agencies undertake an exhaustive review of the foreign media for clues about the negotiating positions of conference participants—open-source intelligence work. Most people in the government outside of the secret agencies do not have the time for such review, and they lack ready access to the CIA's Foreign Broadcast Intelligence Service.

With varying degrees of success, the entire range of covert, intrusive intelligence collection—including electronic surveillance, agent insertion, and the theft of documents—is also deployed against foreign negotiators. (Selected allies are excepted.) As with arms control negotiations, the U.S. government tries to come to the bargaining table at international trade conferences with as much information as possible to improve its likelihood of success. Joseph S. Nye, Jr., the NIC chief in 1993–94, gives this example: "The role of intelligence on NAFTA is to be able to get policy makers to think ahead: What's going to happen in Mexico? And you're not going to get that from the U.S.T.R. [United States trade representative] or the U.S. Ambassador alone."[43]

Third, the monitoring of economic sanctions has become increasingly vital to the U.S. government and therefore to the intelligence agencies. Both before and after the Gulf War the United States has needed to carefully sift through the results of sanctions against Iraq. The Bush administration was determined that Saddam Hussein, the Iraqi dictator, would pay a price for his invasion of Kuwait in 1990. Global economic sanctions would demonstrate the resolve of the anti-Iraqi coalition and, Bush hoped, would bring many nations together against Saddam as a part of a "new world order."

Tracking how well the sanctions were working during this period became a high priority in the U.S. national security establishment. Top-secret reports on sanctions were faxed daily from CIA Headquarters to the White House. The CIA assumed the responsibility for coordinating Community-wide ("all-source") intelligence on the progress of sanctions, providing "one-stop shopping" for busy policy officers. These daily summaries were, and continue to be, augmented by "Week in Review" progress reports and "Perspective" studies on the adherence of specific countries to the sanctions. The intelligence community also produced in-depth research reports on the evolving relationships between Iraq and its neighbors.

The monitoring of sanctions to determine who is cooperating, as well as their effects on the economy of Iraq, has been an enormous undertaking, involving the tracking of money, oil, transportation, arms, business activity, and the behavior of individual traders. All Iraqi ships have been closely followed. On the eve of the Gulf War in 1991, the accuracy of this monitoring enabled the U.S.-led coalition to pinpoint violators, and the United States issued some eighteen hundred demarches against those who had broken the sanctions agreement.[44] Ninety percent of Iraq's imports were shut off, along with 97 percent of its exports.[45] Initially the White House hoped the sanctions would inflict sufficient pain on Iraq to force its capitulation and withdrawal from Kuwait without the need for U.S. military intervention. While this objective fell short, the sanctions did (and continue to) inflict great discomfort on Iraq, helping to tame its roguery.

The successful monitoring of the Iraqi sanctions has led to the establishment of interagency sanctions-monitoring teams, housed at CIA headquarters. High among the collection targets for these teams have been the Balkans region and all Sino-Iranian and Sino-Pakistani commercial transactions (with a careful eye out for weapons shipments). The Department of the Treasury is one of the Community's main consumers of information on sanctions violators, as its Office of Foreign Assets Control is responsible for enforcing sanctions.

Fourth, the intelligence agencies have been active in a macroeconomic activity called "foreign acquisitions review." Serving the Committee on Foreign Investment in the United States (an interagency panel, which also includes organizations outside the Community, such as the Department of Commerce), the secret agencies are charged with contributing whatever information they can toward answering the question: How much foreign investment and buying is occurring inside the borders of this nation?

Fifth, the intelligence community is responsible for maintaining a database on disreputable businesses abroad—"bad actors" in the world marketplace guilty of sanctions violations, money laundering, proliferation of fissionable materials and weapons parts, or abetting terrorist organizations. The Federal Reserve Board, the Treasury Department, the Commerce Department, and several other government entities are in a position to feel only part of this elephant; through its global information-gathering, the intelligence community is expected to gain a sense of the whole and to pass on this more complete picture to relevant government officials.

On the basis of intelligence findings, the Treasury Department's Office of Foreign Assets Control (among other government organizations) can inform U.S. banks and firms not to deal with a particular corporation because it is actually, say, a Libyan front for weapons acquisition. Or, when the Department of Defense spots a suspicious cargo ship at sea—perhaps bearing illegal weapons in its hull bound for Iraq—the computers at the CIA can run a check on the parent company in search of earlier improper shipments abroad.

Sixth, the macroeconomic experts at both the CIA and its companion agencies have been drawn into the battle against narcotics. Cooperating with the Center for Counternarcotics (CNC), they have been helpful in tracing the flow of "narco-dollars"—the profits and laundering operations of drug dealers. As a senior CIA economic analyst notes, "Money provides a mirror image of the real world."[46] To use a different image, like a trail of ants leading to the sugar pot, cash flows to and from international banks can tip off intelligence officers to illegal narcotics transactions. In turn, the CNC can sound the alarm for the government's antidrug agents in the Drug Enforcement Administration (DEA). This, at least, is the theory. In reality, the combined efforts of the intelligence and enforcement communities have done little to curb the flow of dangerous drugs to the United States. Only around 10 percent of all illegal drugs are interdicted—although CNC defenders argue that this percentage would probably be even more disheartening without the assistance of the intelligence agencies.

This list of six collection priorities for macroeconomic intelligence is simply meant to suggest a much wider range of economic data gathering carried out by the secret agencies. Throughout the Cold War, and increasingly today, thousands of specialists inside the intelligence community have been engaged in the planning and direction of macroeconomic collection operations, their focus ranging from Russian oil reserves to the price of rubber in Malaysia.

The weapons proliferation problem illustrates how economic topics have become a part of almost every intelligence question, even those dealing with traditional military issues. Measures pursued by the U.S. government to monitor and deter weapons proliferation—each with clear intelligence ramifications—include screening export license applications, spotting foreign companies that buy weapons-related equipment, tracing the transfer of weapons material to outlaw states or groups, and monitoring the storage of weapons and related materials (such as weapons-grade plutonium) within other countries.[47]

This mission alone presents a tremendous challenge for intelligence collection and processing. It requires highly mobile, remote-collection platforms, as well as fixed sensors, seismic arrays, and earth-penetrating radars, plus a cadre of human agents—old-fashioned spies who must now possess much higher levels of scientific sophistication as a part of their tradecraft. It also demands well-trained economists who know how to trace the flow of money for weapons acquisition, understand the implications of export licenses, and can spot the suspicious accumulation of selected raw materials—such as telltale products necessary for building missiles or manufacturing Semtex, the high explosive popular with terrorist groups.

All of these activities are carried out in hopes of providing information to policy officers that might help them in their quest for U.S. economic security (or, in the case of anti-proliferation measures, military security). The spying is done for the good of America's economic security as a whole, not for specific U.S. companies. Obviously, though, the greater the overall economic strength of the United States, the better individual American firms are likely to fare in their international business transactions.

While macroeconomic intelligence is widely regarded as helpful to this nation, a number of tensions exist in this domain between intelligence producers and consumers. For one, some policymakers are unsure exactly how to task macroeconomic collection—that is, they don't know what kinds of economic information they want. Moreover, many continue to believe that the Cable News Network (CNN) can tell them more about international economic questions than the CIA—and with live coverage. (This constant comparison with CNN reporting has driven some intelligence managers to consider forms of real-time economic intelligence reporting—say, an opportunity for policymakers to dial a closed-circuit CIA channel to watch activities at a Libyan chemical plant via satellite!)[48]

Some policy departments are confident that their own economic expertise (often considerable) far outshines anything the secret agencies can provide by way of analysis. They largely dismiss the CIA's economic assessments, sometimes just because they disagree with their own, as happened in disputes between the Agency and the Treasury Department in 1994–95 over the future of the Mexican peso. Nevertheless, even these policy officers and their aides are unwilling to relinquish access to raw intelligence from the intelligence community—particularly SIGINT and HUMINT—however much they may prefer their own interpretations.

Cover

Closely related to intelligence collection is cover—providing a hiding place for U.S. intelligence officers abroad. Their presence overseas has to be concealed, of course, because they are engaged in improper and usually illegal activities, from espionage to counterespionage and covert action. Yet intelligence officers have relatively few places to hide. Some are integrated into the embassy structure, although the Department of State blanches at too much of this, wishing to maintain the purity of its diplomatic corps.

Intelligence officers can pretend they are someone else—traveling journalists, visiting scholars, bartenders, missionaries, or government officials outside the foreign policy apparatus. Yet by and large, these occupational groups abhor being "contaminated" by spies. They fear that if foreign governments suspect that intelligence agents are hiding among them, their own genuine members would be denied visas, harassed, or even unfairly imprisoned as spies. In light of this criticism by journalists and others,[49] the intelligence community has turned toward two venues of cover related to the business world: U.S. corporate camouflage and the use of proprietaries.

American corporations are found throughout the globe, just as American intelligence tries to be. Corporations seem less squeamish about providing cover to intelligence personnel than are others outside the Community. (The Peace Corps and the Fulbright Fellows Program, for instance, have been completely successful in rejecting overtures from the secret agencies for cover opportunities). Eugene Fodor, the president of Fodor's Travel Guides, once proclaimed that he was "glad, and proud, to be of help" in providing cover for CIA activities overseas.[50] In 1974 the *New York Times* reported that two hundred U.S. intelligence officers were posing as businesspeople abroad.[51] Here, then, is another significant linkage between the intelligence community and the business community. The *quid pro quo* is the occasional dissemination of privileged economic intelligence (macro or micro) to a company in return for its provision of cover—not a topic the intelligence community or individual businesses are inclined to discuss for the public record.

No one can dispute, though, the close ties that U.S. businesses and spies have had over the years. After all, much of the hardware used for TECHINT is manufactured by well-known American companies—Lockheed-Martin, TRW, and Northrop, among others. To ensure that the spy machines are built according to the Community's specifications, the secret agencies have had to open their most closely held technological secrets to these companies. Virtually all of the National Reconnaissance Office's employees are also in private industry; and the CIA has long had close ties to the nation's weapons laboratories, sharing top-secret information on Soviet weaponry and other matters. The spy/business collaboration is well established across a broad plain of manufacturing activities; it becomes a short step for businesses, once entwined, to find themselves pressured into cooperating with the intelligence community to provide foreign cover.

The question of proprietaries points to a murkier connection between the spy world and the business world. These are fake businesses abroad run by intelligence organizations—travel agencies, book publishers, commuter airlines

(Southern Air Transport is one example on the public record), taverns, even brothels. The companies may be nothing more than a name plate on the door and a business card; or they may be full-fledged ("backstopped") commercial enterprises secretly operated by the CIA, making money and providing a hiding place for intelligence officers.

With proprietaries, the CIA goes beyond seeking cover inside a U.S. company; it *becomes* a U.S. company. All profits accrued by those engaged in a program of "non-official cover"—NOC, pronounced "knock" and referring to case officers operating outside of embassy cover—are supposed to revert to the federal treasury. Some critics, though, have claimed that the auditing of these so-called notionals is shoddy at best—a charge adamantly denied by America's top intelligence managers and overseers.[52] NOCs are placed in legitimate businesses overseas, as well, if the CEOs will have them.

Analysis

If collection of global information lies at the heart of the intelligence process, analysis is its brain. As the historian Carl Becker noted long before the U.S. government had much in the way of sophisticated intelligence analysis, "Left to themselves, the facts do not speak . . . for all practical purposes there is no fact until someone affirms it."[53]

The information that pours from around the world into offices throughout the intelligence community must be sorted out and interpreted by experts trained to understand the meaning of events in foreign places. A leading economic intelligence officer at the CIA offers this perspective on her job:

> Those of us on the economic side are not in competition with the *Wall Street Journal*. We try to provide information on broad economic trends. Our consumers include, for example, the National Economic Council, the U.S.T.R., and the Commerce Department. The NEC is a new institution [established in 1993] and had to be convinced that we can be useful to [its members]. The kind of support we now give is probably divided fifty-fifty between day-to-day, direct "tactical" intelligence and the longer-term finished intelligence that we have always done. We do about one [National Intelligence] Estimate a year on the economic intelligence front—not our most important contribution.[54]

This analyst expressed a wariness over "the new trend" toward daily reports, finding current-intelligence reporting on economic matters both "time-consuming and very people-intensive." She continued: "An answer generates another question. . . . It generates a lot more work for us than just sitting back and writing an Estimate. It requires briefings and trips downtown, which are also very time-consuming. In this era of downsizing, we've had to redouble our efforts to make sure we're working on the *right* intelligence—streamlined to meet the needs of the consumer."[55]

The neophyte National Economic Council has already displayed a strong dependence on macroeconomic intelligence. As a senior CIA official told a reporter, "Just about every day, [NEC Deputy Director] Bo Cutter is asking the CIA for information on economic issues. The National Economic Council is treating the CIA like an extension of its own staff."[56]

From the very beginnings of modern intelligence in the wake of World War Two, the analysis of economic data has been a central part of the daily reporting and more in-depth research prepared by U.S. intelligence officers for the government's decisionmakers. The anti-Communist struggles that engulfed Western Europe after the war occurred not only in the mountains of Greece and Yugoslavia but also in the labor unions of Italy, France, and other key nations of the Western alliance. Analyses on the economic health (that is, the pro-West, laissez-faire orientation) of these labor unions was a top priority in the U.S. government. Moreover, soon after its creation the intelligence community turned rapidly toward the analysis of economic trends inside America's rising nemesis, the Soviet Union—especially in an effort to understand its armament capabilities. For, as a senior intelligence analyst has emphasized, "one must study a nation's economy if one wishes to know its military."[57]

Analysis, though, is fraught with difficulties, whether the subject is politics, military affairs, or economics—even at home, let alone in a foreign country. Commenting on the difficulties of making foreign intelligence assessments, former DCI Richard Helms has wryly commented, "How many people got the [1992 American] presidential election right? And we have an open society! I rest my case."[58]

While much of the U.S. intelligence reporting on economic matters has been first rate—tracing the flow of petrodollars, for example, as well as anticipating OPEC investment strategies and monitoring world crop production—it has also been subjected to criticism from time to time. When he was in the House of Representatives, Les Aspin routinely berated the CIA for overestimating the Soviet military through a faulty economic analysis of its resource allocations.[59] Also controversial during the Cold War was the Agency's interpretation of Soviet and worldwide oil supplies, made public by the CIA in a rare declassification of oil estimates.[60] Attacks from other government agencies, members of Congress, and economic specialists in the academic world centered on the CIA's forecasting models, which critics found deterministic and simplistic. While intelligence analysts predicted constant real prices for oil and fixed levels of production, for instance, some witnesses who testified on the subject in congressional hearings anticipated precisely the opposite outcomes.[61]

Some of the criticism seems to have been overstated, but even a balanced critique by the staff of the Senate Select Committee on Intelligence pointed to a number of errors in the CIA oil projections for the USSR. These projections were revisited and corrected by the Agency in the wake of this unusual public debate over an intelligence estimate.[62] The "oil debate" represented a remarkable—and healthy—public airing of views on an important subject, providing policy officers with a much richer understanding of the issue than reliance on the intelligence community alone would have allowed.

The most damaging critique of macroeconomic intelligence came at the end of the Cold War. Critics were appalled that the intelligence community had failed in one of its primary responsibilities: forecasting major outcomes in the USSR. Senator Daniel Patrick Moynihan led the attack with a scathing appraisal that ended with a call for the abolition of the CIA.[63] In response, DCI Robert Gates declassified a parade of Agency documents demonstrating how the CIA had reported in close detail the decline of the Soviet economy throughout the 1980s—though without going so far as to predict its actual collapse.[64]

While the bold Moynihan barrage caught the attention of the media, the DCI's rebuttal was better documented and more compelling—if less interesting to the press corps. Gates pointed out that no one—in the U.S. government, in academe, or even in the Kremlin—had, or could have, anticipated the precipitous fall of communism in the Soviet Union. Another senior intelligence professional noted, "Predicting the fall of the U.S.S.R. was not the most important assignment for the CIA; knowing about the Soviet military's capabilities and intentions was the key task—and we did that well."[65]

Given the importance of the debate over the quality of intelligence assessments of the USSR, I examine this topic more closely in the next chapter. Suffice it to say here that despite the black eye from Senator Moynihan, policymakers in the Bush and Clinton administrations turned increasingly to the secret agencies for macroeconomic intelligence.[66] Above all, presidents and their aides have continued to seek backup information for international trade talks, as well as economic analysis on individual countries, including the effects of the sanctions in place against Iraq, Bosnia, and Cuba.

A recent illustration of the significance of macroeconomic intelligence comes from the crisis over the Mexican peso. In December 1994 the State Department convened some fifty intelligence officers, scholars, and Wall Street financiers to discuss the future of the Mexican economy. The mood among the experts was upbeat.[67] Just three days later the economy of Mexico went into a dangerous tailspin. A peasant uprising in the southernmost state of Chiapas, an impoverished jungle region, frightened foreign investors. The panic led to a run on Mexican stocks and bonds, quickly drawing down Mexico's reserves in defense of the overvalued peso. The Clinton administration anxiously bypassed a recalcitrant Congress and, by executive fiat, stitched together a $53 billion loan package—a makeshift lifeline tossed out to Mexico's sinking economy.

Earlier, in mid-1994, an NIE had warned that political instability in Mexico was on the rise. This was not exactly a daring prognostication, since in March the leading contender for the Mexican presidency, Luis Donaldo Colosio, had been assassinated. Missing from the analysis, though, was any indication that the country's economy was about to enter a disastrous free-fall. The intelligence reporting from the Community accurately predicted the electoral victory of Ernesto Zedillo, who had replaced Colosio as the candidate of the ruling party, the Institutional Revolutionary Party (PRI); but as one senior official told the *Washington Post*, "It didn't tell you that if he kept driving straight, he would fall off a cliff."[68]

Some early warnings were around elsewhere, however. A few officials inside the Treasury Department worried aloud about Mexico's excessive reliance on short-term loans, and they kept a wary eye on the simmering unrest in Chiapas. Outside the government, the economist Rudiger Dornbusch of the Massachusetts Institute of Technology also pointed to impending disaster as early as February 1994.

Yet nothing was done. Treasury officials, who bore the most criticism for failing to anticipate the crisis, sought refuge in a two-pronged defense. First, the magnitude of the collapse in Mexico was impossible for anyone to foresee. Second, decisions made by the Mexicans in the early stages of the crisis (such as flooding the economy with new credit) greatly exacerbated the problem but were beyond U.S. control. Insiders, though, pointed to the problem of "clientitis." Foreign policy officials in the Clinton administration—and particularly in Treasury—had become so tied personally to outgoing Mexican president Carlos Salinas de Gortari (who was trained in economics at Harvard University and was the key proponent of his country's participation in NAFTA) that they were reluctant to criticize the overvalued peso. It was "just too clubby an atmosphere," commented Dornbusch.[69]

A further complication arose from efforts by Mexican officials to paint a rosy picture to conceal their crumbling economy. They delayed releasing to overseers in the International Monetary Fund (IMF) accurate figures about the true economic situation. Only later did the IMF discover that Mexican reserves had fallen to a perilously low $7 billion by mid-December, in an ongoing attempt to defend the peso without devaluation. When this strategy failed in the midst of the Christmas holidays, the Mexican government finally gave up and allowed the peso to float.

Throughout this turmoil President Clinton had little solid information to guide his decisions. It was another sobering reminder of the limits faced by intelligence and policy officers in trying to cope with a world that will neither stand still nor reveal much of itself as it spins through time.

Administration officials drew an important lesson from the failure. Information in the various departments and agencies bearing on the Mexican crisis had been inadequately shared and coordinated throughout the government— the same failure that had allowed the Japanese attack on Pearl Harbor and led to the formation of a *central* intelligence agency in the first place. Intelligence officials failed even to meet with policymakers in the Treasury and State Departments until the early stages of the crisis, as various government entities in Washington reacted in isolation from one another. "Neither the Treasury nor the Federal Reserve," notes the historian Ernest R. May, "had a comfortable relationship with the intelligence community."[70] The tight intertwining of political and security issues in the post–Cold War era would clearly require officials to work together more closely in the future, across the traditional organizational lines of diplomacy, intelligence, and economic policymaking.

Counterintelligence

Far more damaging to the CIA than its failure to pinpoint the precise end of the Cold War has been its counterintelligence failures, most conspicuously in the Ames case. In the economic realm the main responsibility of counterintelligence officers is to protect U.S. government officials with economic portfolios from intelligence operations directed against them by hostile secret services. For example, if Treasury officials were to fly overseas on a foreign airline for an international trade conference, the prudent CI officer would check the interior of the aircraft for hidden cameras in the ceiling that might photograph U.S. documents as officials studied them during the flight. (This is widely rumored to have happened to American diplomats on an Air France flight, courtesy of French intelligence.) At the conference site CI officials would check hotel and meeting rooms for electronic surveillance devices.

Counterintelligence officers are also on the lookout for an "economic Ames" who might be selling to other nations America's economic intelligence secrets, such as negotiating strategies for international trade agreements. Most aggressively, a penetration operation might be run against an economic adversary in an effort to plant an American spy—a "mole"—in the midst of its negotiating team, say, as an economic consultant. The purpose of a CI penetration is not so much to gather intelligence against the adversary (this is the assignment of the CIA's Operations Directorate) but to find out who is trying to spy on America and how, then blocking that effort. In short, all the counterintelligence tricks-of-the-trade used to protect America's military secrets have the same relevance for the protection of economic secrets and are used similarly.[71]

Efforts to protect U.S. government officials against foreign spying lead to a connection between macro- and microeconomic intelligence. Here is where these two worlds, kept at arms length at other times, have tentatively embraced one another. Testifying before Congress in 1992, DCI Gates said that in the most extreme cases counterintelligence measures are necessary to "protect our economy from those who do not play by the rules."[72] The CIA and the FBI work together to inform U.S. companies who are the targets of foreign intelligence services, he disclosed. "In coordination with the FBI, we inform an individual company as we detect an intelligence operation directed specifically at it over-seas. In all such cases, we take care to protect sources and methods. This some-times requires that the information be provided in a generic fashion, but we usu-ally find a way to tell the company what it needs to know to take corrective action."[73]

In 1995 the FBI reportedly lodged protests in Paris after counterintelligence officers uncovered operations by the French secret service against IBM and Texas Instruments.[74] Indeed, the FBI and the CIA have had a lengthy history of aiding U.S. businesses against the operations of hostile intelligence services that seek access to U.S. high technology, pricing data, customer lists, contract bids, sales figures, and marketing plans.[75]

According to a State Department press release in 1995, when its officials are told of a foreign government's counterintelligence operation against an Amer-ican firm, "it is generally the Department's policy to act on this knowledge whenever possible by alerting U.S. companies adversely affected."[76] The de-partment may also deem it appropriate to make a demarche against any coun-try whose intelligence service is misbehaving in this manner.

On another front, the FBI started a program in 1974 called Developing Es-pionage and Counterintelligence Awareness (DECA), which alerts defense contractors as well as other businesses to the dangers of foreign intelligence services and advises them on how to defend themselves.[77] Further, the Clinton administration established the National Counterintelligence Center (NACIC) in 1994, intended to coordinate Community-wide information to warn Ameri-can businesses about hostile foreign intelligence operations. As with their mi-croeconomic intelligence needs, however, U.S. firms had already recruited many former counterintelligence professionals from the secret agencies to guide them on defenses against foreign espionage.

The Canadian Security Intelligence Service (CSIS) employs economic counterintelligence operations, too, but, as with current U.S. policy, only to block espionage operations run by "foreign intelligence services or a surrogate for foreign governments."[78] When there is no government involvement—usually the case—individual Canadian businesses, like their American counterparts, are mostly left to fend for themselves against foreign competitors.

In the United States, debate continues over whether the intelligence community ought to be more involved with American corporations in CI efforts to thwart strictly business-against-business (industrial) espionage. So far, however, the business/intelligence barrier has held—except (similar to microeconomic intelligence) when a relevant tidbit of counterintelligence related to an American firm happens to be passed along to one of the U.S. secret agencies by a foreign agent. "We do not *actively* pursue intelligence on espionage activities carried out against U.S. firms by foreign firms," explains a CIA official. "We focus on efforts directed by foreign governments. However, when an agent comes across evidence of spying by a foreign business, we pass this information along to the relevant policy department in the [U.S. government]."[79]

Covert Action

Economic intelligence has sometimes involved covert action. In its attempts to undermine or destroy hostile regimes, the United States has viewed economic systems as vulnerable targets for secret operations. During the Kennedy administration the CIA concocted a plan to ruin the economy of Cuba by lacing its sugar exports with a foul-tasting chemical—a scheme the president halted at the last minute.[80] Over the years the intelligence agencies have had an active program of testing biological and chemical substances for destroying foreign crops and livestock, though where and when these substances have been used—if at all—remains shrouded in secrecy.[81] In the war against North Vietnam the CIA helped mine enemy ports to disrupt commercial trade and incoming shipments of weapons. It also experimented with weather-altering methods to upset Vietnamese agricultural cycles and attempted to make the Ho Chi Minh Trail slick with chemicals to disrupt the shipment of military and commercial goods—though neither of these efforts had much success.[82]

During the Nixon administration, in operations against the socialist candidate (later president) of Chile, Salvador Allende, the CIA relied heavily on economic disruption—particularly the clandestine instigation of truckers' strikes to impede the flow of commerce throughout Chile. The DCI at the time wrote in his notes from a White House meeting that a primary objective of the anti-Allende campaign in Chile was to "[m]ake the economy scream," and the U.S. ambassador vowed in secret cables to Washington that "not a nut or bolt will be allowed to reach Chile under Allende."[83] In a remarkably close secret relationship between a U.S. corporation and the CIA, International Telephone and Telegraph offered the Nixon administration $1 million or more under the table to assist the covert action in Chile, because ITT feared that Allende would expropriate its holdings in Chile.[84]

Two decades later the Reagan administration pulled out most of the clandestine economic stops against the Sandinista regime in Nicaragua, including the bombing of power plants and the mining of port facilities by CIA operatives.[85] According to one report, the administration also directed the CIA to manipulate world oil prices in an effort to ratchet up the pain level for the Soviet Union by ruining its lucrative petroleum exports. (Apparently this effort met with some success, but at the same time, critics maintain, it devastated the U.S. oil industry.)[86]

The CIA possesses a vast propaganda capability as well.[87] One can conceive of its worldwide "media assets" being used to blacken the reputation of America's economic competitors. The Agency once proposed doctoring U.S. scientific journals to lead Soviet scientists down a false and costly technology research path—a propaganda covert action with an obvious parallel for the industrial world.[88] Counterfeiting foreign currencies is another CIA skill, potentially useful for creating monetary havoc by sowing inflation in an adversary's economy.

This is but a small sampling of operations that have been or could be used by intelligence agencies to disrupt foreign industry. One conclusion is certain: the significance of an adversary's economy to its survival has not been lost on policymakers or the "special activities" experts in the CIA's Operations Directorate.

INTELLIGENCE AND THE INDUSTRIAL BASE

Another topic draws together the worlds of business and intelligence in the United States: concern for the future industrial base of surveillance hardware production. As Robert Kohler, a vice president at TRW, has persuasively stated, the erosion of dollars for national security as a part of the effort to reduce government spending has endangered the livelihood of defense industries vital for the construction of technical intelligence systems—satellites, worldwide listening facilities, reconnaissance aircraft—that have given the United States an undisputed edge in strategic information gathering. "Since 1990," he writes, "the five major companies developing collection systems for the intelligence community have reduced their work force involved in these programs by nearly 75 percent."[89]

Emphasizing the importance of technical intelligence, Kohler poses a telling question about Operation Desert Storm. "What price do we assign the information that Saddam's forces were still in place and facing forward as the left flank of the Coalition's military force executed its pincer movement?"[90] The obvious answer: this information had enormous value.

Kohler's message underscores another basic point having to do with the symbiotic relationship between business and intelligence in still another arena. Just as the two can benefit from exchanges of information about circumstances overseas (How risky is investing in China at the present time? What has been the effect of reunification on German banks?) and about counterintelligence threats (What methods does a foreign secret service use against Microsoft?), so have they shown a common interest since the end of the Cold War in promoting intelligence hardware projects before executive and legislative budget officials. Legislators are also well aware that TECHINT programs can mean jobs back home, and they have joined in this familiar alliance—the "iron triangles" of government long documented by political scientists, though new to the arena of intelligence policy.

Industry and intelligence have joined forces as well on the high-tech battlefield of "information warfare." Together they seek to shield fiber-optic cables from SIGINT thieves and U.S. computer facilities from hackers (a favorite new kind of intelligence agent recruited by modern intelligence services), while at the same time developing America's technical capabilities for penetrating and sabotaging the electronic and other communications facilities of adversaries.

The focus of America's secret agencies on economic subjects has been an important part of their work throughout the modern era. Whether collection, a quest for improved cover abroad, analysis, counterintelligence, or covert action, policymakers have insisted on a wide range of economic intelligence activities. Moreover, the secret agencies have frequently turned to the business community for assistance, and vice versa (especially for counterintelligence protection).

What is new about the current debate is the concentration on the question of the degree to which the intelligence community and the business community should become even more deeply intertwined with one another. Should America's secret agencies also help U.S. firms spy on their competitors? Should they provide counterintelligence assistance even in cases of strictly business-against-business espionage when no foreign intelligence agency is implicated?

The most controversial issue is whether the intelligence community should spy on foreign firms, then give this information to American companies. Imagine that a wealthy Middle Eastern country seeks a $20 billion telecommunications contract to help modernize its oil industry and government communications facilities. Several nations—France, Japan, Germany, England, and the United States—enter bids for this lucrative deal. Unbeknownst to any of the competitors, the Middle Eastern country is leaning toward (let us say) the German bid, but for only one reason: its service component is the most attractive. What if the CIA or the NSA could find out about the German bid before the final contract is let, reporting the intelligence to the Department of Commerce, which could then pass it along to the American company involved in the bidding? The American company might quickly decide to sweeten the service component of its bid and possibly move ahead of the Germans during the final phase of the negotiation.[91]

As Stansfield Turner has noted, the chance to have a "higher probability of winning" through a little help from the CIA is sorely tempting.[92] Edward Luttwak, the well-known strategist, puts the case more strongly still: entry of the Agency into the realm of microeconomic espionage is just a matter of time. "The reality," he says, "is that the CIA will get into this in a pragmatic, organic kind of way."[93]

Yet for others, this pathway leads to unbridled spying against business firms in allied nations—perhaps even the use of dirty tricks (covert actions) that could result in trade wars and, worse, shooting wars. More preferable is the nurturing of trade relations that are cooperative in spirit and helpful to all, cobbled together with international agreements against microeconomic intelligence operations. As a former senior CIA analyst has emphasized, in the language of game theory, "Economic relations should be viewed as multiperson, positive-sum games, not two-person zero-sum games."[94]

From this less belligerent point of view (far too innocent for someone like Luttwak), strictly informal, voluntary consultations between American businesspeople and intelligence officials over macroeconomic collection and analytic issues are entirely appropriate. How good are the new port facilities in Ogafanoga? Can you help with cover? Is this your interpretation of probable Saudi oil pricing? These are useful lines of inquiry that only businesspeople may be able to answer effectively. Appropriate, too, are warnings to businesses about hostile intelligence operations aimed against them—the current practice.

Nor can one gainsay the joint lobbying of Congress by business and intelligence interests on behalf of funding for technical systems—all (for better or for worse) a routine part of pressure-group democracy in the United States.

Still, if one seeks better international trade cooperation rather than the unleashing of a subterranean war of economic spies, some ties between business and intelligence seem questionable. Paid intelligence collection, for example, is espionage, plain and simple—highly risky for businesspeople abroad, just as it is for anyone else. As for the intelligence community's targeting a foreign automobile manufacturer in hope of stealing its designs or sales strategies, the CIA presently has few assets in the foreign business sector to rely on, and developing them would be a long and difficult task. Moreover, which of the U.S. auto companies should receive this information, even if it could be purloined? And if an agent of the CIA or the NSA were caught red-handed in a foreign penthouse office at midnight, would the inevitable rupture in relations between the United States and the target nation have been worth it?

That American businesses have shown virtually no interest in an espionage partnership with the intelligence community also speaks volumes against the idea. The larger American corporations, at the least, are no doubt capable of their own business snooping and have been at it much longer than the intelligence community. Further, some U.S. firms have expressed concern that the CIA could end up spying on them—the return of Operation CHAOS, this time in the corporate boardroom. Finally, economic covert actions to destroy foreign crops or livestock lie so far away from the traditional values of the American people as to be at face value inappropriate. The same is true for the bombing of power plants and the mining of harbors—except under a formal declaration of war.

Some aspects of economic intelligence could be strengthened, however. At present, microeconomic intelligence that is inadvertently derived from routine espionage operations is treated in too ad hoc a fashion. Precise guidelines need to be established to indicate exactly when the secret agencies should pass on this intelligence to policymakers, and through what systematic means (if at all) it should then be filtered down to the relevant American businesses.

In the domain of counterintelligence, a more systematic procedure is required for warning American businesses about foreign espionage directed against them. If through their normal economic intelligence activities the CIA or its companion agencies should learn of a foreign espionage operation targeted against a specifically American corporation, it would be irresponsible not to disseminate this intelligence via the National Counterintelligence Center to the targeted business (duly protecting sources and methods)—whether the espionage has been sponsored by a hostile intelligence service or by a foreign business.

It would be helpful to the American people, as well, for the intelligence community to make every effort (within the constraints of protecting sources and methods) to release to the public as much information as possible on matters of economic intelligence—including selected satellite imagery.[95] The American business community and independent economic analysts could certainly benefit from the Community's rich economic databases; and external critiques, like those that took place in the 1970s with respect to Soviet oil resources, are healthy for the Community in its avowed search for truth.

"Our national security is inseparable from our economic security," Secretary of State Warren Christopher told the Senate Foreign Relations Committee on November 4, 1993. That is why America's intelligence agencies will continue to pay close attention to the conduct of macroeconomic intelligence activities. Yet a concern for economic security should not lead to the adoption of unwarranted microeconomic operations urged by those who evidently place the short-term profit margin above all other considerations.

It must be remembered, too, that America's struggle against faltering economic competitiveness will require much deeper remedies than the intelligence community can possibly provide. The United States must continue to rebuild its aged industrial infrastructure, and its citizens must improve their foreign-language skills if they hope to make inroads into overseas markets. A hundred young American businesspeople studying Japanese, reading the Tokyo business papers, and interacting with their counterparts in Japan are far more likely to keep this country informed about Japanese economic issues—and stimulate the opening of new business opportunities in Japan for U.S. firms—than a score of spies or a thousand wiretaps.

Moreover, the open agencies in the federal government, along with American business associations, can do more than they have so far to seek out international economic data by aggressively exploiting open sources. Virtually all of the economic data on the American market gathered by Japan is said to be obtained through open sources.[96] America's intelligence agencies can only help at the margins, chiefly through the collection and analysis of macroeconomic data and more robust counterintelligence assistance for U.S. companies—not through microeconomic intelligence operations that could easily wreck America's relationships with valued allies.

CHAPTER 7

AN ASSESSMENT OF AMERICAN INTELLIGENCE

From one vantage point the Cold War may be thought of as a subterranean World War Three that pitted America's secret agencies against their Soviet counterparts, the KGB and the GRU. The charge given to the U.S. intelligence establishment by the president and the Congress in 1947 was to employ the tradecraft of espionage for acquiring the best information possible about the capabilities and intentions of the USSR and other hostile powers.

Above all, America's leaders sought reliable guidance on the military strength and objectives of the Communist empire—tightly kept secrets of the highest order. Insights into Moscow's economic, political, and societal dimensions—anything that could make the enemy less opaque—were considered important, too, although secondary to its rising military might. By the 1960s the Soviet arsenal of intercontinental ballistic missiles, tipped with enough nuclear warheads to incinerate hundreds of U.S. military bases and population centers, had concentrated America's attention.

Moreover, American officials expected their secret agencies to take up covert action as a weapon for countering the Kremlin's attempts to woo or coerce the allegiance of the Third World. Counterintelligence would serve as the instrument to protect America's secrets and, if possible, to burrow deeply into the enemy camp in search of Soviet spy stratagems against the United States. This chapter attempts to evaluate the most fundamental question about America's intelligence agencies during the Cold War: How well did they protect the United States against the Soviet Union? The evaluation will center on the three primary missions for which the U.S. intelligence community was responsible: collection and analysis, counterintelligence, and covert action.

ANALYSIS

The chief subject domains of collection and analysis are the military, economic, political, and social dimensions of the Soviet Union. Each domain lends itself to a finer sifting. This chapter concentrates mainly on the Soviet military, America's primary concern, which can be parsed according to a series of critical questions. How well did the intelligence community monitor and assess Soviet weapons development and military capabilities, the adherence of the USSR to arms accords, and the Kremlin's intentions to use military force?

The other domains similarly branch into subtopics. In the economic realm, for example, one could examine the quality of intelligence on agricultural production in the USSR, forecasts of Soviet oil reserves, and the Community's understanding of basic economic indices of material well-being inside the Communist empire. The political domain would encompass intelligence on the Soviet leadership succession, Communist party decisions reached behind the closed doors of the Kremlin, and the vitality of Communist youth movements in Tallin or Tashkent. The social dimension would include intelligence on incidents of public protest, labor unrest, and other manifestations of mass alienation; vodka and cocaine consumption; the spread of AIDS; criminal activity; and, if broadly defined, even the rising levels of pollution in Soviet rivers and forests. One could write a book on each of these domains. The objective here is simply to examine some of the more prominent successes and failures experienced by the intelligence community as it sought to monitor Soviet affairs.

On selected military issues the achievements of America's secret agencies against the Soviet target were commendable. They may have even helped the United States avoid an overt—and likely nuclear—third world war. This is an accomplishment of inestimable value. Yet across the board of the subject domains the results were uneven. Sometimes the secret agencies succeeded, sometimes they did not. Moreover, the record is marred by errors of fact and interpretation by intelligence analysts and self-delusion among policy officers that caused them to reject sound Community assessments—twin demons that have bedeviled the intelligence services of the United States and every other nation.

One would expect the strongest case for U.S. intelligence success from 1945 to 1991 to come from activities directed against the Soviet military target. This is, after all, where a majority of America's intelligence resources were directed during the Cold War. Within the CIA, the leading units with responsibility for understanding the Soviet military were the Office of Scientific and Weapons Research (OSWR) and the Office of Soviet Analysis (SOVA), both located in the Directorate of Intelligence (DI).[1] Also playing key roles were the Arms Control Intelligence Staff (ACIS, attached to the DCI's Office) and the National Photographic Interpretation Center (NPIC, a part of the Directorate of Science and Technology).

Tracking Soviet Weapons Development

The DI contributed in two important ways to an understanding of Soviet weapons development. First, it served as a valuable interlocutor between the producers of intelligence—each of the secret agencies and across the "INTs"—and the government's intelligence consumers, including negotiators for the Strategic Arms Limitation Talks (SALT) and Pentagon strategic planners. Through an ongoing dialogue with policy officers, DI analysts helped determine what information decisionmakers required. Then the analysts worked with the Directorate of Operations (DO), the Directorate of Science and Technology (DS&T), and companion entities in other parts of the Community to craft the collection methods appropriate to these requirements.

Second, the DI worked closely with the technical weapons wizards in the DS&T, as well as with HUMINT managers in the DO, to establish models of the precise measurements that would form the foundation of its weapons analysis—based on empirical facts rather than the intuitive speculation about Soviet arms that characterized the opening stages of the Cold War. These measurements would come from a careful massaging of open sources, augmented by maturing capabilities of IMINT (observed Soviet activity) as well as SIGINT, HUMINT, and MASINT (reported activity).

Foreign material acquisition was important, too. Soviet weapons systems were stolen whenever possible and reverse-engineered. According to an experienced CIA analyst, "Foreign-material collection played a great role in our ability to make accurate assessments of performance—the real capabilities of systems—and often monitor the changes that were made, which reflected changes in the underlying intentions for which the forces were to be used."[2] The direct-measurement programs under SIGINT and MASINT provided especially good intelligence on missiles and submarines. The acquisition of the desired measurements was aided significantly during the 1960s and 1970s by the willingness of some nations abutting the USSR to provide the United States access to territory near Soviet weapons-testing ranges. The NSA's listening posts in Iran captured valuable military intelligence for years, until they were shut down by the Iranian revolution in 1979.

After considerable fumbling around in the early years of the Cold War (the "dark age" of modern American intelligence),[3] the secret agencies began to establish a reliable baseline of knowledge about Soviet weaponry, from the first stages of development through testing, deployment, and operations. An array of clandestine collection methods (SIGINT in particular) provided the United States with a fairly comprehensive understanding of the Soviet nuclear control systems as well. This knowledge in turn had an effect on decisions regarding America's own weapons planning—for example, the insights necessary to develop a Pershing II missile that could destroy the Soviet command structure in time of war.

These efforts to monitor Soviet weaponry were aided by a realization in the 1980s that most of the technology going into these armaments had origins in the West—technology already well understood by America's intelligence experts. Further, throughout the Cold War, HUMINT assets in the Soviet Union—although "few and far between"[4]—proved vital to focusing attention on the likely pathways the Kremlin might take in terms of technological development.

The reliability of U.S. estimates regarding the Soviet military target depended greatly on the extent of America's own technological advances in the science of intelligence collection. In the 1950s, concedes a senior DI manager, "We weren't very good at all."[5] Fortunately, the intelligence community achieved a number of technological breakthroughs that led to higher plateaus of collection capability and, as a result, to richer databases that permitted a more accurate analysis of the number and capability of Soviet bombers and missiles.

The most well-known advances occurred in IMINT, with the construction of a series of high-flying, camera-laden platforms: the U-2 reconnaissance airplane (1956–60), followed by the launching of surveillance satellites under the CORONA program (beginning in 1960) and the maiden voyage of the SR-71A "Blackbird" spy plane (in 1964).[6] The CORONA satellites photographed all Soviet medium-range, intermediate-range, and intercontinental ballistic missile launching bases, as well as Soviet construction sites for submarine and surface fleets. Indeed, the first successful CORONA mission in 1960 photographed 1.5 million square miles of the USSR and Eastern Europe—a greater yield than the previous thirty U-2 missions over the Soviet Union.[7] The

CORONA program also provided imagery of aircraft factories and airbases, and its photographs allowed more reliable estimates of the Soviet ground order of battle as well.

The series of CORONA satellites, codenamed KEYHOLE or KH, possessed increasingly sophisticated cameras. Launched in 1962, KH-4 (for instance) carried advanced stereoscopic cameras. These unblinking eyes in space uncovered Soviet anti-ballistic missile (ABM) sites, which allowed the U.S. Strategic Air Command (SAC) to plan more secure attack routes into Soviet territory for B-52 strategic bombers in case of war. CORONA also yielded detailed military mapping data for the vast Soviet expanse. As the 1960s unfolded, the Community continued to improve the panoramic vision of its surveillance cameras and introduced the use of color film in satellite photography.

Advances in SIGINT collection technology led to further leaps forward in coverage of Soviet military targets in the early and late 1970s, as did all-weather, radar-based intelligence platforms in the 1980s.[8] The first major wave of SIGINT satellite innovations in the early 1970s gave the NSA an improved capacity to capture Soviet microwave communications intelligence (including telephone conversations among Kremlin elites), as well as a better reading of Soviet rocket and aircraft telemetry during test flights along the Black Sea—a quantum jump in collection against Soviet weapons capabilities.[9] The telemetry intelligence was especially important for assisting the Department of Defense in its development of weapons countermeasures. The progress continued. The NIEs published on the USSR in 1981, 1983, and 1985 are enormously more insightful than earlier estimates, in no small part as a result of the deeper knowledge gleaned from the increasingly sophisticated TECHINT collection platforms developed by the intelligence community in cooperation with the U.S. Air Force and private-sector manufacturers.

Qualitative improvements in analysis, such as the maturing skills of photointerpreters assigned to Soviet military targets, supplemented the TECHINT breakthroughs. The most important analytic advance was an evolving ability of the Community to engage in all-source analytic "fusion." Slowly (if incompletely) overcoming bureaucratic rivalries and distrust, the intelligence agencies began to integrate their findings during the 1980s—a vital synergism that brought about a more holistic view of Soviet military advances. "It all started to come together in a critical mass," recalls a DI analyst from this era, "to help the intelligence analyst and the policy maker understand what was happening."[10]

This improved analysis of Soviet weapons systems was by no means a smooth progression. It was flawed by cycles of over- and underestimating. The most egregious errors occurred in the early years of high anxiety about what might be happening behind the Iron Curtain—before the advent of the more advanced (and more plentiful) collection platforms. A combination of Soviet deception, American gullibility about the USSR's having near superhuman weapons capabilities (reinforced by the Sputnik achievement in 1957), U.S. Air Force alarmism, and the opaqueness of the Iron Curtain itself led to uncertainty and fear in the West. The first reaction was to overstate the power of the enemy. By the end of 1961 improved TECHINT revealed that the United States had in fact been vastly overestimating Soviet military progress.[11] Then, however, the pendulum swung in the other direction as the intelligence community started to underestimate Soviet ICBM production. As Wohlstetter once observed, "Overestimating had become disreputable."[12]

Nevertheless, the learning curve for America's secret agencies generally arced upward during the Cold War in a trajectory of improving capabilities against the Soviet military target. Specific examples of achievement and error are presented in figure 7.1.

Monitoring Arms Accords

During the course of the Cold War, America's policymakers became increasingly dependent on the intelligence community for data on arms accords. This nation's SALT negotiating strategies, for instance, rested on data assembled by the CIA based on all-source collection and analysis. Moreover, because of their valued expertise in monitoring Soviet compliance to arms agreements, U.S. intelligence officers (especially those on the Arms Control Intelligence Staff) found themselves sitting at the negotiating table alongside State Department officials drafting treaties with the USSR. The growing capabilities of U.S. intelligence surveillance allowed Washington to know whether the Soviet Union was honoring the provisions of SALT and other weapons agreements reached during the Cold War years. As William E. Burrows writes, this nation's intelligence collection platforms had a reassuring capacity to detect Soviet "cheating on a significant scale."[13]

The success of the Community in monitoring Moscow's compliance to arms treaties depended overwhelmingly on the capacity of the United States to collect telemetry on Soviet weaponry—the performance data from test flights, usually relayed by radio from the missile or aircraft to a ground station. Progress was a matter of trial and error. During the first two decades of the Cold War the intelligence agencies went from knowing precious little

Figure 7.1   Selected U.S. Intelligence Community Successes and Failures with
Respect to Soviet Weapons Development and Military Capabilities

SUCCESSES

1940s

Soviet defector provides accurate information on Soviet long-range bomber program
closely tracks Soviet A-bomb and H-bomb progress, including almost immediate (but
not prior) knowledge of first Soviet A-bomb detonation in 1949

1950s

obtains imagery of USSR ballistic-missile test ranges
accurately estimates the level of Soviet strategic threat facing the United States
resolves "bomber gap" and "missile gap" controversies with U-2 and satellite imagery,
confirming that gaps favored U.S.
closely tracks buildup of Soviet medium-range bombers
acquires data on Soviet aerospace activities, including an accurate forecasting of
Sputnik

1960s

satellites monitor military developments across the entire USSR, aiding in early
warning, nuclear-test monitoring, rapid communications, and mapping of Soviet
territory
forecasts first operational Soviet ICBM
Penkovsky provides valuable documents on Soviet weapons systems
anticipates MIRV development, correctly skeptical about Soviet achievement of operational MIRVs (contrary to Nixon administration belief)
acquires understanding of Soviet ICBM silo-hardening levels
acquires considerable data on Soviet order of battle

1970s

acquires understanding of Soviet submarine specifications
tracks further Soviet ICBM silo hardening
tracks nuclear and ballistic-missile research and development readiness
tracks Soviet technological developments

1980s

builds rich database on weapons production and testing, as well as on accuracy and explosive power of warheads
discovers deep underground leadership facilities near Moscow (which leads to U.S. nuclear retargeting to hold Kremlin at risk and therefore bolster deterrence)
acquires data on Soviet armor
tracks Soviet submarines
monitors Soviet laser/ABM research and development
acquires more sophisticated data (from telemetry) on missile launch weight, throw

Figure 7.1 (*continued*)

weight, manner of propulsion, and number, accuracy, and explosive power of war-heads

provides more detailed maps of the USSR, including location of military facilities

debunks view that Soviets had developed a directed-energy beam weapon

1990s

dramatic improvements in U.S. consumer-producer dialogue regarding intelligence needs

FAILURES

1940s

estimates that USSR will not have nuclear weapons until 1954

1950s

knows little about Soviet bombers and missiles; forced to rely on extrapolations, often
    leading to worst-case analyses

presents inflated estimates on the numbers of Soviet bombers and ICBMs

loses several U-2 surveillance aircraft and crewmen

flies U-2 aircraft only sporadically over USSR, providing uneven coverage

1960s

initially overestimates, then underestimates production of Soviet ICBMs

presents muddled estimates on Soviet BMD versus SAM systems

presents muddled estimates on state of MIRV development

rates *Pueblo* spy ship mission as low risk (North Korea apprehended the ship and crew
    in 1968)

fails to process vast storehouses of SIGINT on USSR

sometimes waters down NIEs to reach Community consensus

1970s

is unable to break Soviet encryption of missile telemetry for a time

acquires little knowledge of Soviet chemical and biological weapons

underestimates Soviet submarine-launched ballistic missiles

underestimates size of Soviet defense expenditures

wrongly assumes Soviets will dismantle old missiles (SS-7s and SS-8s)

submits to Nixon administration view that Soviets seek first-strike capability (despite an
    NIE to the contrary)

1980s

lags in forecasts of improvements in Soviet missile accuracy

continues to lack close dialogue with U.S. policymakers over intelligence needs about the USSR and its military establishment to having a mountain of data. U-2s, SR-71s, satellite imagery, NSA antennae around the Soviet perimeter, and eavesdropping from space together provided a rich mix of independent sources of intelligence on Soviet armaments. Added to this TECHINT cornucopia came an expanding corps of expert analysts who had been poring over data on Soviet weapons for many years and who were at the same time becoming more proficient at integrating all-source intelligence. The key successes and failures of the Community with respect to arms control are outlined in figure 7.2.

The intelligence community's most significant accomplishment during the Cold War was the development of remarkable satellite surveillance capabilities—a science in which the Soviets also excelled.[14] Coupled with the deterrent threat, these surveillance capabilities on both sides no doubt helped to keep a third world war at bay by significantly lowering the chances of a nuclear or conventional blitzkrieg by either superpower. In Burrows's words, "Space reconnaissance and surveillance reduced the element of strategic surprise to practically nil."[15]

Moreover, the intelligence community properly chided the view—widespread during the edgy first years of the Cold War—that the Soviets intended to destroy the United States in a hail of nuclear-tipped bombs and missiles. If indeed America's secret agencies helped to avert an armageddon—a propo-

Figure 7.2 Major U.S. Intelligence Successes and Failures with Respect to American-Soviet Arms Accords

Successes

Assesses accuracy of Soviet claims at the negotiating table, including SALT I and II, the Intermediate-range Nuclear Force (INF), Strategic Arms Reduction Talks (START), and conventional arms agreements

Verifies implementation of arms treaty provisions (compliance)

Challenges deviations from treaty agreements

Reveals violations of the Anti-Ballistic Missile (ABM) Treaty–most notably, the Krasnoyarsk large phased-array radar for ballistic missile early warning in the mid-1980s

Failures

CIA is perceived to have an "arms-control bias" by some policy officers, including the director of the Office of Management and Budget–and later DCI–James R. Schlesinger and Secretary of Defense Melvin Laird in early 1970s

DIA and military service units are perceived to distrust the arms-control process, consistently providing "worst-case" scenarios of possible violations

sition that cannot be proven but is plausible and even compelling—then the billions of dollars spent on their behalf were clearly worth the investment.

Divining Soviet Military Intentions

In contrast to this relative success in understanding Soviet weapons capabilities and arms treaty compliance, the record on forecasting the use of force by the USSR is far more troubling. The intelligence community warned President Carter of a possible Soviet attack on Afghanistan in 1979 (based on imagery and NSA intercepts), but otherwise the secret agencies failed to anticipate several major Soviet military aggressions: Hungary in 1956, Cuba in 1962 (although DCI McCone did warn of missile emplacements on the island, even if his analysts disagreed), and Czechoslovakia in 1968. Earlier, in 1950, the Community had also failed to forecast the Korean War.

The intelligence community does take credit, though, for avoiding a U.S.-Soviet war in the Middle East in 1967, by reassuring President Lyndon B. Johnson that the USSR did not intend to go to war. Further, the agencies learned in the 1980s of a contemplated invasion by the Soviet Army into a (still undisclosed) nation in Eastern Europe. This led to back-channel warnings from Washington to Moscow against the use of force, and the Kremlin backed down. The Community also succeeded in closely tracking Soviet military units during the last days of the USSR, allowing analysts to forecast that the 1991 coup attempt against President Mikhail S. Gorbachev was likely to fail.[16]

As for Czechoslovakia in 1968, Soviet leaders themselves apparently put off invasion plans several times before deciding to proceed. This indecisiveness made the Kremlin's intentions extremely difficult to follow, even with HUMINT sources. Moreover, reliable imagery that disclosed the mustering of Soviet troops along the Czech border came a week too late to be of use[17]—an illustration of the importance of rapid data retrieval and processing. "In recent years, near real-time imagery has made a big difference," one senior CIA analyst has matter-of-factly observed.[18]

Sophisticated imagery would surely have been helpful during America's closest brush with nuclear war: the Cuban missile crisis of 1962. As a study in the shortcomings of American intelligence at the height of the Cold War (mixed with some notable accomplishments, too), the missile crisis warrants closer examination.

The litany of intelligence failures that transpired during those perilous weeks began with a Special National Intelligence Estimate published on September 19, 1962.[19] The SNIE anticipated that the Soviets were more likely to establish a submarine base in Cuba than to place medium-range ballistic missiles (MRBMs) there. As a post-mortem of the crisis prepared by the President's Foreign Intelligence Advisory Board (PFIAB) concluded, the CIA lacked a sense of "urgency or alarm" about developments in Cuba throughout the early stages.[20] Moreover, from September 18 to October 2 reports from refugees and CIA agents were "not of sufficient credibility to warrant their being used in intelligence publications."[21] In fact, according to a memorandum prepared by DCI McCone, of 3,500 HUMINT reports "only eight in retrospect were considered as reasonably valid indicators of the deployment of offensive missiles in Cuba."[22]

Compounding the dearth of reliable information on activities in Cuba was an unfortunate time lag between the first appearance of reliable HUMINT in late September and the ordering of U-2 overhead flights across Cuba to verify the HUMINT reporting. This delay resulted from a combination of factors: unfavorable weather, organizational disruption during the transfer of command over U-2 flights from the CIA to the Air Force, and, perhaps most important, a hesitancy by Secretary of State Dean Rusk to breach Cuban air space with a spy plane—a violation of international law (a subject he had taught as a young professor at Mills College).

When U-2 coverage finally commenced, the overflights led to one of the greatest contributions to American security ever made by the intelligence community. The U-2 photographs provided irrefutable evidence to President John F. Kennedy that the Soviets had indeed placed MRBMs in Cuba. Still, the intelligence agencies never even remotely suggested to the president that the Soviets may have brought tactical nuclear weapons onto the island—a possibility that surely would have weighed during the ongoing deliberations in the White House over whether the United States should invade Cuba. Nor was reliable empirical evidence ever forthcoming from the Community about whether strategic nuclear warheads, each with a yield of from two to five megatons, were on the island for placement on the MRBMs—although the CIA did caution in its reporting to the president that they could be there.

With the end of the Cold War and a filling in of our knowledge about the crisis, it now appears that in fact 102 tactical nuclear warheads were in Cuba—including twelve for Soviet Luna missiles, ninety for tactical cruise missiles, four in the form of nuclear mines, and six for the IL-28 bombers in Cuba.[23] This last set of warheads comes as a particular surprise, since the notion that these bombers might have a nuclear capability was rejected out of hand by U.S. intelligence officers at the time.

Most astonishing of all, up until the midst of the crisis the Soviet military commander in Cuba, General Issa Aleksandrovich Pliyev, may have had authority over the use of the tactical nuclear weapons—a risky devolution of war powers away from Kremlin control.[24] On October 22 that order evidently was rescinded by the Kremlin, restoring authority over the weapons to Premier Nikita Khrushchev. (For a chronology of the crisis, see Appendix B.) Moreover, researchers have learned that on October 26 the Soviet commander in Cuba "ordered Soviet [strategic] nuclear warheads in Cuba dispersed and moved closer to their launch vehicles"[25]—a highly provocative action that also managed to escape the attention of America's concentrated intelligence surveillance of Cuba.

In retrospect, some of the CIA's estimates and recommendations prepared during the crisis seem questionable as well. Agency analysts and managers reached rash conclusions that were laced with policy advocacy going well beyond the norm of neutrality in American intelligence reporting. One CIA product, for instance, declared that "the USSR would not dare to resort to general war"—even though Dean Rusk and Secretary of Defense Robert S. McNamara considered war a distinct possibility.[26] Further, DCI McCone minced no words in his advocacy of a "massive surprise attack" on the MRBM sites if, after a warning to Cuban premier Fidel Castro and the Soviets, the missiles were not dismantled within twenty-four hours.[27] The DCI gave this policy advice without consideration of the possibility that the strategic nuclear weapons the CIA thought could be on the island might well be used in retaliation against the U.S. invasion force gathered on the eastern seaboard of the United States or against other mainland targets.

In a follow-up memorandum after a meeting with Secretary McNamara and others on October 17, 1962, McCone acknowledged that a surprise air attack would "in all probability" escalate into an invasion of Cuba.[28] As McNamara has emphasized, it is now clear that an invasion "would have been an *absolute disaster* for the world."[29]

Further, not until mid-October—at the midpoint of the crisis—did the CIA correct the misjudgments of its September SNIE. Throughout these tense weeks intelligence analysts were more inclined to offer hunches based on the past Soviet pattern of caution than they were to give proper emphasis to the empirical indicators of what the Soviets were actually doing in Cuba: engaging in highly risky behavior. To his credit, McCone thought otherwise. As early as September his intuition told him the Soviets might try to place missiles in Cuba, and he so informed the president. It took the hard evidence of U-2 imagery, however, to convince Kennedy that the Soviets were indeed willing to go to the brink.

The Cuban missile crisis was a sobering event. The USSR, the premier target for American intelligence, managed, without notice by the U.S. secret agencies, to slip more than a hundred tactical nuclear weapons onto an island just ninety miles off the coast of the United States; to turn control of these weapons over to a local Soviet commander, again without the awareness of the intelligence community; and, at the height of the crisis, to move the MRBM strategic warheads from their storage sites and place them near their launch vehicles.

On the positive side, the Community eventually had been able to warn the president about the Soviet MRBMs in Cuba, cautioning that the missiles might soon be equipped with strategic warheads able to strike any American city east of the Mississippi River. Moreover, the president received this alert—first from the DCI, expressing his own private hunch, then from HUMINT and irrefutable U-2 photographs—in time for him to ponder options other than a "surgical" airstrike against the missile sites or an all-out invasion. However distressing the shortcomings of intelligence during the Cuban crisis, this warning in itself was an extremely significant contribution to national security.[30]

Nineteen sixty-two, it should be noted, was still early in the evolution of America's surveillance capabilities. The United States could perhaps fare better today in a similar crisis. Certainly it enjoyed nearly transparent intelligence coverage of the Persian Gulf during Operation Desert Storm in 1991— although the slow buildup to that war distinguishes it from the short-fused Cuban crisis, allowing time for the necessary intelligence platforms to glide into place. But America's relative blindness toward some parts of the globe even today tempers optimism. Referring to North Korea, for example, DCI John M. Deutch has observed, "This is a society—let me leave aside the issue of [a] nuclear weapons program—where we are in my mind remarkably ill-informed."[31]

Intelligence officials point to other specific achievements of collection and analysis against the Soviet military target. The Community accurately forecast the unlikelihood of imminent Soviet military action against Western Europe during the 1948 Berlin blockade. It anticipated the Sputnik launch, which heralded the capacity of the Soviet Union to reach the United States with long-range missiles.

Further, the CIA retrieved some useful data from its operation in the 1970s to raise a wrecked Soviet submarine from the ocean floor—even though the vessel cracked in half as it was being hoisted and the best part fell back into the sea.[32] Throughout the Cold War the Community closely monitored the development of the USSR's conventional weapons systems, from MIG aircraft to Soviet tanks, with HUMINT (especially in Eastern Europe) playing an even greater part in these successes than in the strategic realm.

The Disintegration of the Soviet Union

As for the other subject domains, the record of successful collection and analysis is more uneven. The issue of whether the intelligence community understood and forecast the degree of economic and political decay inside the USSR during the final days of the Cold War warrants special attention.

Among some observers (most audibly Senator Daniel Patrick Moynihan), the feeling is widespread that the intelligence community drastically underestimated the state of decay in the Soviet Union during its last years. In the end game of the Cold War (so the argument goes), America's secret agencies failed to realize that President Gorbachev's economic reforms were genuine, that he faced serious political trouble from opponents—even a coup—and that one of his rivals, Boris N. Yeltsin, was a rapidly rising force. Senator Moynihan and other critics concluded that the time had come to turn the intelligence function over to the Department of State. The CIA had failed in its cardinal mission: to anticipate events in the Soviet Union.[33]

Even if all this were true, obsequies for the CIA would be premature. After all, America's secret agencies were hardly alone in their failure to forecast the abrupt Soviet disintegration. Virtually everyone else—policymakers, scholars, think tanks, the media—missed the impending fall of the USSR. The renowned Sovietologist Adam Ulam noted in 1987, for instance, that Gorbachev "has not become general secretary to preside over the liquidation of the Communist empire."[34]

Focusing on the issue of alleged CIA incompetence, a team of academic specialists presented this testimony before a congressional panel of inquiry looking into the demise of the Soviet Union:

> Neither the CIA nor academic specialists were particularly prescient, for example, in anticipating the outcome of Gorbachev's policies of *perestroika* and *glasnost* [economic and political reform]. The research community as a whole failed to consider the collapse of communism as a possible scenario. . . . [W]e believe that much of the criticism to date is based on twenty-twenty hindsight. In our view, the best that can be expected is for policy makers to be given a range of outcomes or a set of scenarios to which broad probabilities are attached. Although the CIA did fail to predict the catastrophic developments in the Soviet economy at the end of the 1980s, it did begin to alert its clients to a serious and continuing slowdown in the Soviet economy and an increasing competition for resources much earlier.[35]

Highlights from the CIA's attempts to monitor the economic, political, and social decline of the USSR underscore the difficulty of persuading policy officers to accept intelligence that runs counter to their own predilections.[36] As early as 1977 the CIA pointed to the chronic slowdown of the Soviet economy, and by 1981 it had labeled the USSR the "world's most underdeveloped country."[37] A year later the NIO for the Soviet Union tried to report that the Communist empire could not "forever sustain [its] defense burden."[38] The DIA and the CIA's upper echelons blocked this language, evidently viewing the Soviet Union as a much stronger adversary than did the Community's chief Soviet expert.

By 1986, however, SOVA analysts were prepared to stage a rebellion of sorts. Bucking the views of the White House, the DIA, and the CIA's seventh floor, they declared in their own reporting—unrestrained by interagency NIE negotiations and the worst-case views of the military—that the Community's estimates on Soviet military spending were excessively high.[39] This argument quickly raised suspicions, recalling the time in 1977 when the CIA had to concede that it had underestimated Soviet military spending by a factor of two.[40]

Undaunted by the skepticism, the SOVA upstarts extended their semi-radical critique into 1987 with an unorthodox assessment of Soviet president Gorbachev. The CIA leadership—including then DDCI Robert M. Gates (himself a former SOVA analyst) and DCI William H. Webster, an "outsider" with a law-enforcement background who was inclined to defer to Gates on Soviet matters—considered Gorbachev largely a remnant of the old order. In contrast, several (though not all) SOVA analysts looked upon him as a genuine reformer who was apt to bring about lasting changes in the USSR. Indeed, as early as 1985 a SOVA report stated, "[W]ith his own people in place, Gorbachev should be able to build a consensus behind the more far-reaching proposals that he has only hinted at to date."[41] As analysts, managers, and policy officers began to choose sides in this debate, the stage was set for bureaucratic warfare inside SOVA, among CIA managers, and between the Agency and the Reagan administration over the meaning of events rapidly unfolding in Moscow.

In the early skirmishes the SOVA "radicals" pressed their case that the USSR was in serious economic distress. One of their papers in 1988 cited a series of gloomy economic statistics from the Soviet Union, including an 18 percent rise in the price of meat.[42] Further, SOVA advanced the judgment that the Soviet president might have to "impose unilateral cuts" on defense spending.[43] Gaining acceptance of even this rather guarded prognostication took some doing, though, as the report moved along on an almost nine-month journey from first draft to final publication—not exactly a timely presentation of the views held by those CIA analysts who were following events in the USSR most closely.

In SOVA frustration rose over the delays and, more aggravating still, the tendency toward outright rejection of its views by the White House. In 1988 SOVA analysts complained vociferously to their managers about "self-deception" in the Reagan administration; the White House refused to acknowledge that the "evil empire," as the president had characterized the USSR in 1986, might actually be undergoing reform. Some SOVA and CIA managers were sympathetic to these complaints; others, including Robert Gates, continued to agree with the White House perspective most of the time.[44]

Finally, in December 1988 the breach between elements of SOVA and CIA management had an airing on Capitol Hill during hearings on the Soviet situation.[45] At the same time the SOVA radicals received a convincing affirmation of their thesis: at the UN, Gorbachev announced a unilateral cut of 500,000 Soviet troops—a stunning public acknowledgment of Moscow's acute economic distress.

Nevertheless, Secretary of Defense Richard Cheney in the new Bush administration continued to reject SOVA's reports on the permanency of the Gorbachev reforms.[46] Forging ahead despite the high-level disregard (not to say disdain) for their reporting, SOVA analysts raised another new argument in 1989 that also had little support among either the CIA's managers or the administration (where Robert Gates now served as deputy assistant to the president for national security affairs). At first, the analysts had pushed the controversial view that Gorbachev's reforms were real; now they proceeded to argue that Gorbachev himself might be in trouble politically and, further, that the Communist leader of Moscow, Boris Yeltsin, loomed as a significant challenger to the incumbent Soviet president.

It was "far from certain," warned a SOVA paper, "that [Gorbachev] will be able to control the process he has set in motion."[47] The analysis gave Gorbachev only a fifty-fifty chance of retaining the support of the Congress of People's Deputies—unless he made a hasty retreat from his reforms.[48] This forecast stood out in sharp relief from the views of the rest of the Community, which gave Gorbachev a minimum of three or four more years in power.[49]

The SOVA perspective on Gorbachev's future grew steadily more pessimistic. One of SOVA's senior analysts was especially glum about Gorbachev's political longevity.[50] After months of persistence, his judgment finally made it into the estimates process as a dissenting footnote to the text of an NIE on the Soviet Union. Yet the notion that Gorbachev could be in imminent trouble was once more rejected by the White House, on the advice of Secretary Cheney at the Defense Department and Gates at the NSC.

Throughout most of 1989 administration officials dismissed SOVA as too anti-Gorbachev and too pro-Yeltsin. National security aides—though evidently not the president himself[51]—remained skeptical that Gorbachev's reforms were much more than rhetoric. Then, in November, the Berlin Wall fell, severely undermining the status quo orientation of the hard-liners in the Bush administration. Now even Gates and Cheney were prepared to acknowledge that Gorbachev might be losing control.[52]

In 1991 SOVA analysts issued a series of strong forecasts warning that Gorbachev faced serious political trouble, including a possible coup attempt. "The centrally-planned economy [of the USSR] has broken down irretrievably," SOVA warned in April. "[P]reparations for dictatorial rule have begun . . . military, MVD [the Soviet Ministry of Internal Affairs], and KGB leaders are making preparations for a broad use of force in the political process." SOVA analysts believed, however, that attempts at a putsch were likely to fail. "The number of troops that can be counted on to enforce repression is limited," they concluded. Even if momentarily successful, a coup would not halt "the pluralistic forces from emerging in a dominant position before the end of the decade."[53]

In May SOVA presciently forecast these dire prospects for the USSR:

- No matter what happens, the current political system in the Soviet Union is doomed. . . .
- Time is working against the [anti-Gorbachev, anti-Yeltsin] traditionalists. . . . The longer force is not used, the weaker their position will become. . . .
- Even if Gorbachev manages to remain, his domination of the Soviet political system has ended and will not be resurrected.

The analysis continued: "To take the tough steps they believe are necessary to forestall a reformist victory, at any point hardliners may try to remove Gorbachev and install their own regime. The danger would be greatest if they believe Gorbachev is selling out their interests to the republics."[54]

Though conceding Gorbachev's weakness, the Bush administration nonetheless rejected the sense of urgency SOVA was attempting to communicate in 1991.[55] These detailed SOVA analyses seem to have been lost on Senator Moynihan and other Monday morning quarterbacks, although they have been a matter of public record since 1988.

On August 18, 1991, a putsch was led against President Gorbachev by a cabal of high-ranking Soviet military officers. It failed quickly, with Boris Yeltsin standing as one of many courageous opponents in Moscow. While neither the CIA nor anyone else in the world had predicted the precise day of the coup attempt, SOVA analysts certainly had seen it coming—and imminently. Indeed, one analyst had ingeniously tied the date of a possible coup to an impending "union treaty" designed to given greater autonomy to the Soviet republics—a move that was anathema to the old military guard.[56] True to this forecast, the coup plotters arrested Gorbachev shortly before he was to sign the treaty. This insightful analysis never emerged from the layers of management at SOVA, unfortunately, until after the aborted coup.

The report would probably have been dismissed by the administration anyway. No more than President Reagan's advisers, the Bush national security team could never seem to face the prospect of radical change in the Soviet Union. President Bush and his aides appeared genuinely stunned by the attempted overthrow of Gorbachev, despite all the warnings they had received from SOVA analysts.

Facing the reality after the coup attempt that his political support had all but evaporated, Gorbachev resigned on December 25, 1991. The Soviet Union went into free fall, disintegrating into its constituent republics. After much political turmoil Yeltsin emerged as the leading candidate to capture the newly configured Russian presidency.

Autopsy

What can be learned from this review of the CIA's attempts to monitor the Soviet Union during what proved to be its dying days? The analytic process clearly was flawed. For all of their subsequent achievements in tracking the Soviet decline, SOVA analysts in 1987 flatly ridiculed the notion raised by a military participant at an NSC deputies meeting that Gorbachev "was destroying [the Communist] system."[57]

Moreover, a SOVA director from this period has acknowledged that his shop "never really looked at the Soviet Union as a *political* entity."[58] Instead, SOVA tended to focus excessively on arms control issues. Had SOVA analysts given more attention to the political and social unrest in the USSR, they might have caught the signs of disintegration sooner and perceived them more clearly. The methodological barriers were high, however, for SOVA analysts just as for scholars on the outside. As a 1985 NIE stated, the Community lamented the "severe data problems, particularly the lack of statistics on social trends and pathologies, such as crime rates." Nor could intelligence analysts find "good social theory for describing the behavior of a society that is far from fitting the old 'totalitarian model' but is still ruled by a regime that strives to fulfill many of that model's features."[59]

The former SOVA director also wishes that he had gone outside the intelligence community more often for additional Soviet analysis. "We were wrong for not tapping all the best minds of the country," he reflects, "acting as a Great

Facilitator, instead of relying on ourselves so much to carry out this analysis." Moreover, even though elements in SOVA were far ahead of other CIA components and the Reagan and Bush administrations in realizing that Gorbachev's reforms were genuine, the leaders of the SOVA radicals now concede that they were overly slow and cautious in forecasting Gorbachev's willingness to restructure his regime in 1987–88.[60]

Another point is clear: with respect to Soviet assessments, the Community was a Hydra. The DIA and the CIA were often at loggerheads. Inside the CIA, analysts and managers often disagreed over the meaning of events in the USSR. The SOVA insurgents seem to have offered the most farsighted and accurate judgments, but they quickly ran into trouble on the seventh floor—initially for forecasting the permanency of the Gorbachev reforms and then for estimating that Gorbachev himself was in major political trouble. Neither hypothesis sat well with the Reagan and Bush administrations. Thus, it is misleading to refer to "the CIA" as if it were a single monolith; the Agency can speak with many voices and engages in considerable internal debate—sometimes acrimonious—over the meaning of key world events.

Above all, though, Moynihan and other critics have not paid enough attention to the serious analysis that did emerge from SOVA during the final years of the Cold War. The fact is that SOVA tracked events in the Soviet Union fairly well, including the sharp decline in its economy and the political travail that afflicted President Gorbachev. Robert Gates has offered in retrospect a compelling rebuttal to the Moynihan perspective (even if Gates skips over his own early dismissal of SOVA assessments):

From the beginning, CIA analysis clearly described the chronic weaknesses as well as the formidable military power of the Soviet Union. . . . We did not predict the precise timing of the coup attempt [against Gorbachev in 1991]. However, neither did Gorbachev nor Yeltsin, and indeed, the coup plotters themselves have indicated that they decided to act at the last minute.

So, where did we fall short? First, until early 1989 we did not contemplate that a Soviet communist *apparatchik*—Gorbachev—once in power would unintentionally set in motion forces that would pull the props from under an already steadily declining economic system and bring down the entire political and imperial system in the process. We wrote many assessments describing the growing crisis in the Soviet Union—describing a steady but gradual and open-ended decline, but only in 1989 did we begin to think the entire edifice might well collapse. Even so, we saw it in time to warn policy makers more than two years in advance. . . .

We did not remind policy makers, and ourselves often enough that, from time to time, some things are simply unknowable—even to the protagonists. . . .

Obviously there were deficiencies in the CIA's work on the Soviet Union—

things we did not know and areas where we were wrong. But the body of information, analysis, and warning provided to policy makers and to Congress was of extraordinarily high quality. To claim that U.S. intelligence in general and CIA in particular failed to recognize the systemic weaknesses of the Soviet system, failed to inform policy makers of the growing crisis, or failed to warn of impending collapse of the old order is not consistent with the facts. The years-long messages of decline, failed reform and, beginning in early 1989, of approaching crisis were crystal clear and delivered in many ways, public as well as classified.[61]

Gates might have added that these messages were largely discounted by policymakers and, for a long time, rejected by the CIA's own managers. The Reagan and Bush administrations simply cast aside the disagreeable SOVA analysis—at least until the durability of the Gorbachev reforms had become obvious to all by 1990, and until an ashen-faced Gorbachev returned to Moscow from his dacha on the Black Sea following the abortive coup of 1991.

COLLECTION

Most of the information on the USSR provided to policy officers by the intelligence community during the Cold War came from open sources, such as official statements on Soviet radio, published photographs of military parades in Moscow, and articles in *Pravda* and *Izvestiia*. Other wellsprings of open-source intelligence included the study of technical journals, trade press articles, reports from the CIA's Foreign Broadcast Information Service, and conference proceedings. In short, the work of intelligence officers as highly trained "library scholars" of Soviet affairs was central to assembling the Kremlin puzzle. Once the open pieces were in place, finding the hidden ones was a task that fell to the clandestine collectors, whether HUMINT or TECHINT.

HUMINT

America's secret agencies benefited from human penetrations into the Soviet Union and its puppet regimes. Its success rate against the KGB and the GRU was infinitely better than against the Soviet political and military leadership ranks. The most well known "moles" were Lieut. Col. Petr Semenovich Popov, who was active in the 1950s, and Col. Oleg Vladimirovich Penkovski, who was discovered by the Soviets and executed in 1963. Both men provided valuable data on the capabilities of Soviet rocketry and other military subjects. Penkovski's reporting aided Community analysts in identifying and monitoring Soviet missile deployments in Cuba during the 1962 crisis.

The initial sightings of MRBMs in Cuba came from HUMINT sources, which provided accurate coordinates for subsequent U-2 reconnaissance flights—though one should keep in mind that 99 percent of the HUMINT reporting from Cuba at this time proved inaccurate! Moreover, as we now know, during the Cold War virtually all of America's agents in Cuba were evidently "doubled"—that is, discovered and turned back against the United States as spies for Cuba—as was the case in East Germany. This astonishing record of HUMINT failure was capped by the Ames affair and the loss of the CIA's agents in Moscow over the past decade.[62]

Early in the Cold War, CIA agents also acquired and distributed Khrushchev's "secret speech" to the Twentieth Congress of the Communist Party of the Soviet Union (CPSU) in 1956. In this speech Khrushchev announced plans to modernize the Soviet military and, more significantly, denounced Joseph Stalin, thus handing the CIA ideal anti-Communist propaganda. Some critics have charged, however, that this "successful" collection operation may have faltered when CI Chief James Angleton ordered the speech doctored to the point where it may have lost its credibility. Instead of a truthful revelation on the evils of Stalinism, it may have been seen in Eastern Europe (where Angleton reportedly had his amended version widely disseminated) as merely a CIA deception operation.[63]

Still, the value of HUMINT cannot be gainsaid. Even today, how can one distinguish between a foreign pharmaceutical plant and a laboratory for the production of chemical-biological weapons without having an agent inside the building?

TECHINT

No other nation enjoys the degree of high-tech surveillance capability found in America's intelligence agencies. Were it not for these satellites, reconnaissance airplanes, and other machines that can look and listen with incredible sensitivity around the world, it is unlikely that the arms accords between the two superpowers would have been successfully negotiated. America's spy machines made weapons monitoring feasible, verification reliable, and, as a result, arms control politically palatable. Moreover, in a climate of great uncertainty at the beginning of the Cold War, dire reports on the mass production of Soviet weaponry—of which the Air Force's inflated Soviet ICBM estimates from 1957 to 1964 were just one example—would have doubtless had a major influence on Washington and forced even larger expenditures of taxpayer monies than the staggering sums spent.[64]

In 1967 President Johnson expressed his awe at what TECHINT had contributed to America's well-being. "[W]e've spent about thirty-five or forty billion dollars on the space program. And if nothing else had come out of it except the knowledge we've gained from space photography, it would be worth ten times what the whole program has cost. Because tonight we know how many missiles the enemy has and, it turned out, our guesses were way off. We were doing things we didn't need to do. We were building things we didn't need to build. We were harboring fears we didn't need to harbor."[65]

America's TECHINT platforms were not just in space and arrayed around the Soviet perimeter; they were positioned underground and beneath the seas as well. In one operation that enjoys a high place on the intelligence community's honor roll, collectors tunneled their way into East Berlin and tapped the Soviet military's telephone cables. This SIGINT coup, intelligence officials claim, provided valuable intelligence for the United States from its inception in 1955 until April 1956, when it was "discovered" by the Communists. Critics point out, however, that a Soviet agent in England, George Blake, knew about the operation and no doubt warned his KGB handlers, raising the distinct possibility that Moscow may have used the tunnel tap as a conduit for disinformation.

COUNTERINTELLIGENCE

Although counterintelligence is a vast and convoluted subject, for some observers an evaluation of the intelligence community's success in this mission can be summed up in one four-letter word: Ames. Aldrich Hazen Ames, a CIA officer, was responsible near the end of the Cold War for the deaths of a dozen or more CIA agents in Moscow and more than two hundred blown operations.[66] It is difficult to give high marks to U.S. counterintelligence with this dark stain across the ledger.

Moreover, even though Ames was a counterintelligence disaster for the United States, he was by no means the only one during the Cold War. According to some insiders, the treachery of John A. Walker, Jr., and his spy ring, which sold naval communications secrets to the USSR, could have been even more damaging than the Ames case if war had broken out between the superpowers.[67] The British agents Guy Burgess, Harold "Kim" Philby, and Donald Maclean are further examples of U.S. counterintelligence setbacks. All were close to American intelligence officers during the 1940s and 1950s—especially the debonair Philby, who dined regularly with CI Chief Angleton while stationed in Washington. Each of these British turncoats caused damage to American intelligence before at last being detected in the 1960s.[68]

Other American traitors from the 1980s alone have included Edward Lee

Howard, who defected to the Soviets with considerable knowledge of the CIA's operations in Moscow; William P. Kampiles, a young CIA officer who sold a highly classified KH-11 satellite manual to the KGB; and a number of NSA officials who spied for the Soviets, including the technician Ronald W. Pelton.[69] The CIA also poorly handled several Soviet defectors during the Cold War, among them Anatoli Golitsyn (in the early 1960s), Lt. Col. Yuri Ivanovich Nosenko (mid-1960s), and Col. Vitali Yurchenko, who fled back to the USSR under mysterious circumstances in late 1985.[70]

Notwithstanding these gloomy pages in the annals of modern counterintelligence, a more favorable light on the record deserves consideration. Angleton clearly made serious mistakes. His view of the Sino-Soviet schism as a deception was the most ludicrous, and his casting of suspicion on the loyalty of selected Agency officers without adequate evidence of guilt—ruining some careers by innuendo—the most reprehensible. Yet the tireless research and countermeasures against the Soviet intelligence agencies carried out by Angleton and his devoted staff may well have thwarted a large number of potential KGB and GRU penetrations against the United States during his twenty-year tenure as CI chief (1954–74). Had someone of Angleton's tenacity, intellect, and experience been in charge of counterintelligence at the Agency during the 1980s, Ames may have been discovered much earlier.

Some senior CI specialists also believe that Angleton, or someone using his approach to counterintelligence (see chapter 2), might have done more to limit the number of double agents in Cuba and East Germany during the last decades of the Cold War.[71] If one compares the record of known, successful Soviet penetrations against America's secret agencies to those against Great Britain, France, and West Germany during the Cold War, the shadowy Mr. Angleton and his counterintelligence colleagues throughout the Community deserve more credit than commonly accorded—despite the Ames tragedy.

COVERT ACTION

The broad outlines of the success and failure of covert actions against Moscow and its allies are well known. Chief among the successes claimed by the CIA are:

- money and other assistance to aid the anti-Communist resistance in Europe in the immediate aftermath of World War Two
- resistance to Soviet influence in Latin America
- support for the Marshall Plan

- Radio Free Europe and Radio Liberty, whose broadcasts sought to undermine Communist credibility in the Soviet bloc during the Cold War
- the Congress for Cultural Freedom, which attempted to counterbalance the appeal of Marxism in Western Europe and draw attention to the repression of intellectuals in the Soviet empire
- a literature program in which books and magazines were smuggled into the USSR to give the people a taste of Western life and a chance to read criticisms of the Soviet system
- support for anti-Communist coups in Iran (1953) and Guatemala (1954)
- successful resistance to Communist guerrillas in Laos during the 1960s
- political support for anti-Moscow moderates in Portugal during the Ford administration
- support for the Afghan resistance in the 1980s (including Stinger missiles), which most likely encouraged the Soviets to reconsider continuing the war

This accounting is overwhelmed, however, by a much longer list of setbacks, from the Bay of Pigs fiasco and madcap attempts to kill Fidel Castro through the abandonment of emigre groups in Eastern Europe, the Iran-contra scandal, and the vast sums of wasted resources poured into the sinkhole of the Angolan civil war (among other escapades) in the name of anti-Communism. Often the CIA has promised to support anti-Communist rebels abroad, only to abandon them to a cruel fate. Moreover, the unremitting use of covert action against the USSR— even during periods of detente—may have further chilled the Cold War. As Raymond Garthoff comments, "[T]here was never adequate recognition in American assessments of the need to weigh Soviet threat assessments and concerns over *our* military buildup activities and alliance building and global basing . . . to say nothing of our covert operations in Eastern Europe and even in the USSR, overflights, covert penetrations of coastal waters and the like."[72]

Covert action has proven useful on occasion and will continue to have a supporting role in combating terrorism, weapons proliferation, narcotics, and other national dangers. Yet it has also done more to discredit the intelligence community—and the United States—than anything else, including the Ames case. It has too often become the first line of disgrace. It should be resorted to only sparingly and with the utmost discrimination.

EXPLAINING THE INTELLIGENCE FAILURES OF THE COLD WAR

At the beginning of the Cold War, America's inability to forecast accurately the time when the USSR would acquire an atomic bomb, or to pinpoint how many strategic bombers and ICBMs the Soviets would build and deploy, was a result in large part of the thin intelligence coverage of the enemy's vast territory. This poor database meant uncertainty, which in turn produced widespread disagreement over the Kremlin's true military capabilities and intentions. Understandably preferring to be safe rather than sorry, the intelligence community almost always overestimated the military threat during those initial years.

As early as 1956, however, with the first U-2 flights across the Soviet Union, most intelligence analysts began to realize that the Community's estimates were inflated. Contrary to Air Force hype over a "bomber gap," U-2 photos failed to spot more than a few M-4 Bison or Bear bombers on Soviet airfields. Stimulated in part by a Soviet deception operation that consisted of flying the same few Bisons over and over again in different formations during the 1955 Moscow Aviation Day parade, the bomber gap was a bust. The Air Force had to revise its estimates downward. By this time, though, the arms race between the superpowers was under way. The United States had initiated "a massive effort to defend against attack by Soviet nuclear bombers. More than 2,500 aircraft and 10,000 missiles, many armed with nuclear warheads, were built and deployed at a cost of $330 billion (in adjusted 1995 dollars)."[73]

Not until the United States launched its CORONA satellites were intelligence officers and policymakers able to acquire compelling evidence of how grossly inflated their estimates had been. In 1962 the Community laid out the imagery-based facts in the "first NIE to quantify existing Soviet forces and capabilities with high confidence."[74] The photographs proved that the "missile gap" of 1957–61 favored the United States, just as had been the case with the bomber gap. Both scares had been fed by alarmist, self-serving estimates from Air Force intelligence, along with Soviet propaganda that conveyed the impression of a USSR stronger than it really was.

Thanks especially to more satellites in the skies with high-resolution cameras, complemented by radar sites in Turkey and Iran, improved analysis, and valuable documents from agents, the United States in the 1960s had a much more realistic comprehension of the Soviet threat than during the opening years of the Cold War. Before the Community began to criss-cross the heavens with CORONA satellites, it had disseminated "a series of contradictory estimates"[75] on the Soviet strategic posture—first overestimating, then underestimating the adversary's strength. The new TECHINT by no means resolved all the ambiguities. Fresh debates soon raged over Soviet ABMs, MIRVs, laser weapons, and a host of other arms developments. At least, though, the acrimony over the two weapons "gaps" of the early Cold War had been put to rest by the hard data of IMINT, with concomitant savings in U.S. weapons production. The true paltriness of the Soviet strategic bomber force revealed by imagery permitted, for instance, a cutback in Air Force fighter interceptors.[76]

Additional problems had contributed to the early intelligence overestimates of Soviet bombers and missiles, as well as a tendency to underestimate the production of Soviet ICBMs in the 1970s. First, the intelligence community attributed more geostrategic cunning to the Soviet leadership than later proved warranted. "There was less strategic rationale of why they did things than we thought," recalls an experienced DI analyst. "We tried to find an explanation. Well, some of the explanation had a lot to do with the defense industries."[77] The Soviets, too, had a military-industrial complex that lobbied effectively for weapons programs.

Second, good analysts could disagree over the meaning of weapons data, even when the numbers became more reliable in the 1960s. The Soviet Backfire bomber offers an illustration. The CIA called it a medium-range aircraft, which it probably was meant to be; it was also true, however, as the DIA argued, that if the Soviets operated the bomber in a certain manner—sending its pilots on a one-way, no-refueling, suicide mission—then clearly the range of the aircraft would be much longer. From this perspective, one could begin to think of the Backfire as an instrument of strategic warfare.

The Soviet SA-5 missile of 1963 provides another example. Was it a ballistic missile defense (BMD) or a more innocuous surface-to-air missile (SAM) system? The CIA rejected the BMD theory. Still, if the Soviets had been willing to deploy several thousand of these missiles around the USSR (which they were not, as it turned out), then the system could have become a ballistic-missile defense of sorts after all. Thus, an understanding of the full capabilities of various weapons systems required insight into the intentions of Soviet leaders. This in turn called for high-quality HUMINT from inside the Kremlin—a much more difficult proposition than "bean-counting" ICBM silos from the safety of outer space.

Third, in the case of overestimating Soviet ICBM production, the intelligence community discovered through experience that not every weapons system begun by the USSR made it into full production. Analysts would track the early stages of a Soviet weapons project, then lose it for a time as it fell behind deeper veils of secrecy during its developmental phase. Was the weapon a technology demonstration of some kind or a serious weapon for eventual deployment? To fill in the gap of missing data, the Community was forced to extrapolate forward on what *might* be happening to the system in terms of production. Sometimes a particular weapons system would be merely an experiment, eventually dropped altogether by the Kremlin (or at any rate reduced in its number of production units). Yet uncertainty on the American side woul[d] [often lead to] a worst-case projection, just to be prudent—or, in the case [of military intelli-]gence, perhaps to justify increased spending for U.S. [weapons systems.]

Fourth, through their use of disinformation the [Soviets contributed to peri-]odic analytic confusion within the American in[telligence community. "They] wanted us to believe they were stronger than they [really were," recalls a senior] CIA analyst.[78] The Soviets also practiced decep[tion as a means for jamming] American surveillance platforms. A classic, if comical, exam[ple was their use] of inflated rubber submarines set afloat in Soviet ports in hopes of tric[king U.S.] satellites into an overcount. The Kremlin would then offer to reduce i[ts total] number of "submarines" in exchange for reductions in real U.S. weapons systems. While this feeble ploy failed, other deception operations may have been more successful—a subject still under study by counterintelligence specialists.

Fifth, some topics were so tightly held by Moscow that accurate data were virtually impossible to obtain. The most important instance was nuclear weaponry. "That was impenetrable," recalls a CIA weapons expert. "We knew relatively little about the nuclear business."[79] Most of what the Community reported about Soviet nuclear warheads was based largely on hunches—with little empirical data—derived from a series of open-air tests conducted by the USSR in the 1960s. Analysts were forced to extrapolate from telemetry obtained during missile test flights, along with information on nuclear technology ferreted from open sources and occasional weapons specifications proffered by the rare defector with good access to military documents.

Chemical and biological weapons are further examples of Soviet threats about which the United States had (and continues to have) precious little intelligence. As a senior CIA analyst has said, "I think they got away with a lot of shit there."[80] In contrast, the Community believes it had theater forces in Eastern Europe well figured out, a success attributable (recalls a senior DI analyst) to a "tremendous amount of HUMINT."[81]

The underestimations of Soviet ICBMs in the early 1970s elicit a somewhat different explanation from former Community analysts. "We came to understand that we had underestimated some Soviet weapons developments," recalls one, "because we had not understood until the late 1970s just how much Western technology they had gotten their hands on and were beginning to introduce into their weapons."[82]

The answer to reducing estimating errors resided in better data and more analytical experience. In the opening days of the Cold War, disagreements over enemy armaments were much harder to resolve. As America's intelligence capabilities matured, however, a dispute over weapons data would stimulate a more focused collection effort, which in turn often settled the matter—especially by the 1980s, when coverage of the USSR had reached a high plateau of geographical thoroughness and all-source synergism. This was the case with the missile debate about MIRVs (multiple, independently targeted reentry vehicles) and laser beam weapons. Both challenges had been exaggerated by the Nixon administration and some allied private scientists—including the famous physicist Edward Teller, who insisted (wrongly) that Soviet submarines in the Atlantic possessed X-ray laser weapons that could shoot down American ICBMs soon after their launching.[83]

Perhaps the greatest contribution made by American intelligence with respect to the Soviet military target was to set some boundaries in the debate over the capabilities and intentions of the USSR. As a leading SOVA analyst has said, reflecting back on the experience of the Cold War, "Intelligence data can be wrong, it [sic] can be misleading, it can be incomplete; but, properly understood, it does set some bounds on what is possible."[84]

In the early days of estimating Soviet intentions, the most famous of the DDIs, Sherman Kent, would gather his senior intelligence wise men and sit back in his chair, pipe in hand, and ponder the objectives of the USSR. Then the "force estimators" would wander off and develop projections of Soviet military strength to fit this speculation.[85] In the second half of the Cold War, however, data—hard empirical measurements—became the currency of the realm. Opinions and intuition were insufficient; reliable intelligence from all the "INTs" set the parameters for analytic argument, in the way that IMINT had swept aside Air Force speculation about Bison bombers crowded wing to wing on Soviet airstrips.

INTELLIGENCE LESSONS FROM THE COLD WAR

America's secret agencies are indispensable, however many and troubling their mistakes were during the Cold War. The likelihood that they contributed significantly to warding off a third world war has been enough to earn their keep. This does not mean they are perfect, of course—that is why President Clinton and the Congress created a Commission on Intelligence in March 1995 to explore ways of improving them. The commission report will likely make 1996 a landmark year in the ongoing debate about the uses and accountability of intelligence. As citizens and their public servants in Washington carry on the quest for security within a democratic framework, some final observations on the last fifty years of the American experience may provide a few guideposts.

Collection

The United States remains on an upward technological arc in collection, far ahead of any other nation. New advances in TECHINT, among them near real-time imagery and improved all-source fusion, have brought substantial advances in America's understanding of global events. Yet prowess in IMINT, SIGINT, and MASINT is just one ingredient for success in accurately estimating foreign threats and opportunities. A nation must also carefully comb the world's burgeoning open sources, have well-placed agents abroad, and receive insightful reporting from its diplomats and military attachés.

One of the most vital achievements of U.S. intelligence, second only to the acuity of its vigilance against surprise attack, was to acquire empirical data on Soviet weaponry that set the boundaries for debate over the enemy's capabilities and intentions—a significant advance over the more speculative estimating that took place from 1945 through 1961. This building of weapons databases will continue to be a valued assignment for the intelligence community.

During the Cold War hard data on Soviet weaponry and compliance with arms control agreements were always more reliable than softer data on military intentions or on economic, political, and social questions. This may be less true now. Indeed, knowledge about Russian politics has exploded recently as a result of greater openness, while at the same time Moscow's research on biological weapons is shrouded in secrecy. As during the Cold War, large weapons systems will remain more easily identifiable and thus lead to greater consensus in interagency assessments than weapons of a more concealable character, such as chemical-biological agents.

Analysis

At times over the years, estimates have been contaminated by bias. During the Cold War critics accused military intelligence agencies (most notoriously in the Air Force) of embracing worst-case scenarios that supported funding for their own service countermeasures. At a higher political level, intelligence directors have bowed on occasion to the more powerful secretary of defense and to the wishes of the White House, bending analysis to fit political needs. Another problem has been the leveling of assessments. The search for interagency consensus on NIEs has sometimes watered down the intelligence product to the point of vague generalities of little use to policymakers.

The secret agencies have now learned how to make better use of the synergism that comes from all-source analysis; the walls between the INTs are slowly coming down. Moreover, increased contact between producers and consumers near the end of the Cold War (and since) improved the responsiveness of analysts to the informational needs of policy officers. This trend toward a closer relationship between intelligence and policy is apt to accelerate, for it is widely regarded as long overdue and the only way to make intelligence useful to high policy councils. "We have to run the risk of politicization to make certain that the intelligence being produced is relevant to the critical issues we face," stresses a former DDCI. "If you leave it to its own devices, the intelligence community will write scholarly tomes that can fill your walls."[86]

Many observers—especially in the academic community—would be quick to caution, however, that the politicization of intelligence is a far greater danger than its irrelevance. Clearly one of the most pressing challenges for the contemporary intelligence officer is to build rapport and trust with policy officers in order to understand their information needs without becoming their political handmaidens—a fine balancing act that the vast majority of U.S. intelligence officers already practice.

Counterintelligence and Covert Action

Until human beings become angels, treason will remain a threat to national goals. The United States, therefore, must redouble its efforts to secure those secrets that are central to the nation's defense while always maintaining the highest regard for civil liberties. Still, despite some unfortunate traitors of its own, America appears to have had a better record of counterintelligence success than its major allies.

Covert action will also continue to have a place in the repertoire of American foreign policy, but its dangers must not be overlooked. The (rarely) quiet option should be limited to the most extraordinary circumstances, remembering always that seldom can a nation expect to alter history through secret interventions abroad. Moreover, the long-term consequences of covert actions have seldom been foreseen—and have often proved detrimental to the United States.

THE LIMITS OF INTELLIGENCE

These reflections come to a close with three observations: on mysteries, surprises, and the obstinacy of power. However strong the intelligence contribution may be to the affairs of government, some kinds of information will remain elusive, whether the budget for spying is $30 billion or $130 billion. The mysteries of the world vastly outnumber the secrets; and even some secrets are nearly impossible to pry loose from their hiding places.

Every nation must endure a gap between what it may want to know and what it can actually know. The world is simply too large for any one country to sift. Consider these four individuals who from time to time over the past two decades have been the source of great aggravation to the United States: Mu'ammar Qadhafi, the leader of Libya; Gen. Manuel Antonio Noriega, the former president of Panama; Saddam Hussein, the dictator of Iraq; and Mohammed Farah Aidid, a prominent warlord in Somalia. At key moments the top policy officers of the United States wanted to know the precise whereabouts of these foreign leaders, yet in each case the intelligence agencies were unable to locate them. Each of the foreign leaders had proved craftier than anticipated; each knew many places to hide within his own country; each had well-trained security guards knowledgeable in evasive tactics.

When asked why the intelligence community had been stymied in its searches for Qadhafi and Hussein, a CIA official responded, "We had no vibrant HUMINT source near them to keep us informed of their whereabouts; and, furthermore, their op-sec [operational security] people are masters."[87] Nor today does the United States have much knowledge about the present leader of North Korea, even though this renegade state is considered an intelligence target of the first rank. Is Kim Chong-il a clown, a Caligula, or something in between? A reliable answer has yet to surface on the nation's information stream—from any of its tributaries, open or secret.

All nations will remain vulnerable to intelligence surprises. The desire to know whether the Kremlin intended to invade Czechoslovakia in 1968 and exactly when, or if, Soviet army officers would try to topple President Gorbachev in 1991 is simply unrealistic when the protagonists themselves are unsure until the eleventh hour.

Virtually everyone was surprised by the precipitous fall of the Soviet Union. "While CIA could forecast a looming showdown between the political and economic reform elements and the old line power apparatus, it was not inevitable that the August 1991 reactionary 'putsch' would turn out as it did," a former DDI observes. "There was in fact a period when the outcome hung in the balance, pending the critical 'swing' of the key military units and leaders."[88] Simply but eloquently, Dean Rusk has commented on this vexing reality: "Providence has not provided human beings with the capacity to pierce the fog of the future."[89]

Intelligence can talk truth to power, but power may refuse to listen. Rather than an open mind, policymakers often turn a deaf ear to the secret agencies.

The Johnson and Nixon administrations cast aside warnings from the CIA that the Vietnam War could become a swamp for American foreign policy. During the final throes of the Cold War the Reagan and Bush administrations refused to accept the notion of genuine reform inside the world's leading Communist regime—until the evidence became irrefutable. Here is the central paradox of intelligence: despite the approval of billion-dollar expenditures on incredible machines and skillful agents to gather information from around the globe, those who make decisions will often ignore the findings. This occurs for political or ideological reasons, or sometimes because those at the pinnacle of government are too busy or harried to take in new information. Or they may become over-confident, perhaps to the point of arrogance, in the belief that they can serve as their own directors of central intelligence.

The glittering spy machines have been deficient from time to time, but it is the human dimension that has most confounded the fit between information and decision. Human beings—so laudable for their sense of ethics, for the check they provide against hardware that fails, for their ability to reflect and use judgment—remain susceptible to self-delusion and conceit and liable to reject or distort the very information they profess to value.

DIRECTORS OF CENTRAL INTELLIGENCE

1946	Sidney W. Souers
	Rear Admiral, U.S. Naval Reserve
1946–47	Hoyt S. Vandenberg
	Lieutenant General, U.S. Army (Army Air Forces)
1947–50	Roscoe H. Hillenkoetter
	Rear Admiral, U.S. Navy
1950–53	Walter Bedell Smith
	General, U.S. Army
1953–61	Allen Dulles
1961–65	John McCone
1965–66	William F. Raborn, Jr.
	Vice Admiral, U.S. Navy (Retired)
1966–73	Richard Helms
1973	James R. Schlesinger
1973–76	William E. Colby
1976–77	George Bush
1977–81	Stansfield Turner
	Admiral, U.S. Navy (Retired)

1981–87	William J. Casey
1987–91	William H. Webster
1991–93	Robert M. Gates
1993–95	R. James Woolsey
1995–97	John M. Deutch
1997–	George J. Tenet

Chairs, Senate Select Committee on Intelligence

1976–77	Daniel K. Inouye (D, Hawaii)
1977–81	Birch Bayh (D, Indiana)
1981–85	Barry Goldwater (R, Arizona)
1985–87	David Durenberger (R, Minnesota)
1987–93	David L. Boren (D, Oklahoma)
1993–95	Dennis DeConcini (D, Arizona)
1995–97	Arlen Specter (R, Pennsylvania)
1997–	Richard C. Shelby (R, Alabama)

Chairs, House Permanent Select Committee on Intelligence

1977–85	Edward P. Boland (D, Massachusetts)
1985–87	Lee H. Hamilton (D, Indiana)
1987–89	Louis Stokes (D, Ohio)
1989–91	Anthony C. Beilenson (D, California)
1991–93	Dave McCurdy (D, Oklahoma)
1993–95	Dan Glickman (D, Kansas)
1995–97	Larry Combest (R, Texas)
1997–	Porter J. Goss (R, Florida)

CHRONOLOGY OF THE CUBAN MISSILE CRISIS OF 1962

August 10	DCI McCone dictates memo to President John F. Kennedy expressing his belief that medium-range ballistic missiles (MRBMs) will be deployed in Cuba
August 31	Sen. Kenneth B. Keating tells the Senate that there is evidence of Soviet missile installations in Cuba
September 15	The first SS-4 MRBMs arrive in Cuba
September 19	An SNIE concludes that the Soviets would not place missiles in Cuba
September 21	Soviets warn that an American attack on Cuba would mean war with the USSR
September 31	First reliable HUMINT suggesting presence of MRBMs
October 9	President Kennedy approves a U-2 reconnaissance flight over western Cuba, which is delayed by bad weather
October 14	First U-2 flight over western Cuba
October 15	Photointerpreters identify MRBMs in Cuba
October 16	First unofficial meeting of Executive Committee (EXCOMM)
October 20	President Kennedy approves a quarantine instead of an airstrike

October 22	Authority for pre-delegated control over tactical nuclear warheads evidently rescinded by Moscow*
October 23	First official meeting of EXCOMM
October 26	Strategic warheads moved from storage sites and placed near launch vehicles in Cuba
October 27	Some EXCOMM members continue to urge invasion of Cuba
October 28	Soviet leader Nikita Khrushchev announces that he will dismantle MRBMs
November 31	President Kennedy terminates quarantine

*The research on whether pre-delegation happened for certain and, if so, whether it was rescinded, remains inconclusive. Scholars who have examine the matter closely conclude that for each question the answer is "probably." See James G. Blight, Bruce J. Allyn, and David A. Welch, *Cuba on the Brink: Castro, the Missile Crisis, and the Soviet Collapse* (New York: Pantheon Books, 1993).

NOTES

PREFACE

1. The discipline of intelligence studies is expanding so rapidly that it is a challenge to keep up with all the latest research, separating out the reliable works from the much larger outpouring of dubious speculation about America's secret agencies. The "literature reviews" by authors who purport to have read carefully across the field have to be treated gingerly as well, since some display only a limited understanding of the key works (e.g., John Ferris, "Coming in from the Cold War: The Historiography of American Intelligence, 1945–1990," *Diplomatic History* 89 [Winter 1995], 87–115). Even careful appraisals of the "security studies" discipline frequently overlook the importance of intelligence research. In one lengthy review the author fails to mention even a single publication on intelligence (Stephen M. Walt, "The Renaissance of Security Studies," *International Studies Quarterly* 35 [June 1991], 211–39).

Fortunately for the intelligence researcher, the terrain does have some reliable trail markers. The best of the recent bibliographies include: Marjorie W. Cline et al., *A Scholar's Guide to Intelligence Literature: Bibliography of the Russell J. Bowen Collection in the Joseph Mark Lauinger Memorial Library, Georgetown University* (Frederick, Md.: University Publications of America, 1983); George C. Constantinides, *Intelligence and Espionage: An Analytical Bibliography* (Boulder, Colo.:

Westview Press, 1981); Mark M. Lowenthal, *The U.S. Intelligence Community: An Annotated Bibliography* (New York: Garland, 1994); Neal H. Petersen, *American Intelligence, 1775–1990: A Bibliographical Guide* (Claremont, Calif.: Regina Books, 1992); and, from the dean of intelligence bibliographers and a former CIA legislative counsel, Walter Pforzheimer, ed., *Bibliography of Intelligence Literature* (Washington, D.C.: Defense Intelligence College, 1985).

The student of intelligence and national security will find assistance, too, in the pages of specialized journals that publish research and reflections on intelligence. For an excellent guide to this literature, see Hayden B. Peake, *The Reader's Guide to Intelligence Periodicals* (Washington, D.C.: National Intelligence Book Center Press, 1992). Among the best of these periodicals are the *American Intelligence Journal, Intelligence and National Security,* and the *International Journal of Intelligence and Counterintelligence.* Now and then the *American Journal of International Law, Diplomatic History, Foreign Affairs,* and *Foreign Policy* will also publish something on intelligence and, rarer still, the mainstream academic quarterlies in American history and political science will make a contribution.

A decade ago Lawrence Freedman noted that in the past academe had viewed intelligence studies "as being not quite nice, notoriously frustrating when it comes to sources and full of sensational exposes." He added, however, that as more material became available and scholars began to appreciate the significance of intelligence in twentieth-century diplomatic and military history, research "moved ahead by leaps and bounds" (*U.S. Intelligence and the Soviet Strategic Threat,* 2d ed. [Princeton: Princeton University Press, 1986], xiii). The historian Ernest R. May discerns further, if slow, progress ("Studying and Teaching Intelligence," *Studies in Intelligence* 38 [1995], 1–5). Indeed over the past ten years the importance of intelligence as a serious field of inquiry does seem to have gained credibility, and its rightful place in the field of national security studies is likely to grow.

CHAPTER 1: THE MEANINGS AND METHODS OF INTELLIGENCE

1. *Fact Book on Intelligence,* Office of Public Affairs, Central Intelligence Agency, September 1991, p. 13. A thoughtful intelligence scholar and former commandant of the Defense Intelligence College offers this similar definition: "Intelligence is a dedicated and usually tailored foreign information support service for government policymakers, planners, and implementors" (John Macartney, "How Do *You* Define Intelligence?" *The Intelligencer,* a newsletter for intelligence scholars published by the Association of Former Intelligence Officers, January 1995, pp. 3–4). See also the useful overview of intelligence prepared by the DCI's Public Affairs Staff, entitled *A Consumer's Guide to Intelligence,* July 1995 (Central Intelligence Agency, PAS 94–00010).

2. Abram N. Shulsky, *Silent Warfare: Understanding the World of Intelligence,* 2d ed., revised by Gary J. Schmitt (New York: Brassey's US, 1993), 193. See also Abram Shulsky and Jennifer Sims, "What Is Intelligence?" Monograph, Working Group on Intelligence Reform, 1993. In *Silent Warfare* Shulsky refers to intelligence as "the hard and reliable information that [the secret agencies are] able to obtain and that it

would be irresponsible to ignore" (p. 30). In contrast, Sims recommends a broader definition—"information collected, organized, or analyzed on behalf of actors or decision makers" (p. 2)—which would seem to include the Congressional Research Service as well as the CIA. Closer to the Shulsky perspective, the respected British scholar of intelligence Michael Herman underscores the point that the world contains "subjects specially protected from normal means of information collection. Secret intelligence is the art of penetrating this special protection" ("Intelligence for Beginners," unpublished paper, 1990, p. 7).

3. Although I have never served in an intelligence agency, I have been on the staff of the Senate and House intelligence oversight committees, as well as the Intelligence Commission of 1995, and in these capacities I have read a number of "value-added" studies that remain classified. (No information from classified sources is included in this book.)

4. Author's interview, Washington, D.C., July 17, 1994.

5. The "cycle" described here is less a sequence of discrete phases, one cleanly ending as the next begins, than a complicated matrix of ongoing interactions among intelligence officers and policymakers based on new information. See Loch K. Johnson, *America's Secret Power: The CIA in a Democratic Society* (New York: Oxford University Press, 1989), 77–78; Arthur S. Hulnick, "The Intelligence Producer-Policy Consumer Linkage: A Theoretical Approach," *Intelligence and National Security* 1 (May 1986), 212–233.

6. See Bruce D. Berkowitz and Allan E. Goodman, *Strategic Intelligence for American National Security* (Princeton: Princeton University Press, 1986).

7. See Arthur A. Zuehlke, Jr. "What Is Counterintelligence?" in Roy Godson, ed., *Intelligence Requirements for the 1980s: Counterintelligence* (Washington, D.C.: National Strategy Information Center, 1980), 13–39.

8. See Gregory F. Treverton, *Covert Action: The Limits of Intervention in the Postwar World* (New York: Basic Books, 1987).

9. See Christopher Andrew, *For the President's Eyes Only: Secret Intelligence and the American Presidency from Washington to Bush* (New York: HarperCollins, 1995).

10. On the early history of U.S. intelligence, see William R. Corson, *The Armies of Ignorance: The Rise of the American Intelligence Empire* (New York: Dial, 1977).

11. See R. Harris Smith, *OSS: The Secret History of America's First Central Intelligence Agency* (Berkeley: University of California, 1972).

12. Dean Rusk, testimony, *Hearings, Government Operations Subcommittee on National Security Staff and Operations*, U.S. Senate, December 11, 1963, p. 390.

13. See Roberta Wohlstetter, *Pearl Harbor: Warning and Decision* (Stanford: Stanford University Press, 1962); Rear Adm. Edwin T. Layton, with Captain Roger Pineau and John Costello, *"And I Was There" : Pearl Harbor and Midway—Breaking the Secrets* (New York: Morrow, 1985); Seth W. Richardson, "Why Were We Caught Napping at Pearl Harbor?" *Saturday Evening Post* (May 24, 1947), 79–80; and Alvin D. Coox, "Pearl Harbor," in Noble Frankland and Christopher Dowling, eds., *Decisive Battles of the Twentieth Century* (New York: McKay, 1976), 148.

14. See *Aerospace Daily*, February 24, 1994, p. 292; "Deutch Plans New Direction for CIA," *Jane's Defence Weekly*, July 8, 1995, p. 19; Johnson, *America's Secret Power*, n1:280–81; Walter Pincus, "White House Labors to Redefine Role of Intelligence Community," *Washington Post*, June 13, 1994, A8; and Jim Weiner, "$28 Billion Spying Budget Is Made Public by Mistake," *New York Times*, November 5, 1994, p. 54.

15. On the responsibilities of the DCI, see Glenn Hastadt, "Controlling Intelligence: The Role of the DCI," *International Journal of Intelligence and Counterintelligence* 1 (1986), 25–40; and Stafford T. Thomas, "On the Selection of Directors of Central Intelligence," *Southeastern Political Review* 9 (Spring 1984), 1–59, and "Presidential Styles and DCI Selection," *International Journal of Intelligence and Counterintelligence* 7 (Summer 1994), 175–98.

16. On the CIA, see Johnson, *America's Secret Power;* Rhodri Jeffreys-Jones, *The CIA and American Democracy* (New Haven: Yale University Press, 1989); Victor L. Marchetti and John D. Marks, *The CIA and the Cult of Intelligence* (New York: Knopf, 1994): and John Ranelagh, *The Agency: The Rise and Decline of the CIA* (New York: Knopf, 1974).

17. On the NSA, see James Bamford, *The Puzzle Palace* (New York: Houghton Mifflin, 1984), and David Kahn, *The Codebreakers: The Story of Secret Writing* (New York: Macmillan, 1967). On DIA, see Patrick Neil Mescall, "A Creature of Compromise: The Establishment of the DIA," *International Journal of Intelligence and Counterintelligence* 7 (Fall 1994), 251–74.

18. On FBI intelligence, see John T. Elliff, *The Reform of FBI Intelligence Operations* (Princeton: Princeton University Press, 1979); William W. Keller, *The Liberals and J. Edgar Hoover* (Princeton: Princeton University Press, 1989); and Sanford Ungar, *FBI* (Boston: Atlantic Monthly, 1975).

19. For excellent overviews of the intelligence community, see Mark M. Lowenthal, *U.S. Intelligence: Evolution and Anatomy*, 2d ed. (London: Praeger, 1992); Harry Howe Ransom, *The Intelligence Establishment* (Cambridge, Mass.: Harvard University Press, 1970); and Jeffrey T. Richelson, *The U.S. Intelligence Community*, 3d ed. (Boulder, Colo.: Westview, 1995).

20. Remarks by President George Bush at CIA, November 12, 1991.

21. Remarks to the CIA, July 14, 1995.

22. Dean Rusk, testimony, U.S. Senate, December 11, 1963, p. 390.

23. The hearings were in March 1994; see Eric Schmitt, "Cost-Minded Lawmakers Are Challenging a 2-War Doctrine," *New York Times*, March 10, 1995, A22.

24. Ronald Steel, *Temptations of a Superpower* (Cambridge, Mass.: Harvard University Press, 1995), 103.

25. See "Signals Intelligence & Information War," *American Intelligence Journal* 15 (Spring/Summer 1994).

26. For accounts of airborne and spaceborne intelligence collectors, see the fascinating works by William E. Burrows, *Deep Black: Space Espionage and National Security* (New York: Random, 1986); Dino A. Brugioni, *From Balloons to Blackbirds: Re-*

connaissance, Surveillance and Imagery Intelligence, Professional Intelligence Series, 9 (McLean, Va.: Association of Former Intelligence Officers, 1993); and Jeffrey T. Richelson, America's Secret Eyes in Space: The U.S. Keyhole Spy Satellite Program (New York: Harper & Row, 1990).

27. Raymond L. Garthoff, Assessing the Adversary: Estimates by the Eisenhower Administration of Soviet Intentions and Capabilities (Washington, D.C.: Brookings Institution, 1991), 42.

28. Harold Brown, testimony, Congressional hearings on SALT II in 1979, cited in Burrows, Deep Black, 334–335.

29. Richelson has commented on the importance of these developments in the history of technical espionage: "In the first year of their operation, the CORONA satellites helped dispel America's fear of Soviet strategic superiority that had haunted many Americans since the launch of Sputnik. Since then, they have allowed knowledge to prevail over fear in assessing Soviet capabilities. And the arms limitation agreements of past, present, and future would not be possible without such devices to verify compliance." America's Secret Eyes in Space, vi.

30. Author's interview with senior intelligence analyst, Langley, Va., June 11, 1984.

31. See Kenneth E. Greer, "Corona," Studies in Intelligence, Supplement, 17 (Spring 1973), 1–37, reprinted in Kevin C. Ruffner, ed., Corona: America's First Satellite Program, CIA History Staff, Center for the Study of Intelligence, Central Intelligence Agency, Washington, D.C., 1995, pp. 3–39.

32. On the importance of overt intelligence collection, see "Open Source Intelligence: A Special Edition," American Intelligence Journal 14 (Spring/Summer 1993); and Robert David Steele, "A Critical Evaluation of U.S. National Intelligence Capabilities," International Journal of Intelligence and Counterintelligence 6 (Summer 1993), 173–94, and "Reinventing Intelligence: Holy Grail or Mission Impossible?" International Journal of Intelligence and Counterintelligence 7 (Summer 1994), 199–204.

33. See "Human Source Intelligence: HUMINT," American Intelligence Journal 14 (Autumn/Winter 1992–93).

34. Ephraim Kam, Surprise Attack (Cambridge, Mass.: Harvard University Press, 1988), 62.

35. Remarks to CIA staff, Langley, Va., July 14, 1995.

36. Quoted in Steve Emerson, Secret Warriors: Inside the Covert Military Operations of the Reagan Era (New York: Putnam's, 1988), 20.

37. Author's interview, Washington, D.C., July 14, 1994.

38. Quoted in Burrows, Deep Black, 250.

39. Author's Interview with senior NSA official, July 15, 1994.

40. Ibid.

41. Author's interview with an official in the Office of Public Affairs, Central Intelligence Agency, February 7, 1995.

42. On the process by which estimates are produced, see Berkowitz and Goodman, Strategic Intelligence; Lawrence Freedman, U.S. Intelligence and the Soviet Strate-

gic Threat (Princeton: Princeton University Press, 1986); and John Prados, *The Soviet Estimate: U.S. Intelligence and Russian Military Strength* (New York: Dial Press, 1982). An average NIE takes about eight months to draft—considered by critics far too long for this form of intelligence reporting to have much usefulness to policymakers.

43. *A Consumer's Guide to Intelligence,* July 1995, p. 29.

44. John Sontag, remarks, "Intelligence Research—Approaches to Analysis," Panel IV, Symposium on Teaching Intelligence, Central Intelligence Agency (author's tape-recording).

45. Oral history with Dean Rusk, conducted by Richard Rusk and Loch K. Johnson, December 15, 1984, Athens, Ga.

46. Remarks to the author, Chicago, March 14, 1994.

47. Allan E. Goodman, Symposium on Teaching Intelligence, 1993, author's tape-recording.

48. Author's interview with senior DI official, Washington, D.C., February 7, 1995.

49. Joseph S. Nye, Jr., Symposium on Teaching Intelligence, 1993.

50. David D. Gries, Symposium on Teaching Intelligence, 1993.

51. Author's interview with Richard Helms, Washington, D.C., December 12, 1990.

52. Author's interview with Robert M. Gates, Washington, D.C., March 28, 1994.

53. Jack Davis, "A Policymaker's Perspective on Intelligence Analysis," interview with Ambassador Robert D. Blackwill, *Studies in Intelligence* 38 (1995), 7–15.

54. Lawrence Freedman, *U.S. Intelligence and the Soviet Strategic Threat* (Princeton: Princeton University Press, 1986), 188.

55. Quoted in Walter Pincus, "Senate Republicans Question Elevation of CIA Director to the Cabinet," *Washington Post,* March 15, 1995, A4.

56. Adm. Bobby Ray Inman, interview, *U.S. News & World Report,* December 20, 1982, p. 37. For descriptions by two leading analysts about how they and their colleagues sought to maintain high professional standards in the CIA's Intelligence Directorate, see Douglas J. MacEachin (former deputy director of intelligence), "The Tradecraft of Analysis: Challenge and Change in the CIA," Monograph, Working Group on Intelligence Reform, Consortium for the Study of Intelligence, Washington, D.C., 1984, p. 35; and Jack Davis, "Analysis and Policy: The Kent-Kendall Debate of 1949," *Studies in Intelligence* 36 (1992), *The Challenge of Opportunity Analysis,* Monograph, Center for the Study of Intelligence, 1992, and "Changes in Analytic Tradecraft in CIA's Directorate of Intelligence," paper, International Studies Association, annual meeting, Chicago, February 15, 1995.

57. Stewart A. Baker, "Should Spies Be Cops?" *Foreign Policy* 97 (Winter 1994–95), 43.

58. Author's interview with Pentagon intelligence official, Washington, D.C., July 14, 1994.

59. Gen. H. Norman Schwarzkopf, testimony, Armed Services Committee, U.S. Senate, June 12, 1991.

60. Lt. Gen. James R. Clapper, Jr., "Imagery—Gulf War Lessons Learned and Future Challenges," *American Intelligence Journal* 13 (Winter/Spring 1992), 17.

61. Quoted by Steve Komarow, "'Lesser Conflicts': Big Defense Challenge," *USA Today,* November 1, 1994, p. 8.
62. Quoted by Davis, "Policymaker's Perspective," 8, 10.
63. "Foreign and Military Intelligence," *Final Report,* Vol. 1, Select Committee on Intelligence (Church Committee), U.S. Senate, 1976, p. 78.
64. Peter Wyden, *Bay of Pigs: The Untold Story* (New York: Simon & Schuster, 1979), 315. Former INR Director Thomas Hughes accuses the Kennedy administration's secretary of defense, Robert S. McNamara, of routinely practicing "intimidation" against the bureaucracy with respect to Vietnam; he also cites the journalist David Halberstam's charge that the administration—and especially McNamara—"trashed anyone who tried to report [intelligence] honestly or to dissent." Thomas L. Hughes, "Experiencing McNamara," *Foreign Policy* 100 (Fall 1995), 165, 166.
65. Victor A. Thompson, *Modern Organization* (New York: Knopf, 1961), 91.
66. Steve Chan, "Intelligence of Stupidity: Understanding Failures in Strategic Warning," *American Political Science Review* 73 (March 1979), 178.
67. Thomas L. Hughes, *The Fate of Facts in a World of Men: Foreign Policy and Intelligence-Making,* Headline Series, No. 233 (Washington, D.C.: Foreign Policy Association, 1976), 24.
68. Garthoff, "The Eisenhower Administration," 16, 50–51.
69. Dr. Ray S. Cline in Roy Godson, ed., *Intelligence Requirements for the 1980s: Analysis and Estimates* (Washington, D.C.: National Strategy Information Center, 1980), 79.
70. Based on remarks by senior CIA officials at the Conference on Intelligence, Policy and Process, U.S. Air Force Academy, Colorado Springs, June 6, 1984, and at the Conference on U.S. Intelligence: The Organization and the Profession, Central Intelligence Agency, Langley, Va., June 11, 1984, as well as David M. Kennedy, "The Reagan Administration and the Soviet Pipeline Embargo," Case No. C16–91–1016.0, Intelligence and Policy Program, Kennedy School of Government, Harvard University, 1991, and Seymour M. Hersh, *The Target Is Destroyed* (New York: Vintage, 1987), on the Korean airline shootdown. For additional criticisms of a Reagan Administration bias toward "intelligence to please," see Lee H. Hamilton (chair of the House Permanent Select Committee on Intelligence), "View from the Hill," in *Extracts from Studies in Intelligence* (Langley, Va.: Central Intelligence Agency, September 1987), 68; and the testimony of Secretary of State George P. Shultz, *Hearings of the Joint Select Committee to Investigate Covert Arms Transactions with Iran,* U.S. Congress, July 1987.
71. Hughes, *Fate of Facts,* p. 45.
72. James C. Thomson, Jr., "How Could Vietnam Happen?" *Atlantic Monthly* 221 (April 1968), 52, original emphasis.
73. Yaacov Vertzberger, "Bureaucratic-Organizational Politics and Information Processing in a Developing State," *International Studies Quarterly* 28 (March 1984), 87–88.

74. Theodore H. White, "Weinberger on the Ramparts," *New York Times Magazine* (February 6, 1983), 24.
75. Thomson, "Vietnam," 50.
76. Symposium on Teaching Intelligence, 1993.
77. Quoted by Davis, "Policymaker's Perspective," 12.
78. For a model that depicts the complexity of the American foreign policy process, see Loch K. Johnson, *America as a World Power: Foreign Policy in a Constitutional Framework*, 2d ed. (New York: McGraw-Hill, 1995), 47.
79. Dr. Robert J. Hermann, "Advancing Technology: Collateral Effects on Intelligence," *American Intelligence Journal*, 15 (Autumn/Winter 1994), 10.

CHAPTER 2: THE EVOLUTION OF THE INTELLIGENCE MISSIONS

1. See, respectively, Daniel P. Moynihan, "Do We Still Need the C.I.A.? The State Dept. Can Do the Job," *New York Times*, May 19, 1991, E17; and "Indiana Jim and the Temple of Spooks," *The Economist* 326 (March 20, 1993), p. 34, citing the Clinton Administration's DCI, R. James Woolsey, on new global dangers facing the United States.
2. An experienced intelligence overseer notes, however, that "today collection operations are more controversial—especially against friendly governments." R. Britt Snider, Chief Counsel, Senate Select Committee on Intelligence, remarks, International Studies Association, annual meeting, March 28, 1994, Washington, D.C. (author's notes).
3. The trend lines in the figures presented in this chapter, along with the generalizations that accompany them, are based on extensive interviews from 1975 to 1994 with intelligence officers throughout the Community—well over four hundred (most of whom insisted on anonymity). These interviews have been supplemented by a search through every major scholarly and reliable journalistic work, as well as the unclassified government documents, on intelligence. The most important are Christopher Andrew, *For the President's Eyes Only: Secret Intelligence and the American Presidency from Washington to Bush* (New York: HarperCollins, 1995); James Bamford, *The Puzzle Palace* (Boston: Houghton Mifflin, 1984); Bruce D. Berkowitz and Allan E. Goodman, *Strategic Intelligence for American National Security* (Princeton: Princeton University Press, 1989); Adda B. Bozeman, *Strategic Intelligence and Statecraft* (New York: Brassey's, 1992); Dino A. Brugloni, *From Balloons to Blackbirds*, Intelligence Profession Series, no. 9, 1993; William E. Burrows, *Deep Space: Space Espionage and National Security* (New York: Random House, 1986); Ray S. Cline, *Secrets, Spies and Scholars* (Washington, D.C.: Acropolis Books, 1976); William E. Colby and Peter Forbath, *Honorable Men: My Life in the CIA* (New York: Simon and Schuster, 1978); Arthur B. Darling, *The Central Intelligence Agency: An Instrument of Government to 1950* (University Park: Pennsylvania State University Press, 1990); Christopher Felix, *A Short Course in the Secret War* (New York: Dell, 1963); Lawrence Freedman, *U.S. Intelligence and the Soviet Strategic Threat*, 2d ed. (Princeton: Princeton University Press, 1986); Roy Godson, with Richard Kerr and

Ernest May, "Covert Action in the 1990s," Working Group on Intelligence Reform, Consortium for the Study of Intelligence, Washington, D.C., 1993; Allan E. Goodman and Bruce D. Berkowitz, background paper, in *The Need to Know*, Report of the Twentieth Century Fund Task Force on Covert Action and American Democracy, New York, 1992, pp. 25–80; Rhodri Jeffreys-Jones, *The CIA and American Democracy* (New Haven: Yale University Press, 1989); Loch K. Johnson, *America's Secret Power: The CIA in a Democratic Society* (New York: Oxford University Press, 1989); David Kahn, *The Codebreakers: The Story of Secret Writing* (New York: MacMillan, 1967); Ann Karalekas, "History of the Central Intelligence Agency," in *Supplementary Detailed Staff Reports on Foreign and Military Intelligence,* Church Committee, *Final Report,* Book 4, Senate Rept. No. 94–755, 94th Cong., 2d Sess, 1976; Victor L. Marchetti and John D. Marks, *The CIA and the Cult of Intelligence* (New York: Laurel Edition, 1980); U.S. House Select Committee to Investigate Intelligence Activities (Pike Committee), *Final Report* (excerpts), still classified and printed without authorization in "The CIA Report the President Doesn't Want You to Read: The Pike Papers," *Village Voice,* February 16, 1976, pp. 69–92; Thomas Powers, *The Man Who Kept the Secrets: Richard Helms and the CIA* (New York: Knopf, 1979); John Prados, *Presidents' Secret Wars: CIA and Pentagon Covert Operations Since World War II* (New York: William Morrow, 1986); John Ranelagh, *The Agency: The Rise and Decline of the CIA,* rev. ed. (New York: Simon and Schuster, 1987); Harry Howe Ransom, *The Intelligence Establishment* (Cambridge, Mass.: Harvard University Press, 1970); Jeffrey T. Richelson, *The U.S. Intelligence Community,* 2d ed. (Cambridge, Mass.: Ballinger, 1989) and *America's Secret Eyes in Space: The U.S. Keyhole Spy Satellite Program* (New York: Harper and Row, 1990); Harry Rositzke, *The CIA's Secret Operations: Espionage, Counterespionage and Covert Action* (New York: Reader's Digest Press, 1977); Harrison Salisbury, "Interview with William Colby: The Role of the CIA and That of the Press," *Behind the Lines,* WNET Television, New York, 1975; Theodore Shackley, *The Third Option: An American View of Counterinsurgency* (Pleasantville, N.Y.: Reader's Digest, 1981); "Signals Intelligence and Information War," *American Intelligence Journal,* special issue, Spring/Summer 1994; Gregory F. Treverton, *Covert Action* (New York: Basic, 1987); Stansfield Turner, *Secrecy and Democracy: The CIA in Transition* (Boston: Houghton Mifflin, 1985); U.S. Senate Select Committee to Study Governmental Operations with Respect to Intelligence Activities (Church Committee), *Final Report: Foreign and Military Intelligence,* Book 1, Senate Rept. No. 94–755, 94th Cong., 2d Sess., 1976, and "Alleged Assassination Plots Involving Foreign Leaders," *Interim Report,* S. Rept. No. 94–465 (Washington, D.C.: Government Printing Office, November 20, 1975); and Michael Warner, ed., *CIA Cold War Records: The CIA Under Harry Truman* (Washington,D.C.: Center for the Study of Intelligence, Central Intelligence Agency, 1994). For a thorough bibliography, see Mark M. Lowenthal, *U.S. Intelligence Community: A Bibliography* (New York: Garland, 1994).

From this research, I have attempted to arrive at a judgment regarding the Community's emphasis on various missions and responsibilities each year since 1947.

The graph lines roughly depict the priorities—a "best guess" based on the open-source literature and interviews with insiders. In making these judgments, I have heeded the sage advice of a perceptive scholar of the CIA's history: "The number and extent of the activities undertaken are far less important than the impact which those activities had on the Agency's institutional *identity*—the way people with [the various internal components of the CIA] *perceived* the Agency's primary mission, and *the way policymakers regarded its contribution* to the process of government." Karalekas, "History of the Central Intelligence Agency," p. 45, emphasis added.

4. For an assertion that HUMINT dropped in priority under DCI John McCone (1961–65), see Jeffreys-Jones, *CIA and American Democracy*, 135.

5. See, for example, Marchetti and Marks, *Cult of Intelligence*, 20; Ranelagh, *The Agency*, 220.

6. See Marchetti and Marks, *Cult of Intelligence*, e.g., 68. The trend lines for analysis and HUMINT budgeting presented by Berkowitz and Goodman generally track the ups and downs profiled here, but they place funding for analysis consistently somewhat ahead of funding for HUMINT from 1950 through 1985. See Berkowitz and Goodman, *Strategic Intelligence*, 144.

7. Interview with William C. Sullivan, conducted by John T. Elliff and the author, Boston, June 3, 1976.

8. John I. Millis, letter from Professional Staff Member, Permanent Select Committee on Intelligence, U.S. House of Representatives, to the *Wall Street Journal*, October 12, 1994, A15. An important intelligence official, Richard M. Bissell, Jr. (who played a key role in the development of airborne intelligence reconnaissance), considered HUMINT far inferior in its product to spy planes, satellites, and SIGINT. See Marchetti and Marks, *Cult of Intelligence*, 330.

9. Richard C. Snyder and Edgar S. Furniss, Jr., *American Foreign Policy: Formulation, Principles, and Programs* (New York: Rinehart, 1954), 233. The other functions were to advise the NSC and, a notorious catch-all phrase that opened the door to aggressive covert action and counterespionage operations, "to perform any other duties and functions assigned to it by the [National] Security Council." See the National Security Act of 1947, 50 U.S.C. sec. 403.

10. Tom Mangold, *Cold Warrior* (New York: Simon and Schuster, 1991); David C. Martin, *Wilderness of Mirrors* (New York: Harper and Row, 1980); Robin W. Winks, *Cloak and Gown: Scholars in the Secret War, 1939–1961* (New York: William Morrow, 1987), chap. 6; and David Wise, *Molehunt* (New York: Random House, 1992).

11. John T. Elliff and Loch K. Johnson, "Counterintelligence," Church Committee, *Final Report*, Book 1, 163–78.

12. Author's interviews with James Angleton, Washington, D.C., 1976–77. See also James Angleton and Charles J. V. Murphy, "On the Separation of Church and State," *American Cause, Special Report*, American Security Council, Washington, D.C., June 1976.

13. Author's telephone conversation with James Angleton, September 20, 1980.

14. See *United States Counterintelligence and Security Concerns—1986*, Report No.

100–5, Permanent Select Committee on Intelligence, U.S. House, 100th Cong., 1st. Sess., 1987; and David Wise, *The Spy Who Got Away* (New York: Random House, 1988).

15. See especially Karalekas, "History of the Central Intelligence Agency"; Ranelagh, *The Agency;* Warner, *CIA Cold War Records.*

16. Ranelagh, *The Agency,* 220. See also Harry Howe Ransom, *Can American Democracy Survive Cold War?* (Garden City, N.Y.: Doubleday, 1963), which has a case history of U.S. intelligence in the Korean War.

17. See Church Committee, *Final Report,* Book 1.

18. See Colby and Forbath, *Honorable Men;* David Wise and Thomas B. Ross, *The Invisible Government* (New York: Random House, 1964); Kermit Roosevelt, *Countercoup: The Struggle for the Control of Iran* (New York: McGraw-Hill, 1970).

19. See, for example, Marchetti and Marks, *Cult of Intelligence,* 59.

20. Author's interviews with retired CIA officers, 1984–93. For a supporting argument that covert action soon became predominant in intelligence budgetary outlays—most especially during the Korean War—see Berkowitz and Goodman, *Strategic Intelligence,* 144.

21. See Treverton, *Covert Action,* and Church Committee, "Alleged Assassination Plots."

22. Author's interview, October 10, 1980, Washington, D.C.

23. See Berkowitz and Goodman, *Strategic Intelligence,* 40; Leslie Gelb, "Overseeing of CIA by Congress Has Produced Decade of Support," *New York Times,* July 7, 1986, p. 1; Joseph Lelyveld, "The Director: Running the C.I.A.," *New York Times Sunday Magazine,* January 20, 1985, pp. 16ff; Gregory F. Treverton, "Covert Action and Open Society," *Foreign Affairs* 65 (Summer 1987); and Bob Woodward, *Veil: The Secret Wars of the CIA, 1981–1987* (New York: Pocket Books, 1987), 213. Gelb reports that the incidents of covert action in the waning months of the Carter administration dropped off considerably, while Lelyveld reports just the opposite—that Carter had more covert actions than President Reagan. The distinction may be between numbers of findings and covert-action expenditures. Reagan seems to have approved half as many findings as Carter—though, as Gelb suggests, Carter's frequency dwindled near the very end of his tenure. But Reagan's covert actions were far more expensive and dominated the White House agenda more often.

24. See also Jeffreys-Jones, *CIA and American Democracy,* 235. My interviews in 1993–94 with an expanded set of intelligence officers with covert-action experience during the Reagan-Bush years have caused me to revise upward the levels of CIA commitment to covert action during the 1980s over estimates reported in my *America's Secret Power.*

25. George Bush, letter to the author, January 23, 1994; author's interview with DCI R. James Woolsey, September 29, 1993, Langley, Va.

26. Author's interview with Gordon Oehler, April 1, 1994, Langley, Va.

27. Author's interview with a senior CIA official, April 1, 1994.

28. For the intelligence community's early budgeting, see Snyder and Furniss, *American*

Foreign Policy, 299; for funding in the 1960s, see Marchetti and Marks, *Cult of Intelligence*. The additional funding figures are based on interviews with intelligence personnel.

29. Author's interview with former DCI James R. Schlesinger, June 16, 1994, Washington, D.C.

30. As a result of inflation, dollars in the late stages of the Cold War had about two-thirds the spending value of those in the early stages.

31. See Loch K. Johnson, *A Season of Inquiry: Congress and Intelligence* (Chicago: Dorsey, 1988), chap. 1.

32. Author's interview with Schlesinger, June 16, 1994.

33. Church Committee, *Final Report*, Book 1; Pike Committee, *Final Report*.

34. On Mansfield as a proponent of closer accountability of the CIA during this period, see Henry Kissinger, *White House Years* (Boston: Little, Brown, 1979), 458. See Kissinger, too, on the brief rise in executive accountability over the CIA following the Bay of Pigs (p. 660).

35. See Johnson, *Season of Inquiry*, and Frank J. Smist, Jr., *Congress Oversees the United States Intelligence Community* (Knoxville: University of Tennessee Press, 1990).

36. Johnson, ibid.

37. Between 1990 and 1994 I asked each of the DCIs who served from 1966 to comment on the new oversight system. Among these nine intelligence chiefs, only Richard Helms and William J. Casey viewed the new arrangements as an inappropriate infringement on executive prerogative. Indeed, several of the others, especially Adm. Stansfield Turner and Robert M. Gates, expressed frustration with the unwillingness of legislative overseers to take their duties more seriously (as discussed further in chapter 4).

38. See Gregory F. Treverton, "Intelligence: Welcome to the American Government," in Thomas E. Mann, ed., *A Question of Balance: The President, the Congress and Foreign Policy* (Washington, D.C.: Brookings Institution, 1990), 70–108.

39. The official name of this legislation is the Foreign Intelligence Surveillance Act of 1978, P.L. 95–511, signed October 25, 1978; 92 Stat. 1783.

40. Cited in "Indiana Jim."

41. Author's interview with R. James Woolsey, September 29, 1993, Langley, Va.

42. R. James Woolsey, "National Security and the Future Direction of the CIA," Address to the Center for Strategic and International Studies, Washington, D.C., July 18, 1994.

43. Author's interview with R. James Woolsey, September 29, 1993.

44. Woolsey, "National Security."

45. Loch K. Johnson, "Smart Intelligence," *Foreign Policy* 89 (Winter 1992–93), 53–70.

46. Author's interviews with CIA personnel, April 1, 1994.

47. Author's interview with R. James Woolsey, September 29, 1993.

48. Johnson, "Smart Intelligence."

49. Woolsey, "National Security."

50. William E. Connor, *Intelligence Oversight: The Controversy behind the FY 1991 In-*

telligence Authorization Act, Intelligence Profession Series, no. 11 (McLean, Va.: The Association of Former Intelligence Officers, 1993); Johnson, "Smart Intelligence."

51. Imagery involves the conversion of pictures obtained electronically or by optical means into viewable film, electronic displays, or other forms of media for interpretation by analysts.

52. Related to the author by a seventh-floor skeptic, eyes rolling. Washington, D.C., June 29, 1995.

53. Interviews with DCI William H. Webster, May 2, 1991, Langley, Va., and Robert M. Gates, March 28, 1994, Washington, D.C.

54. See, for instance, Select Committee on Intelligence, "An Assessment of the Aldrich H. Ames Espionage Case and Its Implication for U.S. Intelligence," *Staff Report* (Senate Print 103–90), U.S. Senate, 103 Cong., 2d. Sess., November 1, 1994.

55. Author's interviews with intelligence officers and congressional overseers, 1993–94. In 1995 the House of Representatives voted, by voice, for a 5 percent boost in spending for the intelligence community in fiscal year 1996—a 1.3 percent increase over President Clinton's request. *Washington Post,* September 14, 1995, A17.

56. Author's interview with Robert M. Gates, March 28, 1994. The literature on organizational change tends to support the notion that bureaucracies are more responsive than often supposed; see Hal G. Rainey, *Understanding and Managing Public Organizations* (San Francisco: Jossey-Bass, 1991).

57. Interview with the CIA's deputy director in the Office of Congressional Affairs, April 1, 1994, Langley, Va.

58. See Johnson, *Season of Inquiry*; Smist, *Congress Oversees*; Frederick M. Kaiser, "Impact and Implications of the Iran-Contra Affair on Congressional Oversight of Covert Action," *International Journal of Intelligence and Counterintelligence* 7 (1994), 205–34; Louis Fisher, "How to Avoid Iran-Contras: Review Essay," *California Law Review* 76 (1988), 29–39; Harold Hongju Koh, "Why the President (Almost) Always Wins in Foreign Affairs: Lessons of the Iran-Contra Affair," *Yale Law Journal* 97 (June 1988), 1255–1342; Lawrence E. Walsh, *Final Report of the Independent Counsel for Iran/Contra Matters* (Washington, D.C.: U.S. Court of Appeals for the District of Columbia Circuit, 1994); Theodore Draper, *A Very Thin Line: The Iran-Contra Affairs* (New York: Hill and Wang, 1991); and Peter Kornbluh, "The Iran-Contra Scandal: A Postmortem," *World Policy Journal,* Winter 1987–88, pp. 129–50.

59. Author's interview with the former secretary of defense, Les Aspin, July 6, 1994, Washington, D.C.

60. See, for example, Robert Kohler, "The Intelligence Industrial Base: Doomed to Extinction?" monograph, Working Group on Intelligence Reform, Consortium for the Study of Intelligence, Washington, D.C., 1994.

61. Author's interview with Robert M. Gates, March 28, 1994.

62. Ibid. This important bill, which defined covert action and clarified the reporting requirements for findings (among other things), is the Intelligence Authorization Act,

FY 1991, Pub. L. No. 102–88; 105 Stat. 429; 102d Cong., 1st Sess. See "Statement on Signing the Intelligence Authorization Act, FY 1991," *Weekly Compilation of Presidential Documents* 27 (1991), 1137; and Connor, *Intelligence Oversight.*

CHAPTER 3: THE ETHICS OF COVERT OPERATIONS

1. See the Doolittle report, cited in the Senate Select Committee to Study Governmental Operations with Respect to Intelligence Activities (the Church Committee), *Final Report,* Book I, 94th Cong., 2d Sess., S. Rept. No. 94–755, 1976, p. 9; author's conversations with Dean Rusk, when he resorted to this phrase frequently in explaining the use of covert operations during the Cold War (Athens, Ga., 1980–85), and also in the Church Committee, *Final Report,* Book I, p. 9; Ray S. Cline, a retired CIA officer, in "Should the CIA Fight Secret Wars?" *Harper's,* September 1984, p. 39; and Stewart A. Baker, "Should Spies Be Cops?" *Foreign Policy* 97 (Winter 1994–95), 37.

2. On the frequency of U.S. covert operations since 1947, see Loch K. Johnson, *America's Secret Power: The CIA in a Democratic Society* (New York: Oxford University Press, 1989).

3. Herman Kahn, *On Escalation: Metaphors and Scenarios* (New York: Praeger, 1965), 37.

4. Ibid., 38.

5. On the nonintervention norm, see Lori Fisler Damrosch, "Politics across Borders: Nonintervention and Nonforcible Influence over Domestic Affairs," *American Journal of International Law* 83 (January 1989), 6–13.

6. See *Report of the Special Committee on Principles of International Law concerning Friendly Relations and Co-operation among States,* U.N. Doc. A/6799 (1967), 161, quoted in Damrosch, "Politics across Borders," 10–11.

7. Damrosch, "Politics across Borders," 11.

8. The Reagan administration evidently believed, and wanted to spread the word, that the assassination plot in 1984 against Pope John Paul II had been an operation by the Soviet secret service, the KGB, even though the U.S. intelligence community had no compelling evidence to this effect. See remarks by Donald Gregg, a former CIA officer on the NSC staff, in Loch K. Johnson, "Making the Intelligence 'Cycle' Work," *International Journal of Intelligence and Counterintelligence* 2 (Winter 1986–87), 17. On a CIA counterintelligence scheme to falsify and distribute copies of Soviet premier Nikita Khrushchev's "secret speech" denouncing the Stalin era, see Seymour M. Hersh, "The Angleton Story," *New York Times Sunday Magazine,* June 25, 1978, p. 13.

9. See "The CIA and the Media," *Hearings,* Subcommittee on Oversight, House Permanent Select Committee on Intelligence, 96th Cong., 1st Sess., 1979.

10. Walter Pincus, "CIA Steps Up 'Scrub Down' of Agents," *Washington Post,* July 28, 1995, A25. For a criticism of the CIA's "moral checklist," see Jonathan Clarke, "The CIA Drifts between Fear and Loathing," *Los Angeles Times* (September 3, 1995), M5, who wonders: "If human rights abusers are out, what about pedophiles? Embezzlers? Wife beaters? Delinquent dads?" For Clarke, "the CIA [should] operate according to

one ironclad rule: A relationship [with a foreign asset] will continue as long as there is a net benefit to U.S. interests; when it is not, it will be cut loose."

11. Discussed in "The CIA and Guatemala," *Washington Post,* August 4, 1995, A22.

12. On the advantages and risks of embassy break-ins, see the testimony of former Attorney General John Mitchell, *Huston Plan Hearings,* vol. 2, Church Committee, 94th Cong., 1st Sess. (1975), 123; Richard M. Nixon, response to Interrogatory No. 17, Church Committee, *Final Report,* Book IV; *Supplementary Detailed Staff Reports on Foreign and Military Intelligence,* Church Committee, Book III, 157–58; Church Committee, *Final Report,* Book I, 123; and author's interview with James J. Angleton, former CIA Chief of Counterintelligence, cited in Johnson, *America's Secret Power,* 297–98n5.

13. Damrosch, "Politics across Borders," 10–11.

14. Ibid., 36.

15. On the Son Tay prison raid, designed to free U.S. prisoners of war in Vietnam (unsuccessfully, since the prisoners had been evacuated by the North Vietnamese three weeks earlier—an unfortunate intelligence failure), see Henry Kissinger, *White House Years* (Boston: Little, Brown, 1979), 282; and Benjamin F. Schemmer, *The Raid* (New York: Harper & Row, 1976). On the Iran rescue attempt, see Morton H. Halperin and David Halperin, "The Key West Key," *Foreign Policy* (Winter 1983–84), 114.

16. President George Bush, White House press release, Washington, D.C. (August 15, 1989).

17. On the CIA's paramilitary operations in Laos, see William E. Colby and Peter Forbath, *Honorable Men: My Life in the CIA* (New York: Simon and Schuster, 1978), 191–202; and Victor Marchetti and John D. Marks, *The CIA and the Cult of Intelligence* (New York: Knopf, 1974).

18. See, for example, Jeffrey T. Richelson, *Sword and Shield: The Soviet Intelligence and Security Apparatus* (Cambridge, Mass.: Ballinger, 1986); Roy Godson, ed., *Comparing Foreign Intelligence: The US, the USSR, and the Third World* (New York: Pergamon-Brassey, 1988); and Richard H. Shultz and Roy Godson, *Dezinformatsia: Active Measures in Soviet Strategy* (New York: Pergamon-Brassey, 1984)

19. See, for example, the series of lead articles in *Ethics and International Affairs* 3 (1989); Arthur S. Hulnick and Daniel W. Mattausch, "Ethics and Morality in United States Secret Intelligence," *Harvard Journal of Law and Public Policy* 12 (Spring 1989), 509; Joseph S. Nye, Jr., *Ethics and Foreign Policy: An Occasional Paper,* Aspen Institute Human Studies, no. 1 (1985); E. Drexel Godfrey, Jr., "Ethics and Intelligence," *Foreign Affairs* 56 (1978), 624; and Richard Falk, "CIA Covert Action and International Law," *Society* 12 (1975), 39.

20. See the useful summary of these issues in Michael J. Smith, "Ethics and Intervention," *Ethics and International Affairs* 3 (1989), 1–26.

21. On operational codes, see Loch K. Johnson, "Operational Codes and the Prediction of Leadership Behavior," in Margaret Herman, ed., *A Psychological Examination of Political Man* (New York: Free Press, 1977), 80; for an analytic framework outlining these interrelationships, see Loch K. Johnson, *America as a World Power: For-*

eign Policy in a Constitutional Framework, 2d ed. (New York: McGraw-Hill, 1995), chap. 2.

22. Henry L. Stimson and McGeorge Bundy, *On Active Service in Peace and War* (New York: Octagon Books, 1947), 188. Stimson subsequently disavowed this position, perhaps realizing that America's adversaries were seldom gentlemen.

23. George W. Ball, "Should the CIA Fight Secret Wars?" 37.

24. G. Gordon Liddy, public lecture, University of Georgia, Athens, May 4, 1986, based on author's notes.

25. See, Charles R. Beitz, "Covert Intervention as a Moral Problem," and William E. Colby, "Public Policy, Secret Action," *Ethics and International Affairs* 3 (1989), 48 and 63, 69, respectively.

26. See Michael Walzer, *Just and Unjust Wars: A Moral Argument with Historical Illustrations* (New York: Basic Books, 1977).

27. See, for example, Colby, "Public Policy," 69. Damrosch writes: "[T]he nonintervention norm must not become a vehicle for exalting the abstract entity of the state over the protection of individual rights and fundamental freedoms" ("Politics across Borders," 37).

28. See Smith, "Ethics and Intervention," 21.

29. On proportionality, see Colby, "Public Policy," 65–66.

30. See Gregory F. Treverton, "Imposing a Standard: Covert Action and American Democracy," 27 and 32, and Ralph Buultjens, "The Ethics of Excess and Indian Intervention in South Asia," 82, both in *Ethics and International Affairs* 3 (1989).

31. See Treverton, "Imposing a Standard," and Colby, "Public Policy."

32. Hulnick and Mattausch, "Ethics and Morality."

33. See, for example, Robert C. Johansen, *The National Interest and the Human Interest: An Analysis of U.S. Foreign Policy* (Princeton: Princeton University Press, 1980), 386.

34. See Buultjens, "The Ethics of Excess."

35. Colby, "Public Policy," 69.

36. South Carolina representative L. Mendel Rivers, quoted in Charles McCarry, "Ol' Man Rivers," *Esquire* (October 1970), 171.

37. This transformation can also operate in the reverse direction, as shown by President Carter's switch to a harder line—and a sudden attraction to covert action—against the Soviets following their surprise invasion of Afghanistan in 1979. On Reagan's move away from "evil empire" rhetoric toward more cordial relations with his Soviet counterpart, see the two-part series by John Newhouse, "Annals of Diplomacy: The Abolitionist," *New Yorker* 64 (January 2 and 9, 1989), 37 and 51, respectively. Reagan's first public rejection of the "evil empire" label occurred on May 31, 1988. On Carter's reaction to the Soviet invasion of Afghanistan, see his own account in Jimmy Carter, *Keeping Faith: Memoirs of a President* (New York: Bantam Books, 1982), 471–89.

38. See Jeane Kirkpatrick, "Dictatorships and Double Standards," *Commentary* (November 1979), 34; and, with a far different conclusion, Damrosch, "Politics across Borders."

39. See Loch K. Johnson, "The CIA and the Media," *Intelligence and National Security* 1 (1986), 143. These distinctions between regimes lose much of their force, however, at Threshold Four, where the dangers to innocents are greatly magnified.

40. For Colby, on the decline of the Soviet ideological threat (several years before the *glasnost* era), see "Interview with William E. Colby," *U.S. News & World Report* (July 3, 1978), at 37, 39. On Casey's aggressive approach to the use of intelligence operations, see David M. Alpern, "America's Secret Warriors," *Newsweek* (October 10, 1983), 38; and Roger Morris, "William Casey's Past," *Atlanta Constitution* (August 31, 1987), A11. See also DCI Director Stansfield Turner's higher tolerance for the Marxist regime in Nicaragua than that expressed by his successor, DCI Casey: "From an Ex-CIA Chief: Stop the 'Covert' Operation in Nicaragua," *Washington Post* (April 21, 1983), C1.

41. See Theodore C. Sorensen, *Decision-Making in the White House: The Olive Branch or the Arrows* (New York: Columbia University Press, 1963).

42. Author's conversations with Air Marshal Sir Ewan Jamieson (in charge of New Zealand's counterintelligence at the time of the investigation into the *Rainbow Warrior* bombing), Conference on Military Strategy, Georgia Institute of Technology, Atlanta, August 24–26, 1989.

43. For this story, see Kermit Roosevelt, *Countercoup: The Struggle for the Control of Iran* (New York: McGraw-Hill, 1979).

44. Peter Wyden, *Bay of Pigs: The Untold Story* (New York: Simon and Schuster, 1979).

45. Beitz, "Covert Intervention."

46. On this "Gang of Eight" leading legislators, see Johnson, *America's Secret Power,* 222–29. The 1991 Intelligence Oversight amendments, Title VI of the Intelligence Authorization Act, Fiscal Year 1991, Pub. L. No. 102–88, 105 Stat. 429, 441 (adopted August 14, 1991), continue this procedure; see page 443, 503(c)(2). David L. Boren, president of the University of Oklahoma and a former chairman of the Senate Select Committee on Intelligence, has suggested that in extraordinary times the executive branch should be allowed to report to just the Speaker and Minority Leader of the House and their Senate counterparts—a "Gang of Four," removing the chairman and ranking minority members of the two Intelligence Committees (who were part of the wider Gang of Eight). See Boren's remarks, Association of Former Intelligence Officers (March 28, 1988), quoted in the association's newsletter, *Periscope* (Spring 1988), 8. This same recommendation was advanced in the Minority Report of the Inouye-Hamilton Committees, *Report,* 585. (I am grateful to Donald Milner, a Toronto attorney, for his thoughts on the importance of process.)

47. On the strict adherence to this law before the Iran-Contra violation, see H.R. Rept. No. 705, 100th Cong., 2d Sess. (1988), 54. On the debate over prior notice, see Johnson, *America's Secret Power,* 225–28; *The Need to Know,* Report of the Twentieth Century Fund Task Force on Covert Action and American Democracy, New York, 1992; and W. Michael Riesman and James E. Baker, *Regulating Covert Action: Practices, Contests, and Policies of Covert Coercion Abroad in International and American Law* (New Haven: Yale University Press, 1992).

48. The law states that the report should be forthcoming "in a timely fashion" (the same hazy prescription found in the Hughes-Ryan Act of 1974), but the accompanying legislative history stresses the expectation of a "few days" maximum delay.

49. Baker, "Should Spies Be Cops?" 40.

50. See, for example, "Elliott Abrams Is Guilty," *New York Times* (October 11, 1991), A14, an unsigned editorial that cites the State Department official Elliott Abrams's disdain for Congressional involvement in intelligence supervision. Abrams was convicted of lying to Congress about the illegal supply of weapons to the contras during the Iran-Contra affair. For a more scholarly argument against any serious legislative oversight of intelligence, see Paul Seabury, "A Massacre Revisited," *Foreign Intelligence Literary Scene* 1 (1988), 2.

51. Treverton, "Imposing a Standard," 43.

52. For Poindexter's statement, see *Hearings,* Senate Select Committee on Secret Military Assistance to Iran and the Nicaraguan Opposition and House Select Committee to Investigate Covert Arms Transactions with Iran, 100th Cong., 1st Sess. (1987), 159, chaired by Sen. Daniel K. Inouye and Rep. Lee H. Hamilton, respectively (hereinafter Inouye-Hamilton Committees, *Hearings*).

53. Ibid., 240–41. See also *Report of the Congressional Committees Investigating the Iran-Contra Affair,* S. Rept. No. 216 and H. Rept. No. 433, 100 Cong., 1st Sess. (1987), 333 (hereinafter Inouye-Hamilton Committees, *Report*). For an overview of the Iran-Contra affair, see Theodore Draper, *A Very Thin Line: The Iran-Contra Affair* (New York: Hill and Wang, 1991); Lawrence E. Walsh, *Final Report of the Independent Counsel for Iran/Contra Matters* (Washington, D.C.: U.S. Court of Appeals, District of Columbia Circuit, 1994).

54. See, for example, Vice Admiral Poindexter's testimony, Inouye-Hamilton Committees, *Hearings*; Inouye-Hamilton Committees, *Report,* 16, 339; the Tower Commission Report (1987); and Church Committee, *Final Report,* Book I.

55. As Justice Louis Brandeis put it in 1926, "The doctrine of the separation of powers was adopted by the [Constitutional] Convention of 1787, not to promote efficiency but to preclude the exercise of arbitrary power. The purpose was, not to avoid friction, but, by means of the inevitable friction incident to the distribution of the governmental powers among three departments, to save the people from autocracy." *Myers v. United States,* 272 U.S. 52,293.

56. Fundraising letter to "Fellow American," signed by John M. Poindexter, Rear Admiral, USN (Ret.), and reading in part: "I must now face the liberals' accusations surrounding the 'Iran-Contra affair.' And as I stand, one man, alone against the massive onslaught of liberal special interests who want to imprison me for serving my country, I must turn to you for help" (undated, but received by the author in August 1989).

57. Inouye-Hamilton Committees, *Report,* 431–585 (Minority Report).

58. See William S. Cohen and George J. Mitchell, *Men of Zeal: A Candid Inside Story of the Iran-Contra Hearings* (New York: Viking, 1988); and Elizabeth Drew, "Letter from Washington," *New Yorker* (March 30, 1987), 111. The case against North was dismissed by a U.S. district court in 1991 after the Iran-Contra independent prose-

cutor announced that he would abandon the prosecution because the immunity granted to North by Congress in 1987 (to gain his testimony in hearings) had created too great an obstacle. See David Johnston, "Judge in Iran-Contra Trial Drops Case against North after Prosecutor Gives Up," *New York Times* (September 17, 1991), A1, A12.

59. See the Bush Administration's $9 million request to Congress (September 21, 1989) for open support of the anti-Sandinista candidate in Nicaragua's approaching presidential election, reported in "Bush Seeks $9 Million for Nicaraguan Opposing Ortega in Presidential Bid," *Atlanta Journal and Constitution* (September 22, 1989), A4.

60. See Margaret Scranton, *The Noriega Years: U.S.-Panamian Relations, 1981–1990* (Boulder, Colo.: Lynne Rienner, 1991).

61. The Vance and Clifford testimonies are in Church Committee, *Hearings: Covert Action*, 94th Cong., 2d Sess., 1976, 7:50–55. For the Church Committee's conclusion, see Church Committee, *Final Report*, Book I, 159; for the Inouye-Hamilton Committees' conclusion, see Inouye-Hamilton Committees, *Report*, 383. See also the discussion in *The Need to Know*; and Reisman and Baker, *Regulating Covert Action*.

62. In offering these guidelines, I am not unmindful of Clemenceau's wry comment on President Woodrow Wilson's Fourteen Points: "God gave us his Ten Commandments and we broke them; Wilson gave us his Fourteen Points—we shall see." Quoted in W. A. White, *Woodrow Wilson* (Boston: Houghton Mifflin, 1929), 384.

63. See the former secretary's account in his memoirs, *Hard Choices: Critical Years in America's Foreign Policy* (New York: Simon and Schuster, 1983), 398–413.

64. On U.S. intelligence ties with Noriega, see *Drugs, Law Enforcement and Foreign Policy: Hearings before the Senate Subcommittee on Terrorism, Narcotics, and International Operations*, 100 Cong., 2d Sess. (1989), 234–43; on Barbie, see "Klaus Barbie, Lyons Nazi Leader, Dies," *New York Times* (September 26, 1991), C19; and on CIA ties with organized crime in the 1960s, see Church Committee, *Alleged Assassination Plots Involving Foreign Leaders: Interim Report*, S. Rep. No. 465, 94th Cong., 1st Sess. (1975). On refusing intelligence cooperation with regimes engaged in human rights violations, see Thomas Farer, "Low-Intensity Conflict and International Order: The Prospect for Consensus," paper, U.S. Institute of Peace Project on Strengthening World Order and the United Nations Charter System against Secret Warfare and Low-Intensity Conflict, 1990, p. 63. Professor Farer has emphasized the importance of the second guideline, too, in a U.S. Institute of Peace discussion group of which I was a member in 1990. Professor James Berry of James Mason University has graciously corresponded with me on the proper sequencing of rungs on the escalation ladder and has stimulated helpful revisions.

65. On the phenomenon of banishing intelligence and other experts from high councils when key decisions are being made (and related policymaking pathologies), see Irving L. Janis, *Groupthink: Psychological Studies of Policy Decisions and Fiascoes*, 2d ed. (Boston: Houghton-Mifflin, 1982); Robert Jervis, "Intelligence and Foreign Policy," *International Security Studies* 11 (1986–87); and Betts, "Analysis, War, and

Decisions: Why Intelligence Failures Are Inevitable," *World Politics* (October 1978), 31:61–89.

66. On this theme, see Damrosch, "Politics across Borders," esp. 37–50; and Farer, "Low-Intensity Conflict."

67. However, in the two exceptional cases mentioned here, if the regime leader is killed during the destruction of the chemical-biological and nuclear facilities (in the first instance), or during his or her arrest (in the second instance), this unintended result is defensible in light of the need to protect large civilian and innocent populations—a consequentialist verdict that in these situations seems compelling.

On the illegality of assassinations, see Executive Order No. 12,333, signed by President Ronald Reagan on December 4, 1981; *Public Papers (Ronald Reagan)*, 1981, p. 1128. The order continued a prohibition against assassination initiated by President Gerald R. Ford, Executive Order No. 11,905 (February 18, 1976), *Public Papers (Gerald R. Ford)*, 1976–77, p. 349. Since presidents Bush and Clinton never revoked the order, it remains in force. See W. Hays Parks, "Memorandum of Law: Executive Order 12333 and Assassination," *Army Law* (December 1989), 4. Pointing to Article 2(4) of the U.N. Charter, Parks, chief of the Army's International Law Branch, maintains: "Assassination is unlawful killing, and would be prohibited by international law even if there were no executive order proscribing it" ("Memorandum of Law," 4).

68. Church Committee, *Alleged Assassination Plots.*

69. Author's interview with Stansfield Turner, May 1, 1991, McLean, Va.

70. Roger Fisher, "The Fatal Flaw in Our Spy System," *Boston Globe* (February 1, 1976), A9.

71. Remarks, Rep. Steven J. Solarz, C-Span television broadcast, May 22, 1988.

CHAPTER 4: INTELLIGENCE ACCOUNTABILITY

1. Section 662 (a) of the Foreign Assistance Act of 1974; the language of the law is reprinted in Loch K. Johnson, *America's Secret Power: The CIA in a Democratic Society* (New York: Oxford University Press, 1989), 268.

2. Author's interviews with Les Aspin, July 1994, Washington, D.C. (I was also present at these meetings as a HPSCI staff aide.)

3. For a discussion of the Boland Amendments that passed between 1982 and 1986, see *Report,* Senate Select Committee on Secret Military Assistance to Iran and the Nicaraguan Opposition and House Select Committee to Investigate Covert Arms Transactions with Iran, U.S. Congress, July 24, 1987 (the Inouye-Hamilton Committees); and Henry A. Kissinger, "A Matter of Balance," *Los Angeles Times,* July 26, 1987, p. 1.

4. See Joel Aberbach, *Keeping a Watchful Eye: The Politics of Congressional Oversight* (Washington, D.C.: Brookings Institution, 1990); Loch K. Johnson, "The U.S. Congress and the CIA: Monitoring the Dark Side of Government," *Legislative Studies Quarterly* 5 (1980), 477–500; Fred Kaiser, "Oversight of Foreign Policy: The U.S. House Committee on International Relations," *Legislative Studies Quarterly* 2

(1977), 255–80; Morris S. Ogul, *Congress Supervises the Bureaucracy: Studies in Legislative Supervision* (Pittsburgh: University of Pittsburgh Press, 1976); and Morris S. Ogul and Bert A. Rockman, "Overseeing Oversight: New Departures and Old Problems," *Legislative Studies Quarterly* 15 (1990), 5–24.

5. See, for instance, Richard F. Fenno, Jr., *Watching Politicians: Essays on Participant Observation* (Berkeley: University of California, Institute of Governmental Studies, 1990); and, for an example of this methodology in the intelligence domain, Loch K. Johnson, *A Season of Inquiry: Congress and Intelligence* (Lexington: University Press of Kentucky, 1985).

6. Rep. Otis Pike, *Hearings on U.S. Intelligence Agencies and Activities: Intelligence Costs and Fiscal Procedures* (part 1), House Select Committee on Intelligence, 94th Cong., 1st Sess., 1975, p. 168.

7. Ibid.

8. The official names of the permanent intelligence oversight panels in Congress are the Senate Select Committee on Intelligence (established in 1976) and the House Permanent Select Committee on Intelligence (1977)—referred to as the Senate and House Intelligence Committees. The ad hoc investigative panels include the Pike Committee (officially the Select Committee on Intelligence, serving in 1975–76 and led by Representative Pike); the Church Committee (officially the Senate Select Committee to Study Government Operations with Respect to Intelligence Activities, also serving in 1975–76 and led by Sen. Frank Church); and the joint Inouye-Hamilton Committees (officially the Senate Select Committee on Secret Military Assistance to Iran and the Nicaraguan Opposition and the House Select Committee to Investigate Covert Arms Transactions with Iran, serving in 1987 and led, respectively, by Sen. Daniel K. Inouye and Rep. Lee H. Hamilton). Senator Inouye chaired two committees involved in intelligence oversight. The first, designated in this chapter Inouye Committee I, was the first permanent Select Committee on Intelligence (1976–77); the second, designated here Inouye Committee II, was the Senate Iran-Contra investigative committee (1987). Representative Hamilton fulfilled a similar dual role, chairing the House Permanent Select Committee on Intelligence from 1985 to 1987 (after Boland)—Hamilton Committee I—and, jointly with Senator Inouye, the House Iran-Contra investigative committee in 1987—Hamilton Committee II.

In this chapter these permanent and investigative committees are treated together as part of a continuum of intelligence oversight stretching from 1975 to 1990—the era of New Oversight for intelligence policy. A listing of these various intelligence oversight committees can be found in figure 4.1, along with their dates of service. The House Intelligence Committee—including the Pike and the Hamilton II incarnations—held twenty-seven public hearings from 1975 to 1990 (the period covered in this analysis), twenty-four of which included incumbent or former CIA officials as witnesses. The Senate Committee on Intelligence—including the Church and Inouye II incarnations—also held, coincidentally, twenty-seven public hearings from 1975 to 1990, and again twenty-four included incumbent or former CIA officials as witnesses.

9. Loch K. Johnson, *America's Secret Power: The CIA in a Democratic Society* (New York: Oxford University Press, 1989), 230–31.

10. Respectively, the Aspin Subcommittee (see *Hearings on the CIA and the Media,* Subcommittee on Oversight, U.S. House Permanent Select Committee on Intelligence, 95th Cong., 1st and 2d Sess., December 27, 1977–April 20, 1978); the Bayh Committee (see *Hearings on the National Intelligence Act of 1980,* U.S. Senate Select Committee on Intelligence, 96th Cong., 2d Sess., February 21–April 16, 1980); and the Boland Committee (see *Hearings on Congressional Oversight of Covert Activities,* U.S. House Permanent Select Committee on Intelligence, 98th Cong., 2d Sess., September 20–22, 1983).

11. Woodrow Wilson, *Congressional Government: A Study in American Politics* (New York: Meridian [1885] 1956), 69.

12. A former staff director of the Senate Select Committee on Intelligence, George J. Tenet, who served when David Boren was chairman in the late 1980s, looked upon these participation rates from this benign perspective: "The Senate Intelligence Committee had pretty good participation, but there was a great deal of trust placed in the Chairman and Vice-Chairman. They spent an inordinate amount of time on these issues. I'm not sure that the time devoted by the rest of the Committee members is any different than on any other committee. When things really matter, they're all there. The Chairman and Vice-Chairman have to carry the load on a lot of mundane, arcane matters; but when it matters, they [all] show up" (Author's interview, June 17, 1994, Washington, D.C.). Based on my service on the staffs of the Senate Foreign Relations Committee and the House Foreign Affairs Committee, it would appear that low rates of membership participation in hearings may indeed be the rule across congressional committees rather than the exception.

13. For other studies on the content of congressional hearings, see Steven L. Del Sesto, "Nuclear Reactor Safety and the Role of the Congressman: A Content Analysis of Congressional Hearings," *Journal of Politics* 42 (1980), 226–41; and Michael J. Sicchitano, "Congressional Oversight: The Case of the Clean Air Act," *Legislative Studies Quarterly* 11 (1986), 393–407. A reliability check, patterned after Del Sesto's, was incorporated into this study as a test for coding accuracy, with a reassuringly high compatibility rate of 97 percent between coders.

14. Respectively, Rep. Robert McClory, *Hearings on Proposals to Criminalize the Unauthorized Disclosure of the Identities of Undercover United States Intelligence Officers and Agents,* Subcommittee on Legislation, U.S. House Permanent Select Committee on Intelligence, 1980, 96th Cong., 2d Sess., January 30, 1980, p. 26; and Rep. John M. Ashbrook, *Hearings on Graymail Legislation,* Subcommittee on Legislation, U.S. House Permanent Select Committee on Intelligence, 96th Cong., 1st Sess., September 20, 1979, p. 151.

15. Sen. Barry Goldwater, *Hearings on S.1324, an Amendment to the National Security Act of 1947,* U.S. Senate Select Committee on Intelligence, 98th Cong., 1st Sess., May 16, 1983, p. 201.

16. See Rep. Les Aspin, *Hearings on Disclosure of Funds for Intelligence Activities,* Sub-

committee on Oversight, U.S. House Permanent Select Committee on Intelligence, 95th Cong., 1st Sess., December 27, 1977–April 20, 1978, p. 47; and Sen. Frank Church, *Hearings on the Huston Plan,* U.S. Senate Select Committee on Intelligence, 94th Cong., 1st Sess., September 23, 1975, p. 61.

17. Sen. Frank Church, ibid., p. 59; Rep. Morgan F. Murphy, *Hearings on U.S. Intelligence Agencies and Activities: The Performances of the Intelligence Community* (part 2), U.S. House Select Committee on Intelligence, 94th Cong., 1st Sess., September 12, 1975, p. 664.

18. Edward S. Corwin, *The President: Office and Powers, 1787–1957,* rev. ed. (New York: New York University Press, 1957), 171.

19. In Smist's dichotomy, "investigative" versus "institutional" oversight. Frank J. Smist, Jr., *Congress Oversees the United States Intelligence Community* (Knoxville: University of Tennessee Press, 1990), 19–23.

20. In 1992, Gates succeeded in an unprecedented second try for the DCI position.

21. James M. Lindsay, "Parochialism, Policy, and Constituency Constraints: Congressional Voting on Strategic Weapons Systems," *American Journal of Political Science* 34 (1990), 36–60.; Robert A. Bernstein and William W. Anthony, "The ABM Issue in the Senate, 1968–70: The Importance of Ideology," *American Political Science Review* 68 (1974), 1198–1206; and Richard Fleisher, "Economic Benefit, Ideology, and Senate Voting on the B-1 Bomber," *American Politics Quarterly* 13 (1985), 200–211.

22. The exceptional hardball played by GOP overseers in 1987–88 resulted chiefly from the lengthy critical questioning advanced by three Republican senators outraged by the Iran-Contra scandal: William S. Cohen (Maine), Arlen Specter (Pennsylvania), and Paul S. Trible, Jr. (Virginia).

23. Author's tabulation of *Reader's Guide* index entries from 1947 to 1990.

24. On this phenomenon, see Loch K. Johnson, Erna Gellner, and John C. Kuzenski, "The Study of Congressional Investigations: Research Strategies," *Congress and the Presidency* 19 (1992), 138–56.

25. Harry Howe Ransom, "The Politicization of Intelligence," in Stephen J. Cimbala, ed., *Intelligence and Intelligence Policy in a Democratic Society* (Dobbs Ferry, N.Y.: Transnational Publishers, 1987), 25–46.

26. The measures are drawn from Loch K. Johnson, "Strategic Intelligence: An American Perspective," *International Journal of Intelligence and Counterintelligence* 3 (1989), 323; and Charles W. Kegley, Jr., and Eugene Wittkopf, *American Foreign Policy: Pattern and Process,* 2d ed. (New York: St. Martin's, 1982), 58.

27. Author's interview with George J. Tenet, December 14, 1990, Washington, D.C.

28. See Johnson, *America's Secret Power* and "Legislative Reform of Intelligence Policy," *Polity* 17 (Spring 1985), 549–73.

29. See Harold Hongju Koh, *The National Security Constitution: Sharing Power after the Iran-Contra Affair* (New Haven: Yale University Press, 1990); and Peter Kornbluh, "The Iran-Contra Scandal: A Postmortem," *World Policy Journal* (Winter 1987–88), 129–50.

30. See Johnson, *America's Secret Power*.

31. Author's interview, December 12, 1990, Washington, D.C.

32. Author's interview, December 13, 1990, Washington, D.C.

33. Quoted by Tim Weiner, "C.I.A. Tie to Guatemala Deaths Still Hazy," *New York Times*, July 27, 1995, A10.

34. Johnson, "The U.S. Congress and the CIA," 1980; Ogul, *Congress Oversees the Bureaucracy*, 1976; Harry Howe Ransom, "Secret Intelligence Agencies and Congress," *Society* 12 (1975), 36.

35. Testimony, *Hearings on Congressional Oversight of Covert Activities*, U.S. House Permanent Select Committee on Intelligence, 98th Cong., 2d Sess., 1983, p. 29.

36. Testimony, *Hearings on H.R. 1013, H.R. 1317, and Other Proposals Which Address the Issue of Affording Prior Notice of Covert Actions to the Congress*, Subcommittee on Legislation, U.S. House Permanent Select Committee on Intelligence, 100th Cong., 1st Sess., April–June, 1987, p. 66.

37. See, for example, Louis Fisher, "Foreign Policy Powers of the President and Congress, *Annals of the American Academy of Political and Social Science*, 499 (September 1988), 152; and Michael J. Glennon, "In Foreign Policy, the Court Is Clear: President Is Subject to Will of Congress," *Los Angeles Times*, July 19, 1987, sec. 5, p. 3.

38. Intelligence Authorization Act, Fiscal Year 1991, Pub. L. No. 102–88, 105 Stat. 429, 102d Cong., 1st Sess. (1991); see William E. Conner, *Intelligence Oversight: The Controversy Behind the FY 1991 Intelligence Authorization Act*, Intelligence Profession Series, no. 11 (McLean, Va.: Association of Former Intelligence Officers, 1993).

39. Les Aspin, *Congressional Record*, September 30, 1980, p. 28395. See also the views of Theodore C. Sorensen in *The Need to Know*, Report of the Twentieth Century Fund Task Force on Covert Action and American Democracy (New York: Twentieth Century Fund Press, 1992), 20.

40. For examples of unauthorized paramilitary operations—covert actions—carried out by U.S. military units, see Steven Emerson, *Secret Warriors* (New York: Putnam, 1988). Also John Prados, *Presidents' Secret Wars: CIA and Pentagon Covert Operations since World War II* (New York: Morrow, 1986).

41. See Johnson, *America's Secret Power*, 295n63.

42. Inouye-Hamilton Committees, *Report*, 100th Cong., 1st Sess., November 1987, p. 142.

43. Ibid., 153.

44. Ibid., 158. For persuasive evidence that President Reagan's hand was not "on the helm"—in fact, that he was asleep at the helm—see the final report of the Tower Commission (ordered by the president himself): Tower Commission, *Report of the President's Special Review Board* (Washington, D.C.: Government Printing Office, February 26, 1987).

45. Inouye-Hamilton Committees, *Report*, 100th Cong., 1st Sess., November 1987, 158. Perhaps to the detriment of Poindexter and North, Government 101 was never a part

of the required curriculum at the Naval Academy. In the aftermath of the Iran-Contra scandal, it has become so; not that this requirement is guaranteed to inoculate the government against rogue graduates in the future, but it might help.

46. Author's interview with CIA officer, March 26, 1991, Langley, Va.; recall, too, the supporting statistics from chapter 2.

47. Several examples can be found in Johnson, *America's Secret Power*.

48. Author's interview with DCI Webster, May 2, 1991, Langley, Va..

49. Testimony, *Hearings on Disclosure of Funds for Intelligence Activities*, U.S. House Permanent Select Committee on Intelligence, 95th Cong., 2d Sess., January 1978, p. 106.

50. Testimony, *Hearings on Congressional Oversight of Covert Activities*, U.S. House Permanent Select Committee on Intelligence, 98th Cong., 2d. Sess., September 20, 1983, p. 74.

51. Casey's informal remarks were presented at a conference on intelligence at CIA headquarters, June 12, 1984 (author's notes).

52. Author's interview, December 12, 1990, Washington, D.C.

53. Author's interview, December 12, 1990, Washington, D.C.

54. Author's interview, December 13, 1990, Washington, D.C. This was perhaps true for a time, but William Colby (among others) dismisses the Freedom of Information Act as an important check on the CIA. Recent amendments to the law have exempted the Agency from handing over operational files—and rightly so, in Colby's view, to ensure the protection of sources and methods (Author's interview, January 22, 1991, Washington, D.C.). These are precisely the files, though, where mischief is most likely to be found.

55. Interview, "Carter's Intelligence Chief Sizes Up World's Trouble Spots," *U.S. News & World Report,* May 16, 1977, p. 26. For other important checks not discussed here, see Johnson, *America's Secret Power* and "Smart Intelligence," *Foreign Policy* 89 (1992–93), 67–69.

CHAPTER 5: THE DISTINCTIVENESS OF AMERICAN INTELLIGENCE

1. This is not to say that intelligence always plays a crucial role in foreign policy. Sometimes it is ignored by policy officers or is insufficiently illuminating to be helpful. In his study of warfare from the Roman Empire to Napoleon, Edward S. Creasy concludes that intelligence was critical to the outcome of a major battle only once: at Metaurus, where the Romans enjoyed a victory over the Carthaginians. Cited in David Kahn, "Clausewitz and Intelligence," *Journal of Strategic Studies* (June 1986), 125. In modern times, the Battle of Midway in World War Two is considered a striking example of how good intelligence can provide the edge for victory.

2. For some forays into the realm of comparative intelligence, see Jean-Marie Bonthous, "Understanding Intelligence across Cultures," *International Journal of Intelligence and Counterintelligence* 7 (Fall 1994), 275–312; L. A. Bitencourt Dmilio, "The 'Abertura' in Brazil: The Day-After of the Brazilian Intelligence 'Monster,'"

paper, annual meeting, International Studies Association, April 4, 1992, Atlanta; A. Stuart Farson, David Stafford, and Wesley K. Wark, *Security and Intelligence in a Changing World* (London: Cass, 1991); Glenn P. Hastedt, *Controlling Intelligence* (London: Cass, 1991); Michael Herman, "Assessment Machinery: British and American Models," paper, Conference on Intelligence Analysis and Assessment: The Producer/Policy-Maker Relationship in a Changing World, Canadian Association for Security and Intelligence Studies, October 27, 1994; Jeffrey T. Richelson, *Sword and Shield: Soviet Intelligence and Security Apparatus* (Cambridge, Ma.: Ballinger, 1986); Jeffrey T. Richelson and Desmond Ball, *The Ties That Bind: Intelligence Cooperation between the UKUSA Countries* (Boston: Allen & Unwin, 1985); K. G. Robertson, ed., *British and American Approaches to Intelligence* (London: MacMillan, 1987); Geoffrey R. Weller, "From Intelligence to Policy: The Canadian Case," paper, Fifth Biennial Canadian Studies Conference, Association of Canadian Studies in Australia and New Zealand, Armidale, Australia, July 19, 1990; and H. Bradford Westerfield, "America and the World of Intelligence Liaison," unpublished paper, March 1994.

3. The 50 percent figure is from *ABC Evening News,* September 19, 1995.

4. Remarks, CIA officer, West Point Senior Conference, United States Military Academy, June 9, 1990, West Point (author's notes), and author's interviews with senior intelligence officers in 1994, Washington, D.C.

5. See John Newhouse, "Annals of Intelligence: Changing Targets," *New Yorker,* July 10, 1989, p. 77.

6. Interview with CIA officer with extensive service as a liaison with British intelligence, Washington, D.C., July 14, 1994.

7. See, for instance, the skillful handling of Col. Oleg Penkovsky by the British, discussed in David C. Martin, *Wilderness of Mirrors* (New York: Harper & Row, 1980). The British have also had their mistakes, most painfully and obviously in the counterintelligence field (with such major defectors as Harold "Kim" Philby).

8. See Richard Harris Smith, *OSS: The Secret History of America's First Central Intelligence Agency* (Berkeley and Los Angeles: University of California Press, 1972).

9. On burden sharing, see Westerfield, "America and the World of Intelligence Liaison," who is skeptical about too much reliance on allies for intelligence.

10. Christopher Andrew, "American Presidents and Their Intelligence Communities," paper presented at the Canadian Association of Security and Intelligence Studies (CASIS) Conference on "Intelligence Analysis and Assessment: The Producer/Policy-Maker Relationship in a Changing World," Ottawa, October 28, 1994, p. 7.

11. Reg Whitaker, "The Canadian Security and Intelligence System: Fighting the Last War or the Next?" in Farson, Stafford, and Wark, eds., *Security and Intelligence,* 132.

12. Andrew, "American Presidents," 2–3.

13. Bonthous, "Understanding Intelligence," 292–93.

14. See, for example, "Killing of Wazir Ruthless and Efficient," *Los Angeles Times* (April 22, 1988), A1.

15. Andrew, "American Presidents," 5.

16. Interviews with CIA officials, 1980–94. See also James Bamford, *The Puzzle Palace* (New York: Houghton Mifflin, 1984); William E. Burrows, *Deep Black: Space Espionage and National Security* (New York: Random, 1986); Lawrence Freedman, *U.S. Intelligence and the Soviet Strategic Threat* (Princeton: Princeton University Press, 1986); Jeffrey T. Richelson, *The U.S. Intelligence Community* (Cambridge, Mass.: Ballinger, 1985) and *America's Secret Eyes in Space* (New York: Harper & Row, 1990); and Victor Marchetti and John Marks, *The CIA and the Cult of Intelligence* (New York: Knopf, 1974).

17. Stansfield Turner, *Secrecy and Democracy: The CIA in Transition* (Boston: Houghton Mifflin, 1985); author's interview, May 1, 1991, McLean, Va.

18. Stansfield Turner, "Foreword," in David D. Newsom, *The Soviet Brigade in Cuba: A Study in Political Diplomacy* (Bloomington: Indiana University Press, 1987), p. ix.

19. Quoted by Marchetti and Marks, *Cult of Intelligence,* 70.

20. Herman, "Assessment Machinery."

21. Ibid., 10.

22. Ibid., 12.

23. Author's interview, July 14, 1994, Washington, D.C.

24. See Harry Howe Ransom, "The Politicization of Intelligence," in Stephen J. Cimbala, ed., *Intelligence and Intelligence Policy in a Democratic Society* (Dobbs Ferry, N.Y.: Transnational, 1987), 25–46.

25. Author's interviews with all the DCIs from Richard Helms through R. James Woolsey (with the exception of George Bush), Washington, D.C., and Langley, Va., 1991–1994.

26. Author's interview, September 29, 1993, Langley, Va.

27. Author's interview with Igor Khirpinov, former Soviet diplomat and now an expatriate scholar living in the United States; December 21, 1994, Athens, Ga.

28. See the testimony of Secretary of Defense Caspar Weinberger, *Hearings,* Senate Select Committee on Secret Military Assistance to Iran and the Nicaraguan Opposition and House Select Committee to Investigate Covert Arms Transactions with Iran, U.S. Congress, July 24, 1987 (hereafter the Inouye-Hamilton Committees, after their respective chairmen, Daniel K. Inouye and Lee H. Hamilton).

29. See Loch K. Johnson, "National Security, Civil Liberties, and the Collection of Intelligence: A Report on the Huston Plan," in *Supplementary Detailed Staff Reports on Intelligence and the Rights of Americans, Final Report,* Select Committee to Study Governmental Operations with Respect to Intelligence Activities (Church Committee), Book III, U.S. Senate, April 23, 1976, pp. 921–86; and Loch K. Johnson, *A Season of Inquiry: Congress and Intelligence* (Lexington: University Press of Kentucky, 1985).

30. CIA analyst Arthur S. Hulnick, public lecture, November 20, 1984, University of Georgia, Athens.

31. A senior official in the Operations Directorate, cited in Loch K. Johnson, "Covert Action and Accountability: Decision-Making for America's Secret Foreign Policy," *International Studies Quarterly* 33 (March 1989), 81.

32. See, for example, Michael J. Glennon, "Investigating Intelligence Affairs: The Process of Getting Information for Congress," in Thomas Franck, ed., *The Tethered Presidency* (New York: New York University Press, 1981), 141–52; and Johnson, *Season of Inquiry.* The CIA has never allowed the oversight committees to appraise the competence of its chief analytic document for the president, the *President's Daily Brief.*

33. Walter Pincus, "Deutch under Pressure to Punish CIA Agents," *Washington Post,* July 31, 1995, A6. Deutch became the first DCI ever booed by CIA officers when he announced his strict punishments before a convocation at Langley Headquarters on September 29, 1995. After the meeting, officers in the Latin American Division wore black arms bands in the hallways and the Agency cafeteria.

34. Johnson, "Covert Action and Accountability"; the author's many conversations with former secretary of state Dean Rusk from 1979–83, Athens, Ga.

35. Author's interviews with Angleton, June–December 1975, Washington, D.C.

36. See Loch K. Johnson, *America's Secret Power: The CIA in a Democratic Society* (New York: Oxford University Press, 1989), chap. 6.

37. Ibid., 294n45. These battles took place on the House floor; the oversight committees have also halted or modified some covert actions, not because they have the authority to approve them (they do not) but because it is too risky politically for a president to dismiss the views of members.

38. See Loch K. Johnson, "Controlling the CIA: A Critique of Current Safeguards," *Harvard Journal of Law and Public Policy* 12 (1989), 393–94n134; for the 1980 Oversight Act, see 94 Stat. 1981, title 4, sec. 501, 50 U.S.C. 413 (formally, the Accountability for Intelligence Activities Act).

39. See the testimony of Lt. Col. Oliver L. North, *Hearings,* Inouye-Hamilton Committees, 240–41.

40. See William C. Cohen and George J. Mitchell, *Men of Zeal* (New York: Viking, 1988); and Elizabeth Drew, "Letter from Washington" (dated 22 March 1987), *New Yorker,* March 30, 1987, p. 111.

41. Remarks, "Secrecy and U.S. Foreign Policy," Tufts University Symposium, February 27, 1988 (author's notes).

42. Ray S. Cline, former CIA deputy director for intelligence, remarks, panel on "Controlling Intelligence," annual meeting, American Political Science Association, September 1, 1987, Chicago, original emphasis.

43. William E. Colby, "Gesprach mit William E. Colby," *Der Spiegel,* January 23, 1978 (author's translation), p. 21.

44. Cited in Loch K. Johnson, "The CIA: Controlling the Quiet Option," *Foreign Policy* 39 (Summer 1980), 143.

45. William E. Colby and Peter Forbath, *Honorable Men: My Life in the CIA* (New York: Simon and Schuster, 1978). Shakespeare's Marc Antony would have appreciated the irony of the title.

46. Senate bill S-2525, introduced on February 9, 1978, formally entitled the National Intelligence Reorganization and Reform Act. For the text, see *Congressional Record,*

February 9, 1978, pp. 3110–41. On the reasons for opposition to the charter (some well founded), see David Aaron, testimony, "Congressional Oversight of Covert Activities," *Hearings*, Permanent Select Committee on Intelligence, U.S. House of Representatives, September 22, 1983, p. 98; and Anne Karalekas, "Intelligence Oversight: Has Anything Changed?" *Washington Quarterly* 6 (Summer 1983), 22–30.

47. Rep. Norman Y. Mineta, quoted in the *New York Times*, May 14, 1984, p. 10.

48. Senator Patrick Leahy, interview, *This Week with David Brinkley*, ABC Television, December 14, 1986.

49. See Loch K. Johnson, "DCI Webster's Legacy: The Judge's Self-Assessment," *International Journal of Intelligence and Counterintelligence* 5 (Fall 1992), 287–90.

50. Walter Pincus, "CIA Director Adds 4 Deputies," *Washington Post*, August 1, 1995, A17.

51. Quoted in the Church Committee, *Final Report*, book 1, p. 9.

52. Colby and Forbath, *Honorable Men*; Johnson, *Season of Inquiry*.

53. For these executive orders (respectively, E.O. 11905, E.O. 12036, and E.O. 12333), see *Weekly Compilation of Presidential Documents* 12 (Washington, D.C.: Government Printing Office, 1976), 234–44; *Public Papers of the Presidents of the United States: Jimmy Carter, 1978*, book 1 (Washington, D.C.: Government Printing Office, 1979), 194–214; and *Public Papers of the Presidents of the United States: Ronald Reagan, 1981* (Washington, D.C.: Government Printing Office, 1982), 1128–30. The information about assassination attempts against Saddam comes from interviews with senior intelligence officials in 1991.

54. See Church Committee, *Hearings*, December 4 and 5, 1975.

55. See Loch K. Johnson, "Legislative Reform of Intelligence Policy," *Polity* 17 (Spring 1985), 549–73.

56. See "Should the CIA Fight Secret Wars?" (a roundtable discussion with several national security experts), *Harper's*, September 1984, pp. 39, 44. The realist cited here is Ray S. Cline; the ethicist, longtime diplomat George Ball.

57. Author's interview with Les Aspin, July 14, 1994, Washington, D.C.

58. For the account of KGB practices, see Bob Woodwood, *Veil: The Secret Wars of the CIA, 1981–87* (New York: Simon and Schuster, 1987), 416. The bombing of the Greenpeace ship *Rainbow Warrior* occurred in 1985, and the role of French intelligence in the covert action was told to me in 1986 in an interview with a former New Zealand chief of counterintelligence.

59. See Richard K. Betts, "Analysis, War and Decision: Why Intelligence Failures Are Inevitable," *World Politics* 31 (October 1978), 61–89.

60. See Stansfield Turner, *Secrecy and Democracy*, 116–17.

61. Remarks, Senior Conference, U.S. Military Academy, 1990.

62. Author's interview with Dean Rusk, October 5, 1979, Athens, Ga.

63. Thomas L. Hughes, *The Fate of Facts in a World of Men: Foreign Policy and Intelligence-Making*, Headline Series, no. 233 (Washington, D.C.: Foreign Policy Association, 1976), 48.

64. Testimony of Vice Admiral John M. Poindexter, Inouye-Hamilton Committees, *Hearings,* vol. 8, p. 159.

65. Johnson, *Season of Inquiry,* 57.

66. From a speech presented before an OSS veterans gathering on September 20, 1995, quoted by Phil McCombs, "Wonderful Wizards of OSS," *Washington Post,* September 21, 1995, C2.

67. See Steve Emerson, *Secret Warriors: Inside the Covert Military Operations of the Reagan Era* (New York: Putnam, 1988).

68. Loch K. Johnson, "Smart Intelligence," *Foreign Policy* 89 (Winter 1992–93), 69. See also David D. Dabelko and Geoffrey D. Dabelko, "The International Environment and the U.S. Intelligence Community," *International Journal of Intelligence and Counterintelligence* 6 (Spring 1993), 21–42; "Environment and Security Debates: An Introduction," *Environmental Change and Security Project: Report,* Woodrow Wilson Center 1 (Spring 1995).

69. A promising precedent is the MEDEA ("ma-day-a") project, named after a figure from Greek mythology, which joins the CIA's DS&T and private scientists in a cooperative venture to exploit satellite imagery for useful environmental data. See "Intelligence Authorization Act for Fiscal year 1996," report no. 104–138, part 1, Permanent Select Committee on Intelligence, 104th Cong., 1st Sess., June 14, 1995, pp. 55–57.

70. As the senior minister in charge of German intelligence has pointed out, there exists a hierarchy of topics for intelligence liaison. Military intelligence is the least likely to be shared, while intelligence on narcotics problems, weapons proliferation, and terrorism are promising areas for improved liaison. Author's interview, Bonn, Germany, July 7, 1993.

CHAPTER 6: INTELLIGENCE AND ECONOMIC SECURITY

1. Author's interview with Les Aspin, July 17, 1994, Washington, D.C.

2. Bill Clinton, "A New Era of Peril and Promise," speech to the diplomatic corps, Washington, D.C., January 18, 1993.

3. Loch K. Johnson, "Smart Intelligence," *Foreign Policy* 89 (1992–93), 62.

4. Mark Burton, "Government Spying for Commercial Gain," *Studies in Intelligence* 37 (1994), 18; Mark Clayton, "The Usually Legal Business of Keeping Tabs on the Competition," *Christian Science Monitor* 79 (October 26, 1987), 16.

5. Samuel B. Porteous, "Economic Espionage: New Target for CSIS [Canadian Security and Intelligence Service]," *Canadian Business Review* (Winter 1993), 32–35, and "Economic/Commercial Interests and Intelligence Services," *Commentary,* a Canadian Security Intelligence Service publication, 59 (July 1995).

6. On business-intelligence methods, see George S. Roukis, Hugh Conway, and Bruce H. Charnov, *Global Corporate Intelligence: Opportunities, Technologies, and Threats in the 1990s* (New York: Quorum Books, 1990); and Arthur S. Hulnick, "Business Intelligence: Lessons Learned from the CIA," paper, International Studies Association, annual meeting, Washington, D.C., March 29, 1994, pp. 1–14.

7. Philip Zelikow defines economic intelligence as "information about how those outside of the United States develop, produce, or manage their material goods, services, and resources. The term . . . encompasses the interpretation and presentation of raw knowledge or data as finished reports or analyses offered to inform policymaking consumers." *American Intelligence and the World Economy,* background paper for the Twentieth Century Fund Task Force on Intelligence Policy (no date, but probably 1995), 11. This definition is close to the meaning of *macroeconomic intelligence* in this chapter. See also Randall M. Fort, *Economic Espionage: Problems and Prospects,* monograph, Working Group on Intelligence (Washington, D.C., 1993), 1–29.

8. Cited by Tim Shorrock, "Agency Documents Reveal Cold War Economic Role," *Journal of Commerce,* August 17, 1995, p. 8.

9. Based on interviews with intelligence officers in the CIA's Office of Resources, Trade and Technology (RTT), Langley, Va., April 1, 1994.

10. Zelikow, *American Intelligence,* 1.

11. Statement provided to the author by the DCI's Office of Congressional Affairs, Langley, Va., February 7, 1995.

12. See Richard A. Best, Jr., "The U.S. Intelligence Community: A Role in Supporting Economic Competitiveness?" *CRS Report of Congress,* Congressional Research Service, Library of Congress, December 7, 1990; Joseph C. Evans, "U.S. Business Competitiveness and the Intelligence Community," *International Journal of Intelligence and Counterintelligence* 7 (Fall 1994), 353–62; Mark M. Lowenthal, "Keep James Bond Out of GM," *International Economy* (July/August 1992), 52–54; William T. Warner, "Economic Espionage: A Bad Idea," *National Law Journal* 15 (1993); Jay T. Young, "U.S. Intelligence Assessment in a Changing World," *Intelligence and National Security* 8 (April 1993), 125–39.

13. Remarks, West Point Senior Conference, United States Military Academy, June 9, 1990, West Point (author's notes).

14. This point has been emphasized by H. Bradford Westerfield of Yale University, who sees the whole debate over microeconomic intelligence as a "deceptive cover story," since key U.S. firms have already tacitly privatized the microeconomic espionage function. Remarks, Canadian Conference on Intelligence, Ottawa, October 27, 1994.

15. Author's interviews with CIA economic analysts, April 1, 1994, Langley, Va.

16. Summarized in a letter from Robert D. Steele, a seminar participant, to Senator Arlen Specter, January 23, 1995, and provided to the author by Mr. Steele.

17. Burton, "Government Spying," 20.

18. Frederick P. Hitz, inspector general, CIA, "Industrial Espionage," remarks, French American Chamber of Commerce, Washington, D.C., April 11, 1995, p. 9.

19. Robert M. Gates, remarks, Economic Club of Detroit, Michigan, April 13, 1992, p. 6.

20. Author's interview, Washington, D.C., April 2, 1994.

21. Gates, Economic Club of Detroit, 6.

22. See R. James Woolsey, testimony, Select Committee on Intelligence, U.S. Senate, February 2, 1993, as well as "The Future of Intelligence on the Global Frontier," address to the Executive Club of Chicago, November 19, 1993.

23. Stansfield Turner, "Intelligence for a New World Order," *Foreign Affairs* 70 (Fall 1991), 151–52.

24. Cited in Michael J. Stedman, "Industrial Espionage: What You Don't Know Can Hurt, You," *Business and Society Review* 76 (Winter 1991), 27.

25. Pat Choate, *Agents of Influence* (New York: Knopf, 1990); Christopher John Farley, "When Friends Spy on Friends," *Time* 141, May 17, 1993, p. 13; Count Alexandre de Marenches and David A. Andelman, *The Fourth World War* (New York: Morrow, 1992); Nicholas Eftimiades, *Chinese Intelligence Operations* (Annapolis: Naval Institute Press, 1994); John Mintz, "CIA: French Targeted Secrets of U.S. Firms," *Washington Post* 116, April 27, 1993, C1; Clyde Prestowitz, *Trading Places* (New York: Basic Books, 1988); Peter Schweitzer, *Friendly Spies: How America's Allies Are Using Economic Espionage to Steal Our Secrets* (New York: Atlantic Monthly Press, 1994); William T. Warner, "International Technology Transfer and Economic Espionage," paper, International Studies Association, annual meeting, Washington, D.C., 1994, pp. 1–26.

26. Robert Burns, "Nature of Economic Intelligence at Issue in Overhaul of CIA," *Athens* (Ga.) *Banner Herald,* February 23, 1995, p. 9.

27. Quoted in John Maggs, "From Swords to Plowshares," *Journal of Commerce,* August 18, 1995, p. 1.

28. Ibid.

29. Ibid.; and James Risen, "Clinton Reportedly Orders CIA to Focus on Trade Espionage," *Los Angeles Times,* July 23, 1995, A1.

30. Maggs, "From Swords to Plowshares," 1.

31. Porteous, "Economic/Commercial Interests," 37.

32. Risen, "Trade Espionage," A14.

33. R. James Woolsey, during a question-and-answer period following his address, entitled "The Future Direction of Intelligence," Center for Strategic and International Studies, Washington, D.C., July 18, 1994.

34. See "The Threat of Foreign Economic Espionage to U.S. Corporations," *Hearings,* Subcommittee on Economic and Commercial Law, House Committee on the Judiciary, 102 Cong., 2d Sess., April 29 and May 7, 1992.

35. Woolsey, testimony, U.S. Congress, February 2, 1993.

36. Remarks, West Point Senior Conference, June 9, 1990 (author's notes).

37. Cited in Loch K. Johnson, *America's Secret Power: The CIA in a Democratic Society* (New York: Oxford University Press, 1989), p. 80.

38. Author's interviews with CIA officials, June 1993, Langley, Va.; U.S. Congress, "Threat of Foreign Economic Espionage," 55.

39. Author's interview with a senior CIA economic analyst, April 1, 1994, Langley, Va.

40. Joseph S. Nye, Jr., remarks, Symposium on Teaching Intelligence, sponsored by the Center for the Study of Intelligence, CIA, 1993, Tyson's Corner, Va. (author's notes).

41. See Anthony F. Czajkowski, "Techniques of Domestic Intelligence Collection," *Studies in Intelligence* 3 (Winter 1959), 69–83, reprinted in H. Bradford Westerfield, ed., *Inside CIA's Private World: Declassified Articles from the Agency's Internal Journal, 1955–1992* (New Haven: Yale University Press, 1995), 51–62.

42. Seymour M. Hersh, "C.I.A. Salvage Ship Brought Up Part of Soviet Sub," *New York Times* (March 19, 1975), 1.

43. Remarks, Symposium on Teaching Intelligence, 1993 (author's notes).

44. Author's interviews with CIA officers, 1993–94, Langley, Va.

45. See Robert D. Blackwill and Ashton Carter, "The Role of Intelligence," in Robert D. Blackwill and Albert Carnesale, eds., *New Nuclear Nations: Consequences for U.S. Policy* (New York: Council on Foreign Relations, 1993), 216–52.

46. Author's interview, June 21, 1994, Washington, D.C.

47. See Blackwill and Carter.

48. According to State Department official Phyllis Oakley, Symposium on Teaching Intelligence, 1993 (author's notes).

49. See "The CIA and the Media," *Hearings,* Subcommittee on Oversight, House Permanent Select Committee on Intelligence, 96th Cong., 1st Sess., December 1979.

50. Quoted in Lawrence Van Gelder, "Fodor Denies Being Agent But Says He Helped C.I.A.," *New York Times,* January 9, 1975, p. 1.

51. "Business and Spying Mix, But Not Always," *New York Times,* March 10, 1974, E6.

52. Author's interviews with DCIs and intelligence overseers in the Congress, 1991–94. For criticism of CIA proprietaries, see Victor Marchetti and John D. Marks, *The CIA and the Cult of Intelligence* (New York: Knopf, 1974); Select Committee to Study Governmental Operations with Respect to Intelligence Activities (the Church Committee), *Final Report,* book 1, 94th Cong., 2d. Sess., S. Rept. No. 94–755, June 1976; and, "Iran-Contra Affair," Senate Select Committee on Secret Military Assistance to Iran and the Nicaraguan Opposition and House Select Committee to Investigate Covert Arms Transactions with Iran, *Hearings and Final Report,* 100th Cong., 1st Sess., S. Rept. No. 100–216, H. Rept. No. 100–433, November 1987.

53. Carl Becker, "Everyman His Own Historian," *American Historical Review* 37 (January 1932), 233–34.

54. Remarks, Symposium on Teaching Intelligence, 1993 (author's notes).

55. Ibid.

56. Robert Dreyfuss, "Company Spies," *Mother Jones* (May/June 1994), 18–19. Cutter was responsible for encouraging the CIA to publish a *Daily Economic Intelligence Brief* for the circulation of timely macroeconomic intelligence from around the world, for limited distribution to top-level consumers in the government.

57. Author's interview with a CIA analyst, April 1, 1994, Langley, Va.

58. Remarks, *The MacNeil/Lehrer News Hour,* Public Broadcasting Service, February 14, 1995.

59. See, for example, Les Aspin, "Misreading Intelligence," *Foreign Policy* 43 (Summer 1981), 166–72.

60. See Central Intelligence Agency, "The International Energy Situation: Outlook to 1985," *Estimate,* April 18, 1977, and "Prospects for Soviet Oil Production," *Estimate,* April 25, 1977.

61. Ibid.

62. Ibid.

63. Daniel P. Moynihan, "Do We Still Need the C.I.A.? The State Dept. Can Do the Job," *New York Times*, May 19, 1991, E17.
64. See Robert M. Gates, "CIA and the Collapse of the Soviet Union: Hit or Miss?" remarks, Foreign Policy Association, New York City, May 20, 1992.
65. Author's interview, July 21, 1993, Washington, D.C.
66. See Risen, "Clinton Reportedly Orders."
67. See the account in R. Jeffrey Smith and Clay Chandler, "Peso Crisis Caught U.S. by Surprise," *Washington Post*, February 13, 1995, A1, A16.
68. Ibid., A16.
69. Ibid.
70. Ernest R. May, "Intelligence: Backing into the Future," *Foreign Affairs* 71 (Summer 1992), 65.
71. See Johnson, *America's Secret Power*, 29–35.
72. Robert M. Gates, testimony, "Threat of Foreign Economic Espionage."
73. Ibid.
74. Douglas Waller, "The Open Barn Door," *Newsweek*, May 4, 1992, p. 7. At the macroeconomic level of espionage, the CIA returned the favor in 1995 and was caught, leading to strained relations between the two nations for a time. See William Drozdiak, "France Accuses Americans of Spying, Seeks Recall," *Washington Post*, February 23, 1995, p. 1.
75. Hitz, "Industrial Espionage," 11–12.
76. Press release, Department of State, February 21, 1995.
77. Fort, *Economic Espionage*, 3. In a September 1995 public briefing in Washington, D.C., DECA officials noted that about 70 percent of the espionage against American businesses is by other American businesses, 23 percent by foreign businesses, and 7 percent by hostile intelligence services (author's interview with a participant).
78. Porteous, "Economic Espionage," 34.
79. Remarks to the author, Washington, D.C., November 9, 1994, original emphasis.
80. Tom Wicker et al., "C.I.A. Operations: A Plot Scuttled," *New York Times*, April 28, 1966, p. 1.
81. Author's interviews with intelligence officers, Washington, D.C., summer 1980.
82. Author's interviews with intelligence officers, Washington, D.C., 1980–88.
83. Gregory F. Treverton, *Covert Action: The Limits of Intervention in the Postwar World* (New York: Basic Books, 1987), 105.
84. Eillen Shanahan, "McCone Defends I.T.T. Chile Fund Idea," *New York Times*, March 22, 1973, p. 1. The funding proposal was ultimately rejected by the Nixon administration, which pursued the same objective using CIA contingency funds. See Henry Kissinger, *White House Years* (Boston: Little, Brown, 1986), 667n.
85. "The Iran-Contra Affair," U.S. Congress, November 1987; Tower Commission, *Report of the President's Special Review Board* (Washington, D.C.: Government Printing Office, February 26, 1987).
86. Schweitzer, *Friendly Spies*, 1994.
87. "The CIA and the Media."

88. Author's interview with CIA/DO officer, July 18, 1980, Washington, D.C.

89. Robert Kohler, "The Intelligence Industrial Base: Doomed to Extinction?" monograph, Working Group on Intelligence Reform, Washington, D.C., 1994, pp. 1–22.

90. Ibid., 11.

91. I am grateful to Les Aspin for suggesting this hypothetical example (on February 13, 1995).

92. Cited by Dreyfuss, "Company Spies," 68.

93. Ibid., 68.

94. Remarks, West Point Senior Conference, June 9, 1990 (author's notes).

95. This suggestion was made by the former SSCI chairman Sen. Dennis DeConcini, "The Role of U.S. Intelligence in Promoting Economic Interests," *Journal of International Affairs* (Summer 1994), 57.

96. Remarks by Assistant Secretary of Defense Joseph S. Nye, Jr., "The Economic Role of the Intelligence Community," forum sponsored by the Institute for International Economics, Willard Hotel, Washington, D.C., April 25, 1995 (author's notes).

CHAPTER 7: AN ASSESSMENT OF AMERICAN INTELLIGENCE

1. In the early days of the CIA, SOVA was called the Office of Research and Reports (ORR).

2. Author's interview, Washington, D.C., February 13, 1995.

3. Donald P. Steury (a CIA historian), "The CIA and Strategic Intelligence: Estimates of Soviet Strategic Forces, 1950–62," paper, American Historical Association, annual conference, 1994, p. 7.

4. Ibid., 12.

5. Author's interview, Washington, D.C., July 14, 1994. For excellent chronicles of this floundering, see John Prados, *The Soviet Military Estimate: U.S. Intelligence and Russian Military Strength* (New York: Dial Press, 1982), and Lawrence Freedman, *U.S. Intelligence and the Soviet Strategic Threat,* 2d ed. (Princeton: Princeton University Press, 1986).

6. See William E. Burrows, *Deep Black: Space Espionage and National Security* (New York: Random House, 1986); Jeffrey T. Richelson, *America's Secret Eyes in Space: The U.S. Keyhole Spy Satellite Program* (New York: Harper and Row, 1990); and Kevin C. Ruffner, ed., *CORONA: America's First Satellite Program,* CIA History Staff, Center for the Study of Intelligence, Washington, D.C., 1995.

7. Ruffner, 2, 24.

8. See James Bamford, *The Puzzle Palace: A Report on America's Most Secret Agency* (Boston: Houghton Mifflin, 1982); Burrows, *Deep Black;* Richelson, *America's Secret Eyes in Space.*

9. Author's interview with NSA official, Washington, D.C., February 13, 1995.

10. Author's interview, Washington, D.C., July 15, 1994.

11. The "missile gap" was laid to rest by imagery data presented in NIE 11–8/1–61, entitled "Strength and Deployment of Soviet Long Range Ballistic Missile Forces" and

published on September 21, 1961. For the text, along with other key estimates from 1954 to 1984 (now declassified), see Donald P. Steury, comp., *Estimates on Soviet Military Power, 1954 to 1984: A Selection*, Center for the Study of Intelligence, CIA, December 1994.

12. Albert Wohlstetter, "Optimal Ways to Confuse Ourselves," *Foreign Policy* 20 (Fall 1975), 187–91. Not all of the Soviet weapons systems during the late 1960s and early 1970s were underestimated by the intelligence community. Submarine-launched ballistic missiles (SLBMs), for example, continued to be substantially overestimated from 1965 to 1970. See Freedman, *U.S. Intelligence*, 156.

13. Burrows, *Deep Black*, xvii.

14. See Jeffrey T. Richelson, *Sword and Shield: Soviet Intelligence and Security Apparatus* (Cambridge, Mass.: Ballinger, 1986), 90.

15. Burrows, *Deep Black*, xvi.

16. These examples arose in my interviews with intelligence analysts, Langley, Va., and Washington, D.C., July 14, 1994, and February 13, 1995.

17. Author's interview with senior DIA official, Washington, D.C., July 14, 1994.

18. Author's interview with senior DI analyst, Washington, D.C., February 21, 1995.

19. See James G. Blight, Bruce J. Allyn, and David A. Welch, *Cuba on the Brink: Castro, the Missile Crisis, and the Soviet Collapse* (New York: Pantheon Books, 1993); and the documents in Mary S. McAuliffe, ed., *CIA Documents on the Cuban Missile Crisis, 1962*, History Staff, Central Intelligence Agency (October 1962).

20. James R. Killian, Jr., chairman, PFIAB, Memorandum for the President and Report (February 4, 1963), reprinted in McAuliffe, *CIA Documents*, 363.

21. Ibid.

22. John McCone, Memorandum to the President, February 28, 1963, reprinted in McAuliffe, *CIA Documents*, 374.

23. Blight, Allyn, and Welch, *Cuba on the Brink*, 354.

24. Ibid.

25. Ibid.

26. Special National Intelligence Estimate (SNIE) 11–18–62, "Soviet Reactions to Certain US Courses of Action in Cuba," October 19, 1962, in McAuliffe, *CIA Documents*, 202; my conversations with Dean Rusk, November 24, 1986, and Robert S. McNamara, October 24, 1993, both in Athens, Ga.; and Larry King's interview with Robert S. McNamara, *Larry King Live*, CNN Television, October 21, 1992.

27. John A. McCone, "The Cuban Situation," Memorandum for Discussion Today, October 17, 1962, in McAuliffe, p. 162.

28. John A. McCone, Memorandum, October 17, 1962, in McAuliffe, *CIA Documents*, 162.

29. Quoted in Blight, Allyn, and Welch, *Cuba on the Brink*, 379, original emphasis.

30. For the CIA's effusive commendation of its accomplishments (while overlooking the shortcomings), see Admiral William O. Studeman, DDCI, "Intelligence and the Cuban Missile Crisis Symposium," remarks, CIA Headquarters, October 19, 1992, pp. 4–5.

31. Quoted in "Deutch Plans New Direction for CIA," *Jane's Defence Weekly,* July 8, 1995, p. 19.

32. Author's interviews with senior intelligence officers, Washington, D.C., June 30, 1994.

33. Daniel P. Moynihan, "Do We Still Need the C.I.A.? The State Dept. Can Do the Job," *New York Times,* May 19, 1991,E17.

34. Adam Ulam, "Glasnost, II: Moscow Stalling," *New Republic,* December 7, 1987, p. 12.

35. "An Evaluation of the CIA's Analysis of Soviet Economic Performance, 1970–1990," *Report,* Permanent Select Committee on Intelligence, U.S. House of Representatives, 102d Cong., 1st Sess. (November 18, 1991), 4–5. See also Bruce D. Berkowitz and Jeffrey T. Richelson, "The CIA Vindicated," *National Interest* 41 (Fall 1995), 36–47.

36. See Kirsten Lundberg, "CIA and the Fall of the Soviet Empire: The Politics of 'Getting It Right,'" Kennedy School of Government, Harvard University, Case Program No. C16–94–1251.0, Cambridge, Mass., 1994. See also David M. Kennedy, "Sunshine and Shadow: The CIA and the Soviet Economy," Kennedy School of Government, Harvard University, Case Program No. C16-91–1096.0, Cambridge, Mass., 1991.

37. Lundberg, "CIA and the Fall," 9.

38. Ibid., 11.

39. Douglas J. MacEachin, Memorandum to the DDI, April 22, 1986, with reference to "Gorbachev's Modernization Program: Implications for Defense," Intelligence Assessment (IA), declassified, DI/CIA, March 1986, p. 50.

40. See Berkowitz and Richelson, "CIA Vindicated," 39n5.

41. "Gorbachev's Economic Agenda: Promises, Potentials, and Pitfalls," IA (declassified), DI/CIA, September 1985, p. 18.

42. Lundberg, "CIA and the Fall," 27; and also, earlier, "Gorbachev: Steering the USSR into the 1990s," IA (declassified), DI/CIA, July 1987, p. iii.

43. "Soviet National Security Policy: Responses to the Changing Military and Economic Environment," IA, declassified, DI/CIA, June 1988, p. 28.

44. Author's interviews with former SOVA analysts and DI managers, July 14, 1994, and February 13, 1995, Washington, D.C., and Langley, Va.

45. The transcript is reprinted in "Hearings," *Nomination of Robert Gates,* vol. 2, Senate Select Committee on Intelligence, 102d Cong., 1st Sess., 1991, pp. 516ff.

46. Lundberg, "CIA and the Fall," 32.

47. "Rising Political Instability under Gorbachev: Understanding the Problem and Prospects for Resolution," IA, declassified, DI/CIA, April 1989, p. iii.

48. Recollections of Robert M. Gates, remarks, "CIA and the Collapse of the Soviet Union: Hit or Miss?" Foreign Policy Association, New York City, May 20, 1992, p. 6. A SOVA report declared at the time, "The Soviet Union is less stable today than at any time since Stalin's great purges in the 1930s." "Rising Political Instability under Gorbachev: Understanding the Problem and Prospects for Resolution," iii.

49. Lundberg, "CIA and the Fall," 35.
50. "Gorbachev's Domestic Gambles and Instability in the USSR," IA, declassified, DI/CIA, September 1989, p. iii.
51. Lundberg, "CIA and the Fall," 38.
52. Ibid.
53. "The Soviet Cauldron," SOVA paper, declassified, April 25, 1991, pp. 1, 4–6.
54. "Gorbachev's Future," Memorandum, declassified, DI/CIA, May 23, 1991, pp. 11, 16.
55. As Lundberg perceptively notes, "By the fall of 1990, Bush needed Gorbachev as much as Gorbachev needed him"—a close relationship between two men who were both interested in a stable USSR. "CIA and the Fall," 41.
56. Ibid., 55–56.
57. Ibid., 17n29.
58. Douglas J. MacEachin, SOVA director from 1984 to 1989 (and later DDI), quoted in ibid., 30. One of the few important political forecasts involving the USSR that the CIA claims to have gotten right during the Cold War was the anticipation of a political split between the Soviet Union and China in 1962. Even then, however, the CIA's influential chief of counterintelligence, James Angleton, continued to believe the schism was in reality a deception operation designed to lull the West into complacency. James J. Angleton, comments to the author, Washington, D.C., August 24, 1975, and other times.
59. "Domestic Stresses on the Soviet System," NIE 11–18–85 (declassified), November 1985, p. 1.
60. Douglas J. MacEachin, remarks to the author, Washington, D.C., February 28, 1995.
61. Robert M. Gates, "CIA and the Collapse of the Soviet Union: Hit or Miss?" remarks, Foreign Policy Association, New York City, May 20, 1992.
62. Author's interviews with former CIA intelligence and counterintelligence officers, Washington, D.C., June 1993–February 1995.
63. See Seymour M. Hersh, "The Angleton Story," *New York Times Magazine*, June 25, 1978, pp. 13ff.
64. See Raymond L. Garthoff, "Intelligence Assessment and Policymaking: A Decision Point in the Kennedy Administration," Staff Paper, Washington, D.C., Brookings Institution, 1984, p. 17. The CIA has stated in notes for a museum display of overhead reconnaissance, "The U-2 program provided some of the intelligence data that convinced President [Dwight D.] Eisenhower the missile gap was a myth, thus allowing the West to avoid huge and needless defense expenditures." CIA Museum, exhibit, Central Intelligence Agency, Langley, Va., Spring 1995. Garthoff, "Intelligence Assessment," and former DCI Stansfield Turner, among others, have observed that U.S. policymakers could have effected far greater savings, based on the intelligence provided them, if they had been willing to cut back on funding when the bomber and missile gaps were found to be in America's favor (Garthoff), or when during the Carter administration the president decided to buy more, not fewer, nuclear weapons (Turner). In Turner's view, "what [the NIEs] should have said to him . . . was simply two words: too much. We and

the Soviets both have too much firepower to need any more." Conference on "Estimating Soviet Military Power, 1950 to 1984," John F. Kennedy School of Government, Harvard University, December 2–3, 1994, Cambridge, Mass., cited in *Newsletter*, Center for the Study of Intelligence, 3, Spring 1995, p. 2. This is a reminder that good intelligence does not necessarily result in "good" policy; this second step in the policy process depends on the wisdom and courage of a nation's leaders.

65. Quoted by Burrows, *Deep Black*, vii.

66. See Arthur S. Hulnick, "The Ames Case: HOW [sic] Could It Happen," *International Journal of Intelligence and Counterintelligence* 8 (Summer 1995), 133–54.

67. Author's interviews with intelligence officers, Washington, D.C., July 14–15, 1994.

68. See David C. Martin, *Wilderness of Mirrors* (New York: Harper and Row, 1980).

69. On Howard, see David Wise, *The Spy Who Got Away* (New York: Random, 1988).

70. Ibid.

71. Author's interviews with counterintelligence officials, Washington, D.C., February 13, 1995.

72. Raymond L. Garthoff, "Assessing the Adversary: Estimates by the Eisenhower Administration of Soviet Intentions and Capabilities," Occasional Paper, Brookings Institution, Washington, D.C., 1991, p. 51, original emphasis.

73. Stephen I. Schwartz, letter to the editor, dated August 8, 1995, *New York Times*, August 13, 1995, E14.

74. Raymond L. Garthoff, "Intelligence Assessment and Policymaking: A Decision Point in the Kennedy Administration," staff paper, Brookings Institution, Washington, D.C., 1984, p. 2, in reference to NIE 11–8–62 (issued in July 1962).

75. Freedman, *U.S. Intelligence*, 68.

76. Burrows, *Deep Black*, xvi.

77. Author's interview, Washington, D.C., July 14, 1994.

78. Ibid.

79. Ibid.

80. Author's interview, Washington, D.C., February 13, 1995.

81. Author's interview, Washington, D.C., July 30, 1994.

82. Ibid.

83. Author's interview with senior SOVA analysts, February 14, 1995, who heard Dr. Teller make this argument in several meetings at the Pentagon.

84. Author's interview, Washington, D.C., July 30, 1994.

85. Author's interviews with retired DI analysts, Washington, D.C., February 13, 1995.

86. Bobby Ray Inman, interview, *U.S. News & World Report*, December 20, 1982, p. 32.

87. Author's interview, Washington, D.C., July 30, 1994.

88. Douglas J. MacEachin, untitled and undated manuscript (probably 1995), p. 3.

89. Remark to the author, February 21, 1988, Athens, Ga. Secretary Rusk added: "I've told more than one director of Central Intelligence that when they make their national security estimates, a good many of them ought to begin with the expression, 'Damned if I know, but if you want our best guess, well, here it is,' to alert the policy officer that there cannot be certainty in the matters being discussed."

INDEX